I0820734

Palestine in the Evolution of Syrian Nationalism (1918-1920)

CHICAGO STUDIES ON THE MIDDLE EAST

Center for Middle Eastern Studies
The University of Chicago

Previously published titles:

1. Joel Gordon, *Revolutionary Melodrama: Popular Film and Civic Identity in Nasser's Egypt* (2002)

2. Israel Gershoni and James Jankowski, *Commemorating the Nation: Collective Memory, Public Commemoration, and National Identity in Twentieth-Century Egypt* (2004)

3. Th. Emil Homerin, *The Wine of Love and Life: Ibn al-Fāriḍ's* al-Khamrīyah *and al-Qayṣarī's Quest for Meaning* (2005)

Published on behalf of the
Center for Middle Eastern Studies
By
The Middle East Documentation Center

Palestine in the Evolution of Syrian Nationalism (1918-1920)

Muhannad Salhi

Chicago • Middle East Documentation Center • 2008

Published in 2008 by the Middle East Documentation Center on behalf of the Center for Middle Eastern Studies, The University of Chicago

Pick Hall 201
5828 S. University Avenue
Chicago, IL 60637
http://ChicagoStudiesOnTheMiddleEast.uchicago.edu

Manufactured in the United States of America

ISBN 978-0-9708199-3-2

Library of Congress Cataloging-in-Publication Data

Salhi, Muhannad, 1967-
Palestine in the evolution of Syrian nationalism (1918-1920) / Muhannad Salhi.
p. cm. -- (Chicago studies on the Middle East)
Includes bibliographical references and index.
ISBN 978-0-9708199-3-2 (hc)
1. Palestine--History--1917-1948. 2. Arab nationalism--Palestine. 3. Arab nationalism--Syria. 4. Political parties--Palestine. I. Title.
DS126.S2645 2008
320.5409569109'041--dc22

2008060063

For my son, Laith

CONTENTS

ACKNOWLEDGEMENTS

This study began as a dissertation for the Department of History at the University of Chicago. I would like to thank the members of my committee for all their valuable comments and advice: Rashid Khalidi, Lisa Wedeen, and John Woods. I am grateful to Bruce Craig, Marlis Saleh, and the anonymous reader for Chicago Studies on the Middle East, for their help in the editing of the final manuscript, and to the rest of the MEDOC crew, without each of whom this would not have been possible. I would especially like to thank my dear friend and colleague Olaf Nelson for all his talents in creating the maps and for his tireless work on finalizing the book; I don't know what I would have done without him. Of course, any shortcomings or errors remain solely my own responsibility. Finally, I would like to thank my lovely wife Ruma, for her love and unflinching support.

INTRODUCTION

One of the most enduring political dilemmas in modern history, the Palestine question has no doubt had a tremendous effect on the evolution and development of all nation-states in the Middle East. Directly bound to both the once paramount ideology of Arab nationalism and incorporated into the doctrines of politicized Islamic groups, the loss of Palestine and its consequences have been bemoaned by both secular nationalists and religious "fundamentalists" as one of the greatest "catastrophes"[1] Arabs and Muslims have had to face in the modern age. The magnitude of the Palestinian predicament and its complexity have almost necessarily dictated its tremendous impact on the entire Middle East, thus becoming the ostensible source of most problems in the region and the focus of most political pursuits to this day.

With the end of the European Mandate system in the wake of the Second World War, and since the official independence of the former mandates and the creation of a modern nation-state system (including the state of Israel), the region has experienced three major Arab-Israeli wars in 1948, 1967, and 1973; the Suez crisis of 1956; attacks on Israeli targets by various Palestinian groups sponsored by Arab states; Israeli attacks on Jordan on several occasions in the late 1960s; numerous Israeli attacks and incursions into Lebanon and Lebanese targets, including three full-scale military invasions (1978, 1982, 1993, 1995,[2] and, most recently, 2006) and the occupation of entire regions of Lebanon until 2000; Israeli attacks on Iraq and by Iraq on Israel in 1981 and 1990 respectively; the Israeli occupation of the Sinai peninsula for over a decade, and of Gaza until very recently; and finally the continuing decades-long occupation of the West Bank and the Golan Heights. All these events and the bitter wars they engendered have made the Arab-Israeli conflict one of the longest lasting conflicts of the twentieth century, still unresolved in the twenty-first. Much of modern Middle Eastern history has consequently centered on the turbulent relations between the Arab countries and Israel.

---

[1]The loss of Palestine is commonly referred to as *al-nakbah*, the "catastrophe," in Arabic political literature.

[2]Better known as Operations "Litani," "Peace for Galilee," "Operation Accountability," and "Grapes of Wrath," respectively.

The impact of the Palestine question on the Middle East, however, runs deeper than the Arab-Israeli wars and is certainly not limited to conflict between Arabs and Jews. A dominant factor in the political development of the region, the Palestinian question played a fundamental role in shaping the political identity of the nascent surrounding Arab states. Far from simply being a territorial contest occurring on their borders, the Palestine question struck a deep religious, moral, and patriotic chord in the hearts of most Arabs. The prestigious status accorded the city of Jerusalem in Islam had, for centuries, rendered control of the general region of "Palestine" a prized possession for any Islamic potentate or empire-builder seeking to establish his authority and popularity among the Muslim populace. Its loss in 1948 therefore was a serious blow to both Arab and Muslim prestige and its liberation was portrayed as a prime patriotic and religious obligation.

Objectives

The purpose of this study is to examine the place of Palestine in the development of Syrian nationalism from the inception of Syria as a modern nation-state following the dissolution of the Ottoman Empire at the end of the First World War. This work accordingly investigates the origins of the Southern Syria notion, examines its foundations, and explores the development of the concept of Southern Syria and its place in the Syrian political arena during Syria's first experience of nationhood and semi-independence in the Faysali era from 1918 to 1920. The goal of the study is to demonstrate the extent to which the issue of Palestine/Southern Syria was entrenched in Syrian understandings of nationhood and national identity, thereby shaping the evolution of Syrian national discourse and influencing the orientation of Syrian political development for decades to come.

The first chapter offers the historical background of the situation and introduces the setting in which the Southern Syria notion began to take root and develop. It examines the origin of the concept itself, the background behind it, and the foundations upon which it was based. In order to provide a thorough investigation of this point, this notion is examined first from the general Arab perspective; specifically how the Arabs in Syria and Palestine had come to view themselves as part of one Syrian nation, and the bases on which this was justified. Next, the work investigates the perspective of the previous Ottoman administration and its policies. Finally, it examines this concept of Southern Syria from the European perspective, namely that of the French and British—the powers immediately involved in the region. It explores how French and British administrators viewed Palestine in relation to Syria, how their opinions developed and changed after the end of the First World War, and the influence their perspectives had on the majority of the inhabitants of the region and the course of the future.

Chapter two discusses the place of Southern Syria in the official Arab demands for the future of their country and its place in the evolving Syrian national discourse. It examines the four main Arab conferences that took place in the region during that period, namely the First Palestinian Congress of 1919, the General Syrian Congress of 1919, the Second Palestinian Congress of 1920, and finally the General Syrian Congress of March 1920. It provides a thorough analysis of their demands and how the future status of Palestine was envisioned within Syria and Palestine. It then investigates the background behind each of those congresses, the various motivations behind their demands, the events that played a role in bringing them about, the international and Allied reaction to each of them, and their repercussions.

Chapter three discusses the concept of Southern Syria and its importance and centrality to the general Syrian and Palestinian population. In order to do so this study relies on the survey conducted by the American King-Crane Commission. The King-Crane Commission is deemed extremely valuable in this respect for a number of factors. First, it was an impressive effort in terms of its breadth and scope to determine what the inhabitants of the region genuinely wanted for their future; indeed it was the only endeavor of its kind. Second, an ostensibly impartial American team conducted this survey with no imperial interests in the region of their own. Finally, the American Commission had the avid support and backing of the inhabitants of the region, who were very willing to talk to them and candidly inform them of their wishes and demands. This chapter investigates the background of the commission, the various diplomatic obstacles it had to face, and the reaction it generated among the Allies and the Arab population in the region. It then examines and analyzes the findings of the commission regarding Southern Syria, including its methods and the shortcomings of the survey. Finally, it examines the commission's suggestions and recommendations for a lasting peace and stability in the region based on those findings.

Chapter four discusses the status and centrality of Palestine in Syrian political discourse. The chapter analyzes the extent to which Palestine played a vital role in political development of the Syrian political parties and investigates the reasoning and motivation behind its importance. It is divided into two sections: the first investigates the Palestine question in programs of the official political parties and their demands; the second section examines this question and its place in a number of pamphlets and declarations by various known and unknown political actors. The first section begins by providing an investigation of the major active Syrian political parties and quasi-political groups in that region during the Faysali era; it examines their history and background, their programs and agendas, and the place of Palestine within their political platforms. It also examines the various trends among the developing political parties and their bearing on the question of Palestine. The second section of the chapter examines various pamphlets, *communiqués*, and declarations issued during that period by numerous political actors and groups, some well known and others anonymous. It investigates the nature of their demands and the background behind them, focusing on the status of Palestine and the extent of its significance in Syrian political thought.

Chapter five discusses the Palestine question and the concept of Southern Syria from the standpoint of the Syrian diplomacy during that period. It examines Palestine from the perspective of the Syrian leadership, namely that of Faysal, and its place in the Syrian leadership's political negotiations, statements and treaties, and its impact on the various political actors involved. The chapter investigates Faysal's background and his involvement in Syrian affairs, focusing primarily on his position on Palestine in a public and private capacity. It discusses his official stance in that regard in the international peace conferences comparing it to the position he adopted in his private discussions with British, French, and American officials regarding Palestine. It also examines his various negotiations and treaties with the Zionists and their representatives, his statements to the international press, and his public stance on this issue at home.

The study concludes with an overall assessment of the place of Palestine in Syrian politics during that period, analyzing the degree to which it played a decisive role on Syrian political development and thinking on all levels, with the view to determining to what extent Palestine and its conception as Southern Syrian by the Syrians was a crucial factor in Syrian national development and would continue to influence Syrian political evolution until the present.

Syria and the Palestine Question: an Overview

Occurring at a time when the newly formed Arab states were still very much in the process of developing their concepts of nationhood, the Palestine question left an indelible mark on the overall political evolution within these nations. The issue of Palestine became the Arabs' (and Muslims') primary international grievance, a principal objective of various political groups' patriotic and religious "crusades" to overthrow existing regimes and seize power. As such, the Palestinian cause became a virtual standard by which the various Arab regimes' loyalty to Arab nationalism and Islam could be gauged. More often than not, it was through a particular stance on this very issue that an Arab government could gain or lose popularity and indeed the moral right to rule in the eyes of its own people and the entire Arab populace. As the most obvious means to verify their patriotic and religious credentials, the mention of Palestine by Arab leaders in virtually all their public utterances became ritualistic, as was their constant reassertion of their pledges of loyalty and devotion to its cause. The Palestine issue, moreover, has been one of the single most influential factors in determining the course Arab foreign policy was to take on a global level.

Although the Palestine question affected all the Arab and Muslim nation-states to some extent, it certainly did not affect them to the same extent.

The degree to which the Palestine question played a role in shaping these countries' external and internal politics and the extent of their involvement in the conflict[3] depended on the nature of their cultural and historical ties to Palestine, their geographical proximity to the Holy Land, and ideologies that were most prevalent among the populace. Hence, depending on their location, economic situation, political proclivities, and standing in the region, this issue undoubtedly affected certain countries much more directly, intensely, and uniquely than others. In some cases, it shaped the very character of their national evolution.

Of all the nations affected by the Palestine crisis, Syria provides a most interesting case study. Syria's relationship with the Palestine question is one of the most intimate and complex in the region; the influence of this question on that nation's political development has therefore been extremely far-reaching and profound. Indeed, in many ways Palestine has dominated Syrian political thinking and policy-making decisions from the very inception of Syria as a modern nation following the fall of the Ottoman Empire and Faysal's march into Damascus in October 1918, and since the initiation of that question with the Balfour Declaration of November 1917. This work will help to fill a critical gap by providing focus in a topic that is necessary to any study of modern Syrian political history.

The significance of the Palestine question to Syria becomes clear when examined against the backdrop of the Syrian population's overall struggle to determine their national character and political orientation in virtually all regards. Generally speaking, Syria's experience with nationhood and political independence in the modern era has been at best confused and unstable. Domestically, Syria underwent many crucial changes and experienced a variety of political systems. Initially opting for a constitutional monarchy, roughly based on the British model, Arab and Syrian nationalists endeavored to create a kingdom with Faysal as its head. The French nevertheless had their own plans for the region, putting a swift end to this goal by force of arms in the summer of 1920 at the battle of Maysalun. Syria subsequently fell under French rule under the guise of the recently devised mandate system, created by the Allies at the Peace Conference. Below is a brief history of Syrian political development with regard to the Palestine question.

SYRIAN POLITICAL DEVELOPMENT AND THE PALESTINE QUESTION

With the termination of the French mandate, in the wake of the Second World War, a new Syrian nation-state was founded with a republican parliamentary system based on the French model—a final legacy of the French mandate. Syria subsequently set out to establish its own republican tradition. Syrian ideologues and political adventurers nevertheless constantly presented their

[3]Not to mention the immediate problem of having to harbor the hundreds of thousands of refugees fleeing Palestine following the 1948 and 1967 wars.

own radical alternatives to this system, offering to fulfill general aspirations for "unity" and "independence" through their own single party rule and dictatorships; platforms which, depending on the circumstances, could muster quite an appeal among various sectors of the Syrian populace.

Once it gained its official independence on April 17, 1947, Syria became a central actor in Arab politics and, more importantly, in the struggle with Israel a year later. Almost immediately following the foundation of the State of Israel on May 15, 1948, Syria was one of the first Arab countries to commit its armies to fighting in the first Arab-Israeli war of 1948-1949. Since then it has been a primary participant in four major Arab-Israeli wars (1948-9, 1967, 1973, and 1982) and has become one of the main protagonists in the Arab-Israeli conflict.

From the beginning, Syria, as a political entity, was affected by the loss of Palestine more than most other Arab nation-states, suffering an extensive period of political turmoil and instability as a direct result of the Arab defeat in the 1948 war. Undergoing three successive *coups d'état* in 1949 alone, the country soon became subject to numerous bids by military strongmen each seeking to offer their own "alternatives" by way of establishing personal military dictatorships.[4]

Syria consequently experienced a particularly turbulent period in the wake of the Palestine War (1948-9), during which martial rule prevailed after a number of successive coups established short-lived military regimes. Eventually managing to restrict this direct military involvement in politics, the Syrians reverted, albeit temporarily, to their republican system. Numerous factors, including fierce domestic political rivalry combined with popular enthusiasm for the Egyptian president Nasser and the revered goal of Arab unity he championed, soon prompted certain factions within the Syrian leadership to push Nasser into the short-lived experiment of a socialist Arab union with Egypt.[5] When this failed, the Syrian populace and their leaders, both confused and dismayed at its failure, reverted once again to parliamentary republicanism. This was a turbulent, short-lived period, however, and the state soon fell under the domination of the single party dictatorship of the leftist Baʿth party and its various internal rival factions beginning in 1963.[6]

---

[4]For a general overview of the political history of this period see Patrick Seale, *The Struggle for Syria: A Study of Post-War Arab Politics, 1945-1958* (New Haven, 1986). For a detailed discussion of the military involvement in Syrian politics at this time, see Gordon H. Torrey, *Syrian Politics and the Military, 1945-1958* (Columbus, 1964).

[5]For more on this see Seale, *Struggle for Syria;* Malcolm Kerr, *The Arab Cold War: Gamal ʿAbd al-Nasir and His Rivals 1958-1970* (London, 1971); and Muḥammad Ḥasanayn Haykal, *Mā alladhī jará fī Sūrīyā* (Cairo, 1962).

[6]For more on the history and development of the Baʿth party and its role in Syrian politics, see Kamel Abu Jaber, *The Arab Baʿth Socialist Party: history, ideology and organization* (New York, [1966]); John F. Devlin, *The Baʿth Party: a history from its origins to 1966*

On the "regional"[7] inter-Arab front, Syria was a central actor in what has been termed the "Arab Cold War,"[8] which lasted at least until the death of Nasser in 1970. In an era during which the cherished ideal of Arab unity still reigned supreme, Syria, according to Patrick Seale,[9] became the ultimate prize in the tug of war between the various Arab regimes and their unity schemes. Such schemes included the Jordanian King ʿAbdullah's "Greater Syria" project, Nuri al-Saʿid and the Iraqi monarchy's "Fertile Crescent" project, and finally, the ill-fated progressive socialist Arab Union with Nasser's Egypt. Furthermore, the opposing camps in the Arab Cold War (which were in constant flux due to numerous *coups d'état* and revolutions) invariably sought to woo Syria to their side on various inter-Arab and international issues. In this regard, the Palestine question became a central tenet freely utilized by opposing political groups to support their respective positions. Consequently, each side sought to exploit this issue in their political machinations in an attempt to justify their stance and prove that they were the true bearers of the Arab nationalist banner and hence, that the liberation of Palestine was their ultimate goal.

During the brief Hinnawi era in 1949, for example, when supporters of the projected union with Iraq appeared to be the majority in government, one of the main arguments of the proponents of the Fertile Crescent project was that it would strengthen Syria's defensive position *vis-à-vis* Israel, in addition, of course, to appealing to pan-Arab sentiment by abolishing borders in the Fertile Crescent region. Egypt, in turn, responded with the creation of the Arab League Collective Security Pact, thus providing the project's opponents with a pan-Arab alternative to union with Iraq. As a formal military alliance created under the aegis of the Arab League, it declared that the Arabs should rely only on themselves for defense, thus threatening the security zone system created by the British, and shifting regional balance of power against the Hashemite

---

(Stanford, 1976); David Roberts, *The Baʿth and the creation of modern Syria* (London, 1987); also any of the writings of its main ideologue Michel ʿAflaq, such as *Fī Sabīl al-Baʿth* (Baghdad, 1959), would provide valuable insight into its ideology. On the various inter-party struggles see Itamar Rabinovitch, *Syria Under the Baʿth, 1963-1966: the Army-Party symbiosis* (Jerusalem, [1972]); Steven Heydemann's *Authoritarianism in Syria: Institutions and Social Conflict, 1946-1970* (Ithaca, 1999); and Nikolaos Van Dam, *The Struggle for Power in Syria: politics and society under Asad and the Baʿth Party* (New York, 1996).

[7] According to Arab nationalist terminology, to be adopted and expounded by the Baʿth party (the modern standard-bearer of Arab nationalist tenets) later on, the entire Arab world formed the single "nation" (*waṭan),* whereas all the countries forming its component parts were "regions" (*aqṭār,* sing. *quṭr*).

[8] This term is borrowed from Malcolm Kerr from his book of the same title.

[9] Seale, *Struggle for Syria.*

bloc.[10]

Another example of how the Palestinian issue played a role in the unity considerations and its utilization in inter-Arab politics was at the Shtura conference held in Lebanon in 1962, following Syria's secession from the United Arab Republic. At the conference, the Syrian delegates attacked Egypt for meddling in Syrian internal affairs. Despite the problems they were having with him and his regime, the main accusations the Syrians chose to level against Nasser, however, centered on his position towards Israel and the Palestinian question. They denounced Nasser's evacuation of Sharm al-Shaykh in particular, thus permitting Israel to slip through the Gulf of ʿAqaba and into international waters.[11] Aside from criticizing Nasser for behaving like a dictator, two of Syria's representatives at the conference—al-Mahasini and al-Nafuri—also accused him of handing over Sharm al-Shaykh to the Israelis, permitting ships carrying Israeli cargo to pass through the Suez, allowing the Interpol to patrol the Gaza border, refusing to resist Israel's diversion of the waters of the Jordan river, and avoiding the formulation of any serious plans for regaining Palestine.[12]

In the more global arena of the Cold War, Syria's position was very much determined by Palestinian considerations or, more precisely, by the respective superpower camps' position toward the Arab-Israeli conflict.[13] During the Cold War, Syria's international orientation was governed by its leaders' calculations of which camp would offer the most support in the struggle against Israel and, conversely, the extent of aid and support they were willing to offer its enemy. More importantly, Syrian regimes acted as though it were their duty and obligation to champion and promote the Palestinian cause in their foreign relations.

In his country's first diplomatic contact with Communist China at the Bandung Conference of 1955, for example, the main topic that Syrian Foreign Minister Khalid al-ʿAzm saw fit to broach with the Chinese Premier and Foreign Minister Zhou Enlai at their first meeting, was whether or not the Palestine problem should be discussed at the conference. When the Burmese representative objected on the grounds that no Israeli delegation was present to defend its position, ʿAzm and his representative Ahmad al-Shuqayri (himself a Palestinian) took special care in explaining the Palestinian cause to Zhou

---

[10] Michael Doran, *Pan-Arabism before Nasser: Egyptian Power Politics and the Palestine Question* (New York, 1999), 194-5.

[11] Khālid al-ʿAẓm, *Mudhakkirāt Khālid al-ʿAẓm* (Beirut, 1973), 3: 293-4.

[12] Ibid., 294.

[13] For more on this see Helena Cobban, *The Super Powers and the Syrian-Israeli Conflict* (New York, 1991); also Patrick Seale, *Asad of Syria: the struggle for the Middle East* (Berkeley, 1989).

Enlai.[14] The latter allegedly became very interested in this problem and ended up championing the discussion of Palestine at the conference.[15] The issue of Palestine was therefore central to Syria's understanding and practice of international politics.

Domestically, the Palestine question dominated the Syrian political scene from its inception in the final years of the First World War. All the Syrian political parties proclaimed Palestine as part of Syria and its liberation and unity with Syria were seen as essential patriotic goals. After the fall of the Faysali Kingdom and the institution of the Mandate system, Syrians and Palestinians provided each other with aid and support in their respective rebellions against their Mandate powers.[16] Syrians, such as Fawzi al-Qawuqji, played a role in the military campaigns in Palestine during the revolt of 1936-39 and in the war of 1948, helping to rally public opinion in Syria and enlist Syrian efforts in "rescuing" the southern region of the "homeland."[17]

Syrian politicians and political parties continued to proclaim the liberation of Palestine as their foremost national goal as a means of establishing their nationalist credentials. The Baᶜth party, for example, which would dominate Syrian politics down to the present, adopted the Palestinian flag as their party emblem. Politicians also sought to utilize this issue and their stance on it to their own political advantage. During the initial debates in 1947-48 over the amendment of Article 68 of the Syrian constitution (which restricted the president of the republic to one term in office), for example, president Shukri al-Quwwatli and his supporters argued that his re-election was of primary importance to Syria since he was "a leader in solving the Palestine problem and that he was needed for success in regaining that twice-promised land."[18]

Today, the ruling regime in Syria stands as one of the last remaining bastions of Arab nationalism. Due to their country's geographic position, for decades Syrian regimes consistently proclaimed themselves to be at the vanguard of confrontation"[19] and leaders in what became known as the "rejection front"[20] in the Arab-Israeli conflict, continuing to resist direct negotiations with Israel until 1991. While there has been an uneasy détente between Syria and Israel

---

[14] ᶜAẓm, *Mudhakkirāt,* 2: 382.

[15] Ibid.

[16] Philip Khoury, "Divided Loyalties? Syria and the Question of Palestine, 1919-1939," *Middle Eastern Studies* 21 (July 1985): 324-48.

[17] For more on this see Fawzī al-Qāwuqjī, *Filasṭīn fī Mudhakkirāt Fawzī al-Qāwuqjī 1936-1948*, edited by Khayrīyah Qāsimīyah (Beirut, 1975); also Khiḍr ᶜAlī Maḥfūẓ, *Taḥt Rāyat al-Qāwuqjī* (Beirut, 1973).

[18] Torrey, *Syrian Politics and the Military,* 102.

[19] Better known as *duwal al-muwājahah,* "the confronting nations," i.e., the nations in the direct line of fire against Israel.

[20] *Jabhat al-rafḍ.*

for several years, the Syrian government does not yet officially recognize the state of Israel and Syria continues to provide sanctuary to Palestinian groups who do not support peace with the Jewish state.[21] Syria has also traditionally supported groups in Lebanon, such as the militant Shiite group Hizbullah who are known for their active hostility towards Israeli policies.

Many questions remain, however, regarding why the Palestine question influenced Syria, more than most Arab countries, to the point where it practically dictated the course of its domestic and foreign politics. To what degree can this influence be attributed to Syria's fervent dedication to Arab nationalism, and how much of it was genuine fear of Israeli aggression? Moreover, why were the Syrians so prone to being enticed by the unity schemes offered by the various neighboring presidents, rulers, and potentates during such a crucial period in their history?

While, generally speaking, Syrian commitment to Arab nationalism was deemed beyond reproach (not least from the point of view of the Syrians themselves), there also existed a purely Syrian nationalist movement, functioning and thriving in tandem with the dominant Arabist tide. These Syrian nationalist groups had explicit demands regarding the specific geographical boundaries that constituted the integral Syrian nation. Syrian visions of nationhood, and what were proclaimed as Syria's "legitimate national aspirations," were therefore never fulfilled on any level. Indeed, the modern Syrian Arab Republic forms a truncated and attenuated version of what constituted "Syria" in the eyes of both Syrian and Arab nationalists.

Essentially, Syria's evolution as a modern nation did not begin with its official independence from France in 1947, but rather with its separation from the Ottoman Empire in its final years. Furthermore, according to the national discourse as it developed and subsequently became entrenched in the minds of the majority of Syrians, Palestine was constantly being affirmed as an integral part of the Syrian nation: its southern region. More importantly, both the Arab and Syrian nationalist perspectives supported this notion of "Southern Syria," deeming "Palestine" inseparable from "Syria."

The Southern Syria concept, moreover, did not gain popularity due to a particular regime's propaganda efforts based on its territorial ambitions; rather, it was the initial response of both the Syrian and Palestinian people to the prospect of independence and the concept of nationalism becoming a reality. It was a fundamental nationalist demand confirmed repeatedly by the region's population, who sought to make their wishes explicitly known in as many ways as they possibly could, only to have them summarily ignored and rejected by the Allies. This was a demand whose refusal influenced the course of events in the region until the present day. Even as Palestine nationalism began to grow and develop in a different direction following the fall of the Faysali

[21] Such as, for example, the Popular Front for the Liberation of Palestine (PFLP) and the Democratic Front for the Liberation of Palestine (DFLP).

regime,[22] this notion continued to influence Syrian political thinking. The Palestine question subsequently became a central factor in Syria's endeavors to define its concepts of nationality, in outlining its national objectives and in its overall political development. By offering an analysis of this critical and complex relationship between Syria and the Palestine question, this work fills an important gap in understanding the overall evolution of Syrian nationalism and political history.

SOURCES

For this study, in addition to utilizing the pertinent available secondary literature, I have focused primarily on utilizing Arabic, British, French, and American government documents and resolutions, as well as private correspondence between the major actors and parties involved. I have also examined the personal memoirs of the pertinent actors, the press, the minutes and resolutions of the various conferences, the documents, resolutions, and statements of the various political parties, and pamphlets and resolutions issued by independent political groups. Most of these sources are untranslated and unedited and I have carefully presented them for the English speaking audience.

NOTES ON TRANSLATION AND TRANSLITERATION

Unless otherwise indicated, all translations from the Arabic and French sources are mine, and the method for transliteration used for the Arabic names and terms in the footnotes is the standard system used by the Library of Congress.

[22] Indeed, Musa Kazim al-Husayni, one of the most prominent nationalist leaders in Palestine, would declare barely a month after the fall of the Faysali regime: "Now, after recent events in Damascus, we have to effect complete change in our plans here. Southern Syria no longer exists. We must defend Palestine." Quoted in Rashid Khalidi, *Palestinian Identity: The Construction of Modern National Consciousness* (New York, 1997), 165. For more on the development of Palestinian nationalism, see Khalidi, ibid., and Muhammad Muslih, *The Origins of Palestinian Nationalism* (New York, 1988).

Chapter One

SOUTHERN SYRIA: THE ORIGINS OF A NOTION

While the Palestinian question had a tremendous impact on the entire Middle Eastern region, its repercussions on Syria were profound and complex. Deep-rooted and multi-faceted, Syria's intimate relationship with the Palestine question began with the very inception of that question at the initial stages of the evolution of Syrian national consciousness in the modern understanding of the term. When issues such as independence and nation-state nationalism were brought to the fore in the region with the dissolution of the Ottoman Empire in the wake of the First World War, the inhabitants of Syria and Palestine, regardless of their other political differences and differing loyalties, concurred that region of "Palestine" formed an integral part of the Syrian Arab nation, namely its southern province. This notion and its implications would continue to influence Syrian political development for decades to come.

The novelty of the concepts of nationalism and modern nation-states in a region whose inhabitants were accustomed to being part of a single multi-ethnic empire and consequently saw their identity in terms of other criteria,[1] might partially explain the reason why the majority of Syrians and Palestinians would have preferred the security of an, albeit limited, unity to the precarious isolation of individual independence. The Ottoman Empire not only imposed the rule of a central authority on the region for over four centuries, but it also provided its inhabitants with a unifying bond on numerous levels, not the least of which was a focus for their sense of identity, religious and otherwise. Accordingly, when the Syrians did begin developing their own individual notions of nationalism, national identity, and subsequent nationalist ideologies, they generally tended to extend their focus to encompass the entire Arab "nation," rather than confining their allegiance to Syria and the Syrian region alone.

Even while proclaiming themselves and all other Arabs to be a natural part of this prospective united Arab "nation," however, the Syrians did acknowledge regional differences and distinctions among the various Arab "regions" comprising it. They did not consider Egypt or even neighboring

[1] For more on this see Khalidi, *Palestinian Identity*.

Iraq, for example, to be part of "Syria." Thus, the Syrians had a fairly clear notion of where the boundaries of their own "region" lay and Palestine was deemed an indivisible part of the "Syrian nation" itself,[2] as were Lebanon and Jordan. This concept was neither new nor alien to either the Palestinians or the Syrians, indeed it would become one of the prominent political features of the Faysali era, to be utilized and manipulated by the new reigning powers in the region: the British and French. What then was the origin of this belief and what was the justification for it?

The purpose of this chapter is to provide an introduction to the background of Syria's relationship to Palestine during this crucial juncture in the evolution of its national identity, to investigate the foundations of the notion of "Southern Syria," and discuss the various factors and influences that played a role in endowing this notion with importance as a definitive part of Syria's evolving national consciousness and discourse. The chapter begins by providing a brief historical background of the setting; it then examines the general Arab perspective in the region regarding the Southern Syria notion and analyzes its development; finally, it examines the various external influences that played a role in defining this concept and shaping its development. This chapter also considers the Ottoman administrative arrangements extant in the region up until the end of the First World War and their role in providing the structural foundation for the notion, in addition to the European Powers' role in the region, the developing struggle for power and spheres of influence between them, and their subsequent influence on the development of this notion, particularly in the immediate aftermath of the war.

The Setting

When Faysal triumphantly marched into Damascus on October 3, 1918, he ushered in a new era beyond his expectations and certainly far beyond his control. The war had brought about the fall of the Ottoman Empire and with it the end of a way of life that was centuries old. Faysal's advance on Damascus demonstrated the necessity for reevaluating the extant historical and cultural foundations and the need for shifting the traditional foci of allegiance in accordance with the changing circumstances. It was a new dawn, breathing a new life, begging new questions, and necessitating new demands. The time had finally come to act upon those tenets of Arabism that had been developing for so long, to put them into practice and, more importantly, to deal with all the fears, apprehensions, and suspicions of western imperialism's imminent designs on the region.[3]

---

[2]This point is discussed in further detail in chapters 2, 3, and 4, below.

[3]For a discussion of the development and popularity of the early Arab movement during the late Ottoman period see C. E. Dawn, *From Ottomanism to Arabism: Essays on the Origins of Arab Nationalism* (Urbana, 1973), 122-179; Rashid Khalidi, "Ottomanism and Arabism in Syria before 1914: A Reassessment," in Rashid Khalidi (ed), *The Origins*

In accordance with its status as Arabism's "beating heart," Damascus welcomed its new Arab "conqueror" with open arms, giving him a reception worthy of a king.[4] Since the security blanket provided by the Ottoman Empire for all these centuries had finally been rent by war, leaving nothing in its wake but this young Arab prince to guide the way, the fact that Faysal was neither really a conqueror nor a king was under the circumstances quite irrelevant. He was the representative of the new trend and, in the eyes of most Syrians, the only viable hope for the future.

In the minds of both its original adherents and newly gained supporters, the Arab movement, culminating in the recent Arab Revolt, had been fought to liberate and unite all the Arabs, to revive and rejuvenate their once glorious past.[5] The Arab flag, which now fluttered over Damascus and most "Syrian" cities, was a clear illustration of those Arab aspirations. Its very colors—black, white, green, and red—were emblematic of the Arab historical heritage as represented by the great Islamic Arab dynasties of the past: black symbolizing the banner of the Rightly Guided Caliphs and the Abbasids, white for the banner of the Umayyads, green for the banner of the Prophet, and red for the recent Arab revolt.[6]

Syria therefore euphorically hailed the arrival of the victorious young Arab Amir as he carried the first Arab banner of the modern age and proclaimed a united Arab nation—with Damascus as its capital—as the foremost national goal, thus declaring Arabism the order of the day. Soon enough, however, circumstances would force them to awaken, somewhat rudely, from these Arabist pipe dreams. Almost immediately following the cessation of hostilities, the harsh post-war realities became all too apparent and it was clear to the

---

of Arab Nationalism (New York, 1991), 50-69; and C. E. Dawn, "The Origins of Arab Nationalism," in ibid., 3-30. For a discussion of Ottoman politics and the role of the Arab deputies in the Ottoman parliament see Rashid Khalidi, *British Policy towards Syria and Palestine 1906-1914: A Study of the antecedents of the Hussein-McMahon Correspondence, the Sykes-Picot Agreement and the Balfour Declaration* (London, 1980), 200-359.

[4]Yūsuf al-Ḥakīm, *Sūriyah wa-al-ʿAhd al-Fayṣalī* (Beirut, 1986), 23.

[5]For a detailed account of the Arab Revolt see Amīn al-Saʿīd, *al-Thawrah al-ʿArabīyah al-Kubrá: tārīkh mufaṣṣal jāmiʿ lil-qaḍīyah al-ʿArabīyah fī rubʿ qarn* (Cairo, [1934]); also, T. E. Lawrence, *Seven Pillars of Wisdom: the complete 1922 text* (Fordingbridge, Hampshire, 2004); T. E. Lawrence, *Revolt in the desert* (New York, 1927); Sulaymān Mūsá, *al-Thawrah al-ʿArabīyah al-kubrá: al-ḥarb fī al-Ḥijāz, 1916-1918* (Amman, 1989); and Eliezer Tauber, *The Arab movements in World War I* (London, 1993).

[6]It is also said that the colors of the flag were inspired by a poem, written by Ṣafī al-Dīn al-Ḥillī, in which he states: "We are a nation whose morals and honor prevent us from initiating harm towards those who have not harmed us, white are our deeds, black are our battlefields, green are our pastures and red are our swords." Salmá al-Ḥaffār al-Kuzbarī, *Luṭfī al-Ḥaffār, 1885-1968: mudhakkirātuh, ḥayātuh wa ʿaṣruh* (Beirut, 1997), 77.

Arab nationalists and their new leader that their initial hopes of universal Arab unity were not going to materialize, at least not in the near future. It became imperative therefore, for both the leadership and populace, to begin restricting their thinking and goals to more regional "Syrian" terms—a "Syria" which itself was in serious danger of dismemberment. Consequently, it was crucial that the boundaries of their "Syrianness" be clearly defined on both the physical and intellectual levels in order to be able to function and interact in the new post-war reality.

While it can be argued that a substantial majority of politically-conscious Syrians bowed to the dream of Arab unity and pledged their allegiance to Arab nationalism, political realities nevertheless dictated that even if they were to play an active role in realizing this dream, they still needed to act from a "Syrian" point of departure. In other words, it was incumbent upon them to think first in terms of a feasibly attainable Syria, regardless of its inherent significance to the greater cause of Arab unity, and then in terms of their ultimate goal. The immediate task therefore lay in determining what constituted an integral part of the Syrian "nation", how was this nation to be defined and governed, and, perhaps most importantly, how it could be saved from the transparently eager clutches of the colonialists, and indeed where exactly did "Palestine" figure into this "Syrian" equation.

Despite Faysal and his liberating Arab army's proclamations of unity and independence for all of Syria,[7] the facts on the ground were that the "Syrian region" was already divided into four, allegedly temporary, military administrations or "Occupied Enemy Territory Administrations" (O.E.T.A.), controlled by three different powers. The first (O.E.T.A. East) encompassed the Syrian interior from ʿAqaba to Aleppo and was under Arab control—Faysal's ostensible domain. The second (O.E.T.A. West) encompassed Lebanon and the Syrian coast from Tyre to the confines of Cilicia and was under French military administration. The third (O.E.T.A. South) encompassed Palestine and was under British military control. The final area (O.E.T.A. North), encompassing Cilicia, was also under French control, "but this lay outside the Arab rectangle."[8]

---

[7]See, for example, Faysal's proclamation of an independent Arab state in Syria in the name of his father, the "Sultan Husayn", on October 2, 1918, *al-Sharīf Fayṣal yuʿlin taʾsīs al-dawlah al-ʿArabīyah fī Sūrīyah bi-ism "al-Sulṭān" Ḥusayn,* full text in Dhūqān Qarqūṭ (ed.), *al-Mashriq al-ʿArabī fī Muwājahat al-Istiʿmār: Qirāʾah fī Tārīkh Sūrīyā al-Muʿāṣir* ([Cairo], 1977), 17.

[8]George Antonius, *The Arab Awakening: the Story of the Arab National Movement* (Beirut, 1969), 279. While many Arab and Syrian nationalists vehemently contested this region demanding that it too constituted part of the Syrian and Arab "homeland", Turkey always claimed it as a Turkish region on account of its large Turkish population. It was ultimately given to Turkey by the French on the eve of the Second World War as a price for their neutrality. The Turkish government nevertheless did hold a controversial

While the Arabs could find some consolation in the fact that at least one part of Syria—that encompassing Damascus—was under an Arab administration, in reality, even the area presumably under Faysal's control was largely at the Allies' mercy: it clearly did not exercise full independence nor did its future appear certain. Faysal's only course of action, it seemed, was to try to hold onto as much of Syria as he possibly could in the face of France's determination to seize it all as its own rightful dominion in accordance with their previous agreement with Britain, better known as Sykes-Picot.[9] His task was further complicated by the vacillating position of his British allies—his only real source of political support in the international arena.

The British, for their part, not only had their own definitive plans for at least part of that region, they also made seemingly incompatible promises to three different parties regarding its future: Faysal's father, the Sharif Husayn of Mecca and self-proclaimed "King of the Arabs," the French, and eventually, the Zionists. Above all, the British were forced to consider their promises to the French—the only other superpower in this bargaining frenzy and their staunchest ally during the war—to be the most politically significant and therefore the most binding, their own inclinations notwithstanding. More precisely, it was France which, in the final assessment, was bound to prove the most troublesome to oppose, particularly if it opted to impose its will through direct military action.

Britain's choice to negotiate with the Sharif Husayn of Mecca[10] during the war (through the famous Husayn-McMahon Correspondence[11]) was predicated, among other things, on his religious prestige as a descendent of the Prophet Muhammad and his office as the autonomous governor of the Hijaz—home of the holy cities of Mecca and Medinah. It was a tactical maneuver therefore, that sought to utilize a rebellious Arab Sharif to counterbalance the Ottoman Sultan's own religious prestige as Caliph and undermine his authority both in the eyes of his Arab subjects and their own vast empire's Muslim population.[12]

---

plebiscite in which the population, somewhat predictably, voted to join Turkey. For more on this see Khoury, *Syria and the French Mandate*, 494-514.

[9]The Sykes-Picot Agreement was concluded in London on May 16, 1916. For full text, see Antonius, *Arab Awakening*, 428-430.

[10]Other groups, such as the Syrian Unity Party (*Ḥizb al-Ittiḥād al-Sūrī*) for example, approached the British with similar offers of joining the war effort by revolting against the Ottomans in return for independence, but these negotiations were ultimately not productive since the British had already decided on dealing with the Hashemites. See below (Chapter 4); also see James L. Gelvin, *Divided Loyalties,* 57.

[11]For a full text of the correspondence, see Antonius, *The Arab Awakening*, 413-427.

[12]For a discussion of Sharif Husayn and his dealings with the British and their war aims, see Dawn, *From Ottomanism to Arabism,* 1-68, and 87-121; Abdul Latif Tibawi, *Anglo-Arab Relations and the question of Palestine, 1914-1921* (London, 1977); Elie

Able to unite the Islamic and Arab nationalist causes under his banner, the Sharif Husayn thus emerged as the prime candidate in British eyes for winning the loyalties of an Arab population which was fast becoming disgruntled with the increasingly oppressive rule of the secularist Young Turk regime and their staunchly centralist "Turkification" policies in their provinces. More importantly, Husayn was weak enough to remain fully dependent on British favor in the future. However, the Sharif's success in establishing his popularity and "legitimacy" notwithstanding, Damascus remained as the only natural choice for the capital of the projected "Arab State."

THE ARAB PERSPECTIVE

From its inception as a political entity separate from the Ottoman Empire, Syria, as a recently "liberated"[13] nation—albeit still in the making—struggled to define its geographical boundaries and develop its founding national myths. The Syrian dilemma lay not only in establishing what lay within the realm of Syria's legal dominion as an aspiring sovereign state on the physical level, but indeed in determining how this "Syria" should be defined and how much nationalist loyalty and energy should be expended towards its maintenance and well-being as a unique, separate and distinct national entity.

While dilemmas regarding the direction and focus of nationalist loyalty and patriotism might not plague another newborn nation in a different part of the globe to the same degree, these very issues threatened to destroy altogether the nationalist movement in this region. Ideologically speaking, Arab nationalism was the dominant trend in Syria, a nationalist philosophy espousing the revival and preservation of the cohesive political, geographical, and cultural unity of the entire Arab world.[14] Hence, if Arab nationalism were pursued to its logical conclusion, any "localist" nationalist tendency along

---

Kedourie, *In the Anglo-Arab Labyrinth: the McMahon-Husayn Correspondence and its Interpretations, 1914-1939* (New York, 1976); Mary C. Wilson, *King Abdullah, Britain, and the Making of Jordan* (New York, 1987); William W. Haddad and William Ochsenwald (eds.), *Nationalism in a Non-National State: the Dissolution of the Ottoman Empire* (Columbus, 1977).

[13]The use of the term "liberated" in reference to the status of the territories following the defeat and dissolution of the Ottoman Empire was one used by the Allied Forces, the Arab nationalists, the Syrian political parties, and the Faysali regime, each for their own purposes, as will become evident from their statements in the following chapters.

[14]Perhaps the most eloquent exposition of this ideology, at least at its early stages, can be found in the works of Satiʾ al-Husri; see for example, Abū Khaldūn Sāṭiʿ al-Ḥuṣrī, *Abḥāth mukhtārah fī al-qawmīyah al-ʿArabīyah allatī katabahā wa-nasharahā al-muʾallif fī tawārīkh mukhtalifah 1923-1963* (Beirut, [1974?]); *al-ʿUrūbah bayna duʿātihā wa muʿāriḍihā* (Beirut, 1961); *Mā hiya al-qawmīyah?: abḥāth wa-dirāsāt ʿalá ḍawʾ al-aḥdāth wa-al-naẓarīyāt* (Beirut, [1963]); *Muḥāḍarāt fī nushūʾ al-fikrah al-qawmīyah* (Beirut, 1964), among others.

the lines of "Syrian nationalism" could be viewed as being not only at odds with, but also fundamentally counterproductive to, the greater Arab cause. This seemingly paradoxical situation can be explained by briefly examining the political situation in the region prior to its separation from the Ottoman Empire.[15]

Under Ottoman rule, the Arab provinces, while certainly exposed to western ideas and influences, had generally been somewhat immune to the separatist nationalist fervor that had swept the empire's mainly Christian western provinces. Whether for reasons stemming from loyalty to religion, dynasty, or the establishment as a whole, after four centuries of Ottoman rule, most Arabs believed that they had more to lose by wrecking the Ottoman edifice than to gain by vague promises of independence.

On the one hand, the empire undeniably functioned as the final bastion of Islam against an ever-encroaching Christian west: the ultimate barrier standing between European colonialism and the remaining lands of Islam not presently under their sway. Nor were these Western colonial designs in any way secret; indeed, for decades, there had been an ongoing debate among the European powers, otherwise known as the "Eastern Question," over who should get which of the empire's provinces the minute the "Sick Man" died. (The fact that, up until the war, Britain and France had made it their policy to defend the Empire's existence on the premise of preserving order and maintaining the status quo should be viewed more as a tactic of temporarily delaying the inevitable in the hope of enhancing their own bargaining position in these negotiations.)

On the other hand, those Arabs directly exposed to the notions of "nation" and "nationalism" were generally educated in the West or in western institutions based in the region and, more often than not, belonged to the notable classes which had more of a stake in the empire's continued existence than in its disintegration.[16] They alternatively sought to adopt and adapt these western

---

[15]There are a number of studies that provide a detailed discussion of the history and development of the early Arab movement, for example: Antonius, *The Arab Awakening;* Dawn, *From Arabism to Ottomanism;* Hasan Kayalı, *Arabs and Young Turks: Ottomanism, Arabism, and Islamism in the Ottoman Empire, 1908-1918* (Berkeley, c1997); Khalidi, *The Origins of Arab Nationalism*; Sulaymān Mūsá, *al-Ḥarakah al-ʿArabīyah: sirat al-marḥalah al-ūlá lil-nahḍah al-ʿArabīyah al-Ḥadīthah, 1908-1924* (Beirut, 1977); Bassam Tibi, *Arab nationalism: A Critical Enquiry*, edited and translated by Marion Farouk-Sluglett and Peter Sluglett (New York, 1981); Zeine N. Zeine, *The Emergence of Arab nationalism; with a background study of Arab-Turkish relations in the Near East* (Delmar, N.Y., [1973]), among others.

[16]One particular group who, by virtue of their background and circumstances, were noticeably exposed to western education, ideas, and ideals in the region were the Christian minority. This group's role in the development of the early Arab cultural "awakening," or *al-nahḍah,* towards the end of the nineteenth century certainly cannot be ignored,

political ideas and notions to the Ottoman situation in an attempt to reform and rejuvenate the empire from within, rather than pursuing the course of independence and secession.[17]

The efforts of these Ottoman reformers, Turkish, Arab, and otherwise, were not entirely fruitless and played a role in the institution of the era of *Tanzimat*, a period of reform or reorganization. During this *Tanzimat* era, they managed to introduce various important measures aimed at political and constitutional reform, such as the decrees of *Hatt-ı Şerif of Gülhane* of 1839 and *Hatt-ı Humayun* of 1856 which guaranteed the equality of all the Sultan's subjects before the law regardless of religious faith, the promulgation of the short-lived Ottoman constitution of 1876, and the attempt to create a modern Ottoman-based nationalism—or Ottomanism—with the empire as the central focus of its loyalty.

It was patently clear, more importantly, even to those individuals whose dedication to the principles of Arab nationalism and independence did come to supersede their Ottoman loyalties that, if they were to form a potentially successful independence movement to liberate them from the Empire, outside support and assistance was crucial. Since this assistance, almost inevitably, needed to be sought from the Empire's European rivals—the only powers with the capability and vested interest to offer such help—it meant that, in all likelihood, it would only be offered at an exorbitant price. As Rashid Khalidi states:

---

nor can the names of such people as Butrus al-Bustani, Nasif al-Yaziji and Ibrahim al-Yaziji. While, theoretically speaking, this group certainly may have had more to gain from the establishment of an independent, secular Arab state in which they would be regarded as equal citizens, nevertheless, as a minority, the Arab Christians continued to function, develop, and expound their views and goals in tandem with the Muslim Arab nationalists. Nor, for example, did they endeavor to establish a separate Christian state with the help of the Christian powers, viewing themselves as Arabs first and foremost. The only exceptions, of course, were the Maronite Christians of Lebanon. Lebanon, however, had enjoyed a unique autonomous status under Ottoman rule since 1860 thanks to French intervention and guardianship. It is not surprising therefore, that the Maronites' principal aspiration was to form an independent Lebanese state with a distinctly Christian character under French tutelage, free from any other outside influence or intervention. For a general history of modern Lebanon see Kamal Salibi, *A House of Many Mansions: the History of Lebanon Reconsidered* (London, 1988).

[17]For a study of the different Arab thinkers and trends in thought in the Ottoman Empire from the late 18th through the mid-20th centuries, see for example Albert Hourani, *Arabic Thought in the Liberal Age, 1798-1939* (New York, 1991); Marwan Buheiry (ed.), *Intellectual Life in the Arab East, 1890-1939* (Beirut, 1981); William L. Cleveland, *Islam Against the West: Shakib Arslan and the Campaign for Islamic Nationalism* (Austin, 1985); William L. Cleveland, *The Making of an Arab Nationalist: Ottomanism and Arabism in the Life and Thought of Satiʾ al-Husri* (Princeton, 1971).

> All Arab nationalists in 1914, like the people of Palestine, faced the same dilemma: their understandable inclination to appeal to another Power for assistance against the Turks was necessarily tempered by the knowledge that their benefactor would be sure to demand something in return.[18]

Moreover, if the final objective was achieved and the Ottomans were driven out, the Arabs would ultimately be left at the mercy of these superior Western colonial powers, and would have to contend with their unmistakable aspirations in the region. Consequently, striving for independence was a decision that certainly had to be weighed carefully and was not very likely to find unqualified support among the predominantly Muslim indigenous population.

Once a proto-nationalism did begin to take root in the Syrian region in the latter years of the empire, it generally took the form of an "Arab" rather than a distinctly "Syrian" nationalism, choosing the broader Arab identity as its focus over an even more confined "Syrian" alternative. Furthermore, at least in its initial stages, Arabism was largely a cultural movement, better known as *al-Nahḍah*—the "renaissance," intent on reviving the Arabs' sense of literary heritage, culture, and arts rather than espousing any political goals. Even as it became steadily more politicized, particularly following the Young Turk Revolution of 1908 and the Turkification policies of the Committee for Union and Progress (C.U.P.), it nevertheless remained relatively tame in its aspirations (particularly in comparison to other similar movements within the empire). This early stage of Arabism never demanded complete secession from the Ottomans, but rather limited its demands to more rights, or, at its most ambitious moments, autonomy within the framework of the empire. It remained, moreover, a minority movement, never being able to effectively compete with the greater bonds of Islam and loyalty to the empire and the security it provided.[19]

The brutal policies of Jamal Pasha in Syria (known to its inhabitants as *Jamāl Bāshā al-Saffāḥ*—"Jamal Pasha the Butcher") during the war, however, drove the Arabist societies to become more radicalized until they finally strove for complete independence. The Hashemite-led Arab Revolt of 1916 consequently seemed to be an inexorable conclusion that rose from a different quarter, the autonomous Hijaz.

While it was not the staging point of the Arab revolt, Syria was nevertheless

---

[18] Khalidi, *British Policy towards Syria and Palestine,* 357.

[19] See n. 1, above. This latter fact might explain why a Syrian nationalism of an even more limited focus never took root; for, with the trouble Arabism was having, competing with the loyalties to the firmly established, broad bonds of the great Islamic Empire, an ideology focusing on an even more restricted local Syrian bond would have found even fewer adherents.

intimately bound to Arab nationalism, rendering Damascus the natural choice for the first Arab capital. Indeed, Damascus had developed a well-established tradition and reputation as the hub of Arab nationalism. The secret societies devoted to this cause were generally either founded or had a base in that city, and a substantial majority of the membership in these societies was Syrian.[20] As such, Damascus became known as the "beating heart of Arabism"—*qalb al-ʿUrūbah al-nābiḍ*—and was a meeting place for all the young revolutionary adherents to this new ideology, from Syria as well as other Arab regions.

While outwardly, Arabism was an ideology that ultimately advocated taking control of the destiny of the entire "Arab nation," internally it was Syrian in character. As Philip Khoury wrote:

> Prior to 1914, Arabism was a Syrian-inspired and Syrian-dominated ideology. Syrians, whether political activists operating in Syrian towns, or in Istanbul, or exiled intellectuals sitting in Cairo and Paris, directed the nascent 'Arab movement'. Furthermore, Syrian localist and personal ambitions and conflicts were as much involved in the development of the ideology and its dissemination as were the cultural and political expressions which lent it content.[21]

The connection between Syria and the early Arab nationalist movement was quite profound; Arabism was Syria's initial response to nationalism and nationalist tendencies, and as such, Arab nationalist issues would have a deep resonance in Syria and Syrian politics. The fact that Damascus did become the capital of the first "Arab State" therefore was appropriate to its status and role in the Arab movement.

The Amir Faysal, the Sharif Husayn's third son, now provided the Arab nationalists with a young, dynamic leader for their cause and, initially, it appeared that the Hashemites, through their British connections, might manage to secure the desired goals of Arab unity and independence after all. As leader of the Arab nationalist cause, however, Faysal's following and power base in Syria was drawn primarily from the Arab nationalists, most of whom were young, politically inexperienced, and burning with the zealous fervor of their ideals.[22] Moreover, a number of those young Arab nationalists were not Syrians; to them the greater Arab cause reigned supreme and Syria's interests were at very best in second place. As such, they were the least willing to yield

[20] See, for example, Dawn, *From Arabism to Ottomanism*, 148-179.

[21] Philip S. Khoury, *Urban Notables and Arab Nationalism,* 68.

[22] For a discussion of the socio-economic background of the adherents to the early Arabist movement and their motivations, see Rashid Khalidi, "Social Factors in the Rise of the Arab Movement in Syria," in Said Amir Arjomand (ed.), *From Nationalism to Revolutionary Islam* (New York, 1984), 53-70; cf. Dawn, *From Arabism to Ottomanism*, 148-179.

in circumstances that unfortunately demanded the most concessions and thus proved to be the stumbling block that led to Faysal's ultimate undoing.

Nevertheless, whether dedicated to a comprehensive Arab unity free from all foreign fetters or not, it became clear to Faysal and his Arab nationalist retinue quite early that they had to focus on Syria first, if only as a preliminary step, to create a base of action from which to realize their ultimate goal of unity. With the immediate battle revolving around Syria, the question then became how to define and distinguish "natural Syria"—*Sūrīyah al-ṭabīʿīyah*—from its surroundings. More importantly, where did the boundaries of "Mother Syria"—*Sūrīyah al-Umm*—begin?[23] Where did they end? How would the borders of the new state be drawn? Moreover, how did "Palestine" fit into this picture?

In a region where identities were based on a broad spectrum of personal loyalties and affiliations, including religion, family, clan, village, town, and city, creating a set of geographical borders that would become the focus of all "national" allegiance was not a simple task. Nevertheless, outlining the geographic boundaries that defined "Syria" was not in itself a forbidding endeavor. Preceding Ottoman administrative practices combined with Syria's long historical, cultural, religious, linguistic, and commercial traditions provided a workable structural foundation for determining what areas comprised the Syrian region. Consequently, regardless of the differences among Syrians in terms of their loyalties towards the greater Arab cause, how they defined and envisioned their ultimate goals, and what steps they deemed necessary for their realization, some consensus could be reached among them over what constituted the "Syrian nation" and what should not be compromised at least on this immediate level.

One of the first groups to ascribe to Syria a set of "national" geographic boundaries as a principal part of its political program was *Ḥizb al-Ittiḥād al-Sūrī* (the Syrian Unity Party) founded by a group of Syrian émigrés residing in Egypt in mid-1918, shortly before the war ended. [24] They defined Syria's borders as follows:

> from the Taurus Mountains in the north, from the Khabur until the Euphrates to the east, the Arabian desert until Maydan Salih to the south, and the Red Sea until ʿAqaba, and Rafah until the Mediterranean to the west.[25]

[23] Such terminology as "natural Syria" and "Mother Syria" would subsequently become popular in the writings of *al-Ḥizb al-Qawmī al-Sūrī al-Ijtimāʿī* (the Syrian Social Nationalist Party) and its founder Antun Saʿadah. See for example Anṭūn Saʿādah, *al-Āthār al-Kāmilah* (Beirut, 1978-1989); also of interest is Anṭūn Saʿādah, *Marāḥil al-Masʿalah al-Filasṭīnīyah, 1921-1949* (Beirut, 1977).

[24] For a detailed discussion of this group, see chapter 4, below.

[25] Amīn al-Saʿīd, *al-Thawrah al-ʿArabīyah al-Kubrá,* 1: 41.

Almost a year later, one of the first resolutions of the First General Syrian Congress held in Damascus in June 1919, was to demand independence for Syria roughly within these exact same borders, thereby formally establishing the map of Syria in the evolving Syrian national discourse:

> We ask for complete political independence for Syria within these boundaries. The Taurus system on the North; Rafah and a line running from Al Jauf to the south of the Syrian and the Hejazian line to Akaba on the south; the Euphrates and Khabur rivers and a line extending east of Abu Kamal to the east of Al Jauf on the east; and the Mediterranean on the west. [26]

It is evident from this demarcation of Syrian boundaries that "Palestine" —or what would become the British Mandate of Palestine two years later—was considered an integral part of the incipient Syrian nation, as were Jordan and Lebanon. This was not a one-sided notion on the part of the Damascenes, or the Arab nationalists in Faysal's retinue for example, to increase their immediate territorial gains in the post-war settlement. On the contrary, this sentiment gained widespread support and the full backing of a substantial number of the Palestinian population (and of many Lebanese) as well. [27] Hence, as the question of Palestine began to develop into a major dilemma that would affect the entire Middle East for decades to come, its immediate effects on Syria were threefold.

First was the broader Islamic dimension that held Palestine, and more specifically Jerusalem, in high religious esteem, both as the first *qiblah*[28] and home of the third holiest shrine in Islam, the al-Aqsa mosque (*ulá al-qiblatayn wa-thālith al-ḥaramayn*). The fall of Palestine into non-Muslim hands was considered a blow to Muslim prestige worldwide. On the other hand, the fact that Palestine was designated to become a Jewish homeland was no less of an outrage to Christian Arabs in Syria, Palestine, and elsewhere in the Arab Middle East. [29] The position of the native Jewish community in Syria, at least initially,

---

[26] "Resolutions of the General Syrian Congress at Damascus, 2 July 1919," in J. C. Hurewitz (ed.), *Diplomacy in the Near and Middle East, A Documentary Record: 1914-1956* (Princeton, 1956), 2: 63.

[27] See chapters 2 and 3, below.

[28] Direction towards which the Muslims turn in prayer. Jerusalem was initially the first *qiblah* until superseded in status by Mecca.

[29] This position is clear from the stance of the various Christian patriarchs as well as the secular Christian politicians in the region regarding the foundation of the Jewish State, not to mention the various Muslim-Christian associations in Palestine. The position of the Christian religious leadership towards Faysal, for example, is demonstrated early on by their oath of allegiance to him and to a united Syria (including Palestine) at the Damascus Town Hall Meeting of May 1919 (discussed in more detail below). For a full

appeared to be in favor of unity, independence, and essentially supportive of Faysal and his rule.[30] The Jewish position was logical considering that these communities, though small in number, had long been established in the region, managed to prosper, and coexisted relatively peacefully with their neighbors. As a result, they had much to lose by openly supporting the foundation of a prospective Jewish state of uncertain future, thus jeopardizing their standing within the society by declaring their national solidarity with the rest of their Syrian compatriots.

Second, from the purely Arab nationalist perspective, the Syrians, like other Arab nationalists, were quite loath to see Arab lands divided among the allies under the guise of the Mandate system, a reality that constituted the materialization of their worst nightmare. Syria was nevertheless doubly committed to the Palestinian issue on this level, for a number of reasons. Ideologically speaking, Damascus, as previously mentioned, was the beacon of Arab nationalism; hence, it was incumbent upon the Syrians to be the standard-bearers of its tenets. Conceding Palestine as a Jewish national home, which many saw as a modern foreign colony reminiscent of the Crusader Kingdoms, was simply unacceptable and could not be reconciled in any way with the most fundamental basics of Arab nationalism. Moreover, Syria was to become the first modern "Arab State," flying the first Arab flag, and ostensibly ruled by an Arab nationalist government under an Arab nationalist king, a hero of the Arab revolt. As such, its position and standing dictated certain obligations and responsibilities; Syria, in this new historic role, could not afford to take a compromising stance on Palestine—at least not in any official or public capacity. (After all, Syria's leader technically represented the Arabs and their cause in international circles.) Syria's politics were thus intimately bound to Arab nationalist issues, and the question of Palestine as it unfolded became one of the most pertinent problems in the Arab political arena, a fundamental grievance in a long list of Arab grievances.

Finally, for those who were less inclined to push Syria into taking a

---

transcript in English see *Emir Feisal's Address to the Notables of Syria in the Town Hall of Damascus, the 9 May, 1919, at 3 p.m.*, Enclosure 2 in No. 182, Appendix A, in *Documents on British Foreign Policy, 1919-1939*, edited by E. L. Woodward and Rohan Butler (London, 1952), 4: 268. Perhaps the exception to this rule were the Maronites in Mount Lebanon who were willing to concede the foundation of a Jewish homeland in Palestine and recognize the significance of establishing of a Jewish state in the region as a means of further legitimizing their own unique status and plans for establishing a Christian state in Lebanon.

[30]The position of the indigenous Jewish community, as represented by their Religious Head, can also be gauged by the latter's position at the Damascus Town Hall Meeting (described in more detail below) where he was equally enthusiastic to give Faysal his support and allegiance. In fact his exact statement was, "Our possessions and our souls are in your hands." Ibid., 271.

leadership role in an inter-Arab capacity, and chose instead to focus mainly on Syrian issues and Syrian development, Palestine remained an integral part of their political program. Palestine was deemed an indivisible part of the Syrian nation; consequently, acceding to its severance from the Syrian whole was agreeing to the dismemberment of Syria itself. (Not to mention the fact that this "southern region" of Syria was to become colonized as a home for a foreign minority.) Agreeing to a separate Palestine under a British regime intent upon creating a Jewish state not only meant acquiescing to a temporary division of the Arab lands among the colonial powers, but, more importantly, to the permanent mutilation of the Syrian homeland.

Thus, regardless of religious affiliation, political proclivities, or nationalist inclinations, the prevailing Syrian political climate dictated that Palestine was and needed to be considered part and parcel of any political resolution involving Syria. The Palestinians themselves played a role in the Syrian political process from its inception, and Palestinians such as ʿAwni ʿAbd al-Hadi, Muhammad ʿIzzat Darwazah and ʿIsa al-ʿIsa served Faysal as ministers and members of parliament in Faysal's government from the outset.[31]

Moreover, this sense of internal unity, which included the Palestinians as an essential component, was demonstrated at the historic Damascus Town Hall meeting on May 9, 1919, at which the Palestinians were represented along with all other regions, religious and tribal groups within "Geographic Syria." This meeting, one of the earliest and clearest illustrations of Syrian national solidarity, was attended by delegates from the regions of Hawran, Damascus, Baalbek, Homs, Jabal ʿAmil, Hama, Aleppo, Maʿarat al-Nuʿman, Tripoli, Beirut, Sidon, Amman, Latakia, Salt, Lebanon, and Palestine, the tribes of Amiriyin, Ruwala, the Druze of Hawran, the Druze of Lebanon, and the Kurds of Tripoli, in addition to the Catholic Patriarch of Syria, the Greek Orthodox Patriarch of Syria, the Mutran of the Syrian Catholic Church, and the Religious Head of the Jews.[32]

At this meeting, Faysal addressed all the notables of Syria, requesting their allegiance and approval for his leadership and actions, both past and present. In the course of his speech, Faysal explained his political stance and posed the following questions to his constituents:

> Does the nation depend upon the one that is pleading her cause? Does the nation permit me to handle her internal and foreign affairs, or not? Does the nation back me in speech and in action in all that I do in the country and outside; and does the nation give me all that I ask for without objection or discussion?[33]

---

[31] Khalidi, *Palestinian Identity*, 164.

[32] *Emir Feisal's Address to the Notables of Syria*, 267-8.

[33] Ibid., 268.

The Palestinian delegate was one of the first to respond to Faysal's beckoning, boldly stating, "The blood and the property of the Palestinians are yours."[34] The Palestinians, at least insofar as this delegation represented their views, therefore clearly considered themselves to be part of the Syrian nation.

Southern Syria: Historical Foundations

While the Islamic and Arab nationalist positions in Syria toward Palestine are broad enough to render in terms of opposing the division and colonization of Arab/Islamic lands, the Syrian nationalist position in this regard requires more explanation. How did the Syrians come to view Palestine as an integral part of Syria itself and indeed why would a substantial number of Palestinians have come to share this view?

Traditionally, Palestine fell into the historical geographic demarcation of *Bilād al-Shām*, a term coined earlier than the Islamic conquests. Nevertheless, this term was more of conventional regional distinction and not based on any ideological "nationalist" foundations, and was consequently somewhat vague in terms of specific territorial boundaries.[35]

According to Arab nationalist ideology as it would later develop, the entire Arabic-speaking world formed one indivisible entity and therefore should naturally be united on that basis and Palestine was included with Syria as a part of that Arab whole. Unlike most other Arab states that saw the Palestinian dilemma as an affront to their Arab nationalist and religious sensibilities, the Syrians saw the Palestinian question in its incipient stages as a challenge to Syria's own natural boundaries, a blow at the heart of the prospective state of Syria—constituting the loss of its southern region. "Palestine" therefore possessed a special place in Syrian nationalist discourse, since its loss was perceived not only as a blow against the Arabs and the Arab nationalist ideal, but as an outright division and partitioning of "Syria" itself.[36]

---

[34] Ibid., 269. In fact, the Palestinian delegate was the second to give his oath of allegiance to Faysal. For a full transcript of the address in English, see ibid., 267-272.

[35] Etymologically the term *Bilād al-Shām* derives from *Bilad al-Shamāl*, or "the left-hand region," because, as Bosworth puts it, "in ancient Arab usage the speaker in western or central Arabia was considered to face the rising sun and to have Syria on his left and the Arabian Peninsula, with Yaman (the "right hand region") on his right." C. E. Bosworth, "al-Shām" in *The Encyclopaedia of Islam*, edited by C. E. Bosworth et al. (Leiden, 1996), 9: 261.

[36] It is important to note that this analysis of the Arab nationalist ideological position, as previously mentioned, is one that does not take its full form until years later. At this particular historical juncture, no states as such had formed in much of the Arab world. Furthermore, the sentiment towards Palestine had not yet crystallized to the extent that it would decades later, particularly after the 1936-1939 revolt in Palestine and especially after the Palestine War of 1948.

As a part of the Ottoman Empire, which itself was constantly subject to external pressures in forming its internal policies, the fate of the region encompassing both "Syria" and "Palestine" was largely in the hands of external powers and there were no independent indigenous governments controlling those regions that were capable of making a conscious and unanimous decision to finally unite the two areas, or indeed divide them, based on the direct wishes of their inhabitants. The area was therefore conceptually defined by those external powers, based on their own international political considerations and agreements concluded according to administrative facility. These European powers constantly had the advantage in drawing boundaries and shaping the region according to their own interests, and had a tremendous influence on the indigenous inhabitants' worldview and their concepts of nationality and nationhood. Their perspectives consequently deserve closer examination.

Ottoman Perspective and Structure

As the supreme reigning power for four centuries, the most pertinent influence upon the region had naturally been that of the Ottoman Empire. Under the Ottomans, the "Syrian region" was governed as the *vilayet* of *Şam* (or *al-Shām* in Arabic—"Syria") and, as such, generally included Palestine within the scope of its administration. Palestine, or *Filasṭīn*, as it was known to its inhabitants, was recognized as a geographical region, but not one with distinct boundaries and, except for a very brief period in 1872, was never governed as a whole independently under Ottoman rule.[37] References in Ottoman official correspondence to *Arz-i Filistin* ("Land of Palestine") apparently referred to the area west of the River Jordan[38] (this same area would later become the British Mandate of Palestine in 1922). As a part of the *vilayet* of *Şam* (Syria), the geographic area of Palestine was divided into three *sancak*s: Jerusalem, Nablus, and Acre, each governed by a *mutasarrif*, with subordinates or deputies (*kaymakams*) governing the main towns, such as Jaffa, Gaza, Tiberias, and Safed.[39]

In the late 1880s, however, the v*ilayet* of *Şam* underwent some administrative reorganization; the s*ancak* of Jerusalem subsequently attained more of an autonomous status by becoming a *mutasarriflik* in 1887, with its *mutasarrif* responsible directly to Istanbul. Furthermore, in 1888, a new *vilayet* of Beirut

---

[37]Palestine was governed as an independent *vilayet* for a very brief period in 1872, but the Ottoman administration soon reconsidered their decision and, as a compromise, they created an independent *sanjaq* of Jerusalem including only the southern part of Palestine, which was answerable directly to Constantinople, in 1874. For a more detailed examination, see Alexander Schölch, *Palestine in Transformation, 1856-1882: Studies in Social, Economic and Political Development* (Washington, D.C., 1993), 13-14.

[38]Neville J. Mandel, *The Arabs and Zionism before World War I* (Berkeley, 1980), xx.

[39]Ibid., xix-xx. See also ʿAbd al-ʿAzīz ʿAwaḍ, *al-Idārah al-ʿUthmānīyah fī Wilāyat Sūrīyah, 1864-1914* (Cairo, 1969).

was created and the northern *sancak*s of Nablus and Acre were transferred under its administration.[40] Hence, on the eve of the First World War, southern Palestine was governed from Jerusalem, while the north was governed from Beirut. Nevertheless, as Khoury points out, "between these different units peoples and goods moved back and forth unencumbered by the bureaucratic processes and taxes associated with borders."[41]

With the fall of the Ottoman empire and the absence of a central government in a distant capital to impose such administrative reshuffles, it seems understandable why the inhabitants of that region viewed themselves as one "nation" placing themselves under the purview of a single regional government (based in Damascus or otherwise), provided that on the local level, problems were still addressed in the traditional way: by the local religious representatives, town and village elders, familiar *mukhtārs* (or governmental officials), and the patronage of the local notables. The Ottomans had thus set the conceptual and administrative framework for a united Syria in place.

EUROPEAN PERSPECTIVE, POLITICS, AND TERMINOLOGY

While the Ottomans did rule the "Syrian region" for four centuries, their authority and control were not entirely undisputed and they often succumbed to external European pressures that influenced their official schemes for the administration and management of the area. European involvement, motivated by imperial competition over spheres of interest, became a pertinent factor in the region's development. The European powers' (primarily British and French) perspectives and their understanding of the region ultimately played the most crucial role in endowing it with its final definitive shape—particularly after the Europeans became the region's new masters following the Ottoman Empire's demise.

While Palestine had traditionally been accorded a special status as the "holy land," central to all three major monotheistic religions, the Ottomans had managed, for the most part, to keep it secure from any attempts at direct European control. This looming threat may have played a direct role in ensuring that the Ottoman government never permitted Palestine to be governed as an independent *vilayet* for any lengthy period, thereby allowing all the holy places to fall under the authority of one governor and facilitating the task of European penetration.[42]

Consequently, even when intent on severing Palestine from the larger Ottoman body, the European powers tended to view it conceptually as "Southern Syria," or rather, referred to that whole region vaguely as "Syria." Examples of this viewpoint are found in formal conventions as early as the

[40] Mandel, *Arabs and Zionism before World War I,* xx.

[41] Khoury, *Syria and the French Mandate*, 536.

[42] Schölch, *Palestine in Transformation,* 13-14.

treaty of London of 1840. In the separate act to the convention, in return for withdrawing from Arabia, Adana, and all other Ottoman territories outside of Egypt, Mehmet Ali was promised the "command of the fortress of St. John of Acre, the administration of the southern part of Syria, the limits of which shall be determined by the following line of demarkation [*sic*]:

> This line, beginning at Cape Ras-el-Nakhora, on the coast of the Mediterranean, shall extend from thence as far as the mouth of river Seisaban, at the northern extremity of the Lake Tiberias; it shall pass along the Western shore of that Lake, it shall follow the right bank of the river Jordan, and the western shore of the Dead Sea; from thence it shall extend straight to the Red Sea, which it shall strike at the northern point of the Gulf of Akaba, and the eastern shore of the Gulf of Suez, as far as Suez.[43]

Clearly, the "Pashalic of Acre," described as the "southern part of Syria," comprises what would be considered northern "Palestine" less than a century later by those very same powers.

For their part, the French were clearly determined to preserve this Syrian unity after the war, not because of an overwhelming concern to maintain Syria's national, cultural, or territorial integrity, but primarily because they wanted to swallow Syria whole. From the French standpoint, France's interests in Syria were twofold. First, from the larger global perspective, France felt that Syria was crucial to its imperial interests in the Mediterranean. Despite its position in Algeria, and its important territorial gains in Morocco and Tunisia from 1840 and 1914, France never seemed to forget having lost its grip on Egypt. France desired to increase its power in the eastern Mediterranean and the acquisition of the ports of Alexandretta and Haifa would have greatly facilitated that goal.[44]

Second, from a more specific regional perspective, France believed it had a great deal invested in Syria—certainly more than any other Western power—and by virtue of this relationship that dated back to the time of Louis VII (Saint Louis) and the Crusades in the thirteenth century, it believed that it had thus been endowed with "historic rights" to that region. France's view of her "historic rights" and "investment" are best illustrated by Pichon's arguments, described in the minutes of a secret meeting of the Supreme Council in Paris:

> French intervention in Syria had been frequent, the last instance being the case of the expedition organized in Syria

---

[43]Convention (London) for the Pacification of the Levant: Austria, Great Britain, Prussia, and Russia with the Ottoman Empire, 15 July-September 1840. Text in Hurewitz, *Diplomacy in the Near and Middle East*, 1:117.

[44]Leonard Stein, *The Balfour Declaration* (New York, 1961), 47-55.

> and Lebanon in 1860, which had resulted in the establishment of the status of the Lebanon. France he pointed out, had a great number of hospitals in Syria. There were a great number of schools in many villages, and some 50,000 children were educated in French primary schools. There were also a number of secondary schools and one great university in Beyrout. Moreover, the railway system of Syria was French, and included the Beyrout to Damascus line, and Tripoli-Homs line, which latter it was proposed to prolong to the Euphrates and to unite with the Bagdad system. Altogether it was contemplated to have a system of 1,233 kilometers, of which 683 kilometers had already been constructed. Beyrout was entirely a French port. The gas and electricity works were French, and the same applied to the lighting along the coast. This was not the limit of French enterprise, for France had perfected the agriculture and the viticulture of Syria and had established many factories. No other country had anything like so complete a development in these regions. Hence, France could not abandon her rights. Moreover, France strongly protested against any idea of dividing Syria. Syria had geographical and historical unity.[45]

The French, however, did not view their claims on Syria as a form of encroachment on the rights and liberties of an inherently sovereign nation worthy of independence. On the contrary, France believed Syria to be its rightful domain. As French Prime Minister Alexandre Ribot[46] would comment to the French Chamber, on July 21, 1917:

> We do not desire to annex countries by force, but merely to regain that of which we have been robbed![47]

France's obvious sense of entitlement towards Syria meant that it was not about to compromise on what it viewed to be its legitimate sphere of influence. On the eve of World War I therefore, the French immediately began asserting their claims to what they believed to be their due share in the Eastern Question. Accordingly, in October of 1914, shortly after the entrance of the Ottoman Empire into the war, Georges Lèygues, the Chairman of the Foreign Affairs Committee of the Chamber, while addressing the French Geographical

---

[45] Summary Record of a secret meeting of the Supreme Council at Paris to Consider the Sykes-Picot Agreement, 20 March 1919, text in Hurewitz, *Diplomacy in the Near and Middle East*, 2: 52.

[46] Ribot was also Minister of Foreign Affairs.

[47] [FO 882/22] in *Records of the Hashemite Dynasties: A Twentieth Century Documentary History*, ed. by Alan de L. Rush ([Slough], 1995), 10: 352.

Society, declared his country's position and plans towards Syria, explicitly delineating the boundaries of the territory in question:

> The Mediterranean will not be free for us...unless Syria remains in our sphere of influence. By Syria it must be understood, not a Syria mutilated and discrowned, but Syria in its entirety, that which extends from El Arish to the Taurus.[48]

Britain also recognized the geographical cohesion of the area and the difficulties involved in dividing it. Even insofar as the issue of Palestine was concerned, officially speaking, the British themselves did not necessarily distinguish it as a separate national entity distinct from Syria either. For example, the specific "Foreign Office Handbook" entitled *A Handbook of Syria (including Palestine)*, prepared under the direction of the Historical Section of the Foreign Office for the British delegation at the Paris Peace Conference, a text that is fascinating for its drive towards precision in drawing inherently imprecise boundaries, states:

> In the south the boundary between Egypt and Syria, as drawn in 1906, was nearly a straight line from slightly west of Rafah on the Mediterranean to slightly east of Tabah on the Red Sea. The southern boundary was completed by a line starting south of Akaba and running NE. towards Maʿn and the depression of El-Jafar, separating the vilayet of Damascus from the vilayet of the Hejaz.
>
> In modern usage the expression "Palestine" has no precise meaning. No definition can be got merely by discussing or attempting to follow the limits of territory of the ancient Hebrews. The expression is best taken to be equivalent to Southern Syria and then defined in accordance with geographic and political conditions. On this assumption only the northern boundary presents any special difficulty. On the west side of the Jordan the Līṭāni (Nahr al-Qāsimīyeh) from its western bend to its mouth is a definite physical limit. This boundary may be completed eastwards to the Jordan (Nahr Ḥasbāni) in several ways.
>
> The amount of country east of the line of the Jordan that may be reckoned to Palestine depends chiefly on the political situation in Damascus in relation to Palestine. If Damascus itself be associated with southern Syria the difficulty disappears. All that portion of middle Syria that lies to the east of Jebel esh-Sharqi (Anti-Lebanon) may be easily

---

[48] Stein, *The Balfour Declaration,* 53.

> separated from northern Syria and associated with Palestine. If, on the other hand, only a portion of the country along the Hejaz railway line, south of Damascus, is to be united with Palestine, a satisfactory line between the portion dependent on Damascus and that associated with Palestine is not easily found.[49]

Furthermore, when providing statistics and information, the "Handbook" tends to treat the area as a unitary whole in terms of its inhabitants, its cities, its history, religion, culture, agriculture, and economics, even while the ultimate intention is to create borders and partitions.

Britain was aware of France's definition of '*la Syrie intégrale*' from the outset and, up to this point, had disavowed any political aspirations of its own in that area. This is not to imply, however, that the British were happy or even ambivalent about conceding such a large and strategically sensitive area to France.[50] Hence, during their negotiations with the Sharif Husayn, though clearly well apprised of France's ambitions in Syria, the British were already seeking a "legitimate" means of restraining them. Describing the situation in the autumn of 1915, Lord Maugham[51] stated:

> It may be perfectly true that under the influence of Lord Kitchener and others His Majesty's Government before and after the outbreak of the war were anxious to restrict the French claims on the Levant coast if they could find a legitimate means of doing so. But there is a great difference between desiring an object and attaining it. It can be stated as a fact that at the time of the correspondence [with Hussein] France claimed the Mediterranean littoral as far south as the Egyptian border and as far east as Damascus.[52]

More specifically, the British fully understood that France's interpretation of *la Syrie intégrale* clearly encompassed Palestine. This is plainly articulated by Sir Mark Sykes on April 8, 1917—some seven months before the issuance of the Balfour Declaration—in his statement to the Foreign Office:

---

[49] *A Handbook of Syria (Including Palestine): Prepared by the Geographical Section of the Naval Intelligence Division, Naval Staff, Admiralty* (London, [1920]), 10-11.

[50] For more on this see Khalidi, *British Policy towards Syria and Palestine*, 332-359.

[51] At the time, the Lord Chancellor and the principal British representative on the Anglo-Arab Committee, which in 1939 examined the letters exchanged between Sir Henry McMahon and the Sharif Husayn.

[52] Stein, *The Balfour Declaration*, 54-55.

> At present the great mass of Frenchmen interested in Syria, mean Palestine when they say Syria.[53]

What then prompted this British change of heart regarding a hitherto "established" French sphere of influence? Without discounting Britain's imperial self-image as the "New Rome" as a factor—a vision that would remain incomplete without the possession of the province of Palestine—the British nevertheless had other, more concrete, issues to consider. In the words of T. E. Lawrence:

> The French insist on Syria—which we are conceding to them: there remains Alexandretta...It's going to be the head of the Baghdad line, and therefore the natural outlet for N. Syria and N. Mesopotamia...In the hands of France it will provide a sure base for naval attacks on Egypt—and remember with her in Syria, and compulsory service there, she will be able any time to fling 100,000 men against the canal in 12 days from the declaration of war. The Sinai desert is not really an obstacle in the spring—or at any time when the railway (which is inevitable) is built.[54]

"One cannot go on betting," he concluded, "that France will always be our friend."[55]

On the eve of the war therefore, British interest in Palestine, or Syria for that matter, centered mainly on proximity to the Suez Canal and gaining a dominant position in its vicinity (or indeed preventing anyone else from doing so). After the war, the British aimed at creating a land bridge under their control from the Persian Gulf to the Mediterranean, which would have included Palestine and the eastern part of Syria—in other words, the areas Britain had earmarked for the Arabs and the Jews.[56] Attaining this objective, however, meant changing the international status that the Sykes-Picot agreement had established for Syria and Palestine.[57] Hence, at least one of the reasons behind Britain's Balfour Declaration was to ensure a special status for Palestine as a Jewish homeland and, as such, tentative continued British presence and influence

---

[53] Ibid., 45.

[54] "Letter to D.G. Hogarth, 18 March, 1915," in *The Letters of T.E. Lawrence*, edited by David Garnett (New York, 1939), 193.

[55] Ibid., 194. It is noteworthy that in another letter to Hogarth written a few days later on March 22, Lawrence suggests ways in which "we can rush right up to Damascus, and biff the French out of all hope of Syria. It's a big game, and at last one worth playing." Ibid., 196.

[56] For more on this see Khalidi, *British Policy towards Syria and Palestine*.

[57] For the full text of the Sykes-Picot Agreement see Antonius, *The Arab Awakening*, 428-430.

there. Furthermore, by playing its role as the traditional friend and ally of the Arabs, Britain could maintain its position and influence in Faysal's Arab domain as well. The latter, faced with the looming threat of French colonial expansion on the one hand, administrative inexperience and lack of funds on the other, would doubtless remain helpless without British support.

True to their schemes, the British did initially try to prevent France from moving in on both "northern Syria" and "southern Syria" (Palestine)—an issue which was fast becoming very complicated. The private negotiations that took place between the chief conference delegates in Paris behind closed doors provide a clear illustration of the Allies' conflicting interests, and the problems inherent therein.

In a private meeting on March 20, 1919, at the British Prime Minister Lloyd George's residence in Paris, he declared to Pichon "the League of Nations cannot be used to put aside the bargain with King Hussein in North Syria. It has the status of a treaty."[58] He then asked Pichon if the latter "intended to occupy Damascus with French troops? If he did, it would clearly be a violation of the treaty with the Arabs."[59] Nevertheless, as J.M. Jefferies observantly states:

> True as this was, and notable as was the Premier's acknowledgement of the status of the agreement with King Hussein, yet there was something stupendous in the way that Lloyd George could admonish the French for using the League of Nations to put aside the bargain with Hussein in North Syria, while he and Balfour were making ready to use the League of Nations to put aside the bargain with King Hussein in South Syria.[60]

Pichon, understandably upset, retorted, "France had no convention with King Hussein."[61] This was a British agreement and therefore could not be held to be binding on France. He then claimed that:

> This undertaking had been made by Great Britain (*Angleterre*) alone. France had never seen it until a few weeks before when Sir Maurice Hankey handed me a copy of the text.[62]

---

[58]*Notes of a Conference Held in the Prime Minister's Flat at 23 Rue Nitot, Paris, on Thursday, March 20, 1919, at 3 p.m.,* The Council of Four: Minutes of Meetings March 20 to May 24, 1919, in *Papers Relating to the Foreign Relations of the United States: The Paris Peace Conference, 1919* (Washington D.C., 1946), 5: 7.

[59]Ibid.

[60]J. M. N. Jeffries, *Palestine: The Reality* (London, 1939), 270.

[61]*Papers Relating to the Foreign Relations of the United States,* 5: 7.

[62]Ibid.

To this, Lloyd George responded:

> The agreement might have been made by England alone, but it was England who organized the whole of the Syrian campaign. There would have been no question of Syria had it not been for England. Great Britain has put from 900,000 to 1,000,000 men in the field against Turkey, but Arab help had been essential; that is a point upon which Lord Allenby can speak.[63]

At his beckoning, Lord Allenby declared that Arab help "had been invaluable."[64] Lloyd George then defended his position on the grounds that the Sykes-Picot Agreement itself had been based on a letter from Sir Henry McMahon to King Husayn,[65] and that it was on this same basis that King Husayn had "put all his resources in the field which had helped us most materially to win the victory. France had for practical purposes accepted our undertaking to King Hussein in signing the 1916 agreement."[66] Further, Lloyd George stated that he was "bound to say that if the British Government now agreed that Damascus, Homs, Hama and Aleppo should be included in the sphere of direct French influence we should be breaking faith with the Arabs, and we could not face this."[67] Ironically, he did not seem to feel that His Majesty's Government would have any difficulty "facing" the Arabs on the question of Palestine.

Lloyd George then reminded the French that the Sykes-Picot accords had been signed subsequent to Britain's agreements with Husayn and had contained an extract through which France had technically agreed to the terms of these agreements and hence, Arab independence.[68] To this, Pichon replied that there had never been any contest regarding an independent Arab State, but "how could France be bound by an agreement the very existence of which

---

[63] Ibid., 7-8.

[64] Ibid., 8.

[65] The letter Lloyd George is referring to is the Sir Henry McMahon's second letter to the Sharif Husayn, dated October 24, 1915. For the full text, see Antonius, *The Arab Awakening,* 419-420.

[66] *Papers Relating to the Foreign Relations of the United States,* 5: 8.

[67] Ibid.

[68] The extract Lloyd George is referring to is the following:
"It is accordingly understood between the French and British Governments:
That France and Great Britain are prepared to recognize and uphold an independent Arab State or Confederation of Arab States in the areas A. and B. marked on the annexed map under the suzerainty of an Arab Chief."
According to the "map," Damascus, Homs, Hama and Aleppo were included in the area designated to become part of the independent Arab State. Antonius, *The Arab Awakening,* 428-9.

was unknown to her at the time when the 1916 agreement was signed?"[69] He continued:

> In the 1916 Agreement France had not in anyway recognized the Hedjaz. She had undertaken to uphold "an independent Arab State or Confederation of Arab States," but not the King of the Hedjaz. If France was promised a mandate for Syria, she would do nothing except in agreement with the Arab State or Confederation of Arab States. This is the role which France demanded in Syria. If Great Britain would only promise her good offices...France could reach an understanding with Feisal.[70]

Both Britain and France were thus clearly engaged in a tug of war over the spoils of the Ottoman Empire and, more importantly, in a regional struggle for power aimed at driving the other out so that each could deal with the Arabs directly. In other words, each viewed the other as the primary threat and impediment to gaining ascendancy in the region. Insofar as the Arabs were concerned, both powers believed that an "understanding" with them could be easily reached, once all other obstructive "outside" influences had been eliminated.

With the Ottoman Empire finally destroyed, and a weak, inexperienced Arab regime heavily dependent on British support reigning temporarily in part of Syria, the newly dominant powers in the region sought to capitalize on the situation and maximize their bargaining positions. They meanwhile sought to safeguard their interests by coming to an implicit understanding over spheres of interest. This was particularly true in the case of Palestine. During a visit to London in December 1918, Clemenceau attempted to salvage an already tense situation, and thus prevent it from reaching an impasse, by requesting that the British confirm the 1916 Sykes-Picot Agreement. Speaking on behalf of His Majesty's Government, Lloyd George confirmed that Britain had no problem reaffirming France's position in Syria and Cilicia, but nevertheless made new demands regarding what should be included in the British zone, namely Mosul and Palestine.[71]

Clemenceau wished to resolve this state of affairs in an amicable manner, and on his return, "ordered a scheme of agreement to be prepared, with the inclusion of Mosul in the British zone of influence, and this had been handed to the British Government on the 15th February, 1919."[72] Palestine, however, which was seen to lie within the Syrian region, proved to be more problematic.

---

[69] *Papers Relating to the Foreign Relations of the United States,* 5: 8.

[70] Ibid.

[71] Ibid., 3.

[72] Ibid.

Accompanying their aforementioned proposal, the French sent a letter in which they had "asked for a recognition of the historic and traditional case for including the regions claimed in the French zone,"[73] where "no Government in the world had such a position as France,"[74] namely, geographic Syria.

After making a strong case for Syrian geographic and cultural cohesion and unity, and France's special relationship with that region, the French government "frankly avowed that they did not want the responsibility of administering Palestine, though they would prefer to see it under an international administration. They asked that:

> 1. That the whole Syrian region be treated as a unit:
>
> and
>
> 2. That France should become the mandatory of the League of Nations of this region."[75]

France was therefore clearly trying to reach an understanding with Britain and its new postwar demands. Insofar as Mosul was concerned, France was willing to be accommodating; on the issue of Palestine, however, they were more intransigent. While they were willing to publicly proclaim that they did not desire to control Palestine or include it in their own sphere of interest, they were certainly not content with conceding it to Britain, nor indeed did this imply that they would categorically refuse it if it were offered to them. They could therefore meet the British halfway; officially, they would claim they did not want to administer Palestine, but they preferred that it would be placed under an international administration, in other words that it did not fall directly under undisputed British dominion. They also made it clear in their demands, however, that the Syrian region should be treated as a "unit" and that France should become the League's Mandatory Power for this region. Implicit in this demand is that Palestine, which according to "official parlance"[76] fell under the purview of Greater Syria, should be considered as part of this "unit," and would therefore fall under French responsibility.

Ultimately, the French would be compelled to concede "South Syria"/ Palestine to Britain; compromising on "North Syria," however, would be quite another issue, where force of arms would become the final deciding factor. Meanwhile, a power struggle ensued as each of these two powers sought to gain the upper hand in the region by attempting to drive the other out. They each consequently strove to make common cause with the local nationalists by pretending to be the true champions of their aspirations and blaming the other for all the current ills and disappointments affecting the local population.

---

[73] Ibid., 4.

[74] Ibid.

[75] Ibid.

[76] Antonius, *The Arab Awakening,* 436, n. 1.

The British thus gave support and encouragement to Faysal and his regime in Damascus, whose hatred for France needed no encouragement and was unwavering in the spreading of virulent anti-French propaganda.[77] Assuming that Faysal would always rely on them for support and would be willing to acquiesce in whatever formula they proposed regarding their plans for a Jewish homeland in return for some measure of independence,[78] they could indirectly present themselves as the saviors of the Arabs from French colonial encroachment on their lands.

The French, for their part, embarked on a vigorous propaganda campaign of their own. Appealing directly to the masses in those areas where they enjoyed popular support or where support for the British or Faysal was lukewarm at best, they began openly declaring themselves the only party to have been interested in the true emancipation of Syria, not just from the Ottomans but from Britain as well. After all, they argued, were they not the traditional champions of liberty and justice who had aided the Americans (whom the Syrians now sought as their ideal choice for a mandate power)[79] in their own quest for independence? One clear example of this strategy is found in Georges Picot's[80] speech to the schoolteachers of Beirut on May 13, 1919, in which he states:

> A people once asked the French to help them to gain their independence. The French responded and within a year, the desired end was achieved. These people were the Americans and the country from which they were freed was Great Britain. Having appreciated the help given, the Americans asked what reward they could give. "Have your independence, that is the only reward we seek," said the French. The same attitude is now held towards Syria. To see you independent is what we long for. You have my assurance that France will help you to this end.[81]

---

[77] Yehoshua Porath, *The Emergence of the Palestinian-Arab National Movement, 1918-1929,* 73. Faysal's fears and outright resentment towards the French were no secret; in his written statement to the King-Crane Commission, for example, he describes French rule thus, "she takes off manliness from the people and prevent it from progress and development as a political body..." quoted in *Chief Political Officer, Egyptian Expeditionary Force to Foreign Secretary, London, enclosing statement by Amir Faisal to American Commission*, in *Records of the Hashemite Dynasties,* 10: 220.

[78] This point will be discussed in more detail in Chapter 5, below.

[79] This point will be discussed in more detail in Chapter 3, below.

[80] Co-author of the famous Sykes-Picot Agreement and then head of the civil administration of Occupied Enemy Territory (West).

[81] *Earl Curzon to the Earl of Derby (Paris) No. 876 [88743/2117/44]* in *Documents on British Foreign Policy, 1919-1939*, 4: 275. Such statements naturally outraged the British

The French furthermore directed their agents in Palestine to play on the local population's fears of Zionism by indicating that the blame for the Zionists' presence and power in Palestine lay squarely on Britain's shoulders.[82] Alternatively, they proposed a union between Syria and Palestine, under French tutelage and with France's support and backing, as the sole possible means to counter Britain's nefarious plans and hence as the only viable solution.[83] The notion of southern Syria was thus kept alive, directly or indirectly, not only by the indigenous Arab inhabitants of the region in their various factions and formations, but also by the powers who sought to manipulate them towards their own ends.

Conclusion

In conclusion, this chapter provided an introduction to the historical setting and analyzed the historical foundations behind the conception of Palestine as the southern region of Syria. The Arab inhabitants of the region saw it as an integral part of Syria, based on past historical, geographical, economic, and cultural bonds. Moreover, many saw Syria itself as part of the larger Arab nation that was promised to them by the Allies. The Ottomans traditionally viewed Palestine as a unique province, albeit part of the larger Syrian region. Based on administrative facility, this province, like others in Syria, was divided into smaller administrative units and governed from various centers at various times. Based on these factors, the British and French had also historically recognized the geographic, economic, and cultural cohesion of the Syrian region. France, with its own designs on Syria, sought to maintain its territorial integrity and uphold these claims for unity in order to colonize the region as a whole. Britain had already made incompatible promises to several groups regarding the future of region, had its own plans to control part of it, and wanted to check France's territorial ambitions. The British consequently strove to divide the region into several different entities administered separately by the Allies. Meanwhile, the British and French each supported the notion of Southern Syria and greater Syrian unity for their own ends.

Both the French and the British-backed Arab regime were therefore publicly proclaiming Palestine as constituting an indivisible part of Syria, while in reality, the Syrian nation's future hinged on the outcome of the diplomatic tug of war that ensued between Britain and France and their attempts to outmaneuver each other out of territory and influence in the region, maneuvers which included secret negotiations with Faysal and the Zionists,

---

who viewed them as "an astonishing travesty of the facts." Ibid.

[82] Weizmann, for example, describes "French propaganda" in Palestine as being "active and extensive." See *Dr. Weizmann to Earl Curzon, Paris, February 2, 1920* [17705] in ibid., Doc.132, p. 232.

[83] Porath, *Emergence of the Palestinian-Arab National Movement, 1918-1929,* 74.

among others.[84] Thus, each of these groups had different ideas regarding the future of Syria and the place of Palestine therein. The next chapter provides an in-depth examination of the official Arab perspective on the issue.

[84] See Chapter 5, below.

Chapter Two
THE ARAB STANCE

There were many historical, geographical, and cultural bases for the Southern Syria notion that declared Palestine as an integral part of Syria. The Allies readily utilized this notion for their own imperial purposes in their competition over control of the region. More importantly, there were many solid foundations upon which the Syrians could build a coherent Syrian national identity, within clear geographic boundaries, where a consensus among the indigenous inhabitants could be reached. While such an endeavor was bound to be fraught with certain difficulties—such as separatist tendencies towards full independence under French tutelage in certain parts of Lebanon, for example, and ideological dilemmas among the Arab nationalists regarding Syria's place as an independent entity within the larger "Arab" context—there was nevertheless general agreement over where the borders of the Syrian region lay. One of the areas on which there appears to have been no dispute, at least insofar as the inhabitants were concerned, was Palestine. This issue would hence become a central tenet in the evolving Syrian national discourse and one of the Syrians' primary demands.

Contest over spheres of interest had nonetheless created strange bedfellows in the region: while the British were trying to institute their own plans to divide the area, the French and Arabs were trying to maintain its unity and territorial and cultural integrity, each according to their own objectives. The Allies were engaged in a diplomatic struggle for power in which they naturally sought to utilize all circumstances in order to gain the upper hand. The Arabs attempted to come to the negotiating table as partners with legitimate rights and demands; demands they believed had long been recognized by these same Allies, and which they were now seeking to have formally established and internationally recognized. Far from the diplomatic quagmire of the Peace Conferences in Europe in which their leader and his retinue were embroiled, the Arab inhabitants of the Syrian region sought to make their own voice heard and wishes known.

The purpose of this chapter is to examine the Syrian official stance regarding their future, to the extent that it is represented by those visible, politically active members of society participating in the political process. This chapter seeks to determine their position towards Palestine and the notion of "Southern Syria," and to gauge its place in the evolution of Syrian national discourse. Accordingly, this chapter first provides an examination of the various Arab congresses held in the region during the Faysali era and their backgrounds; second, it analyzes the resolutions and the motivations behind the congresses and the circumstances surrounding them; and finally examines the Allies' subsequent responses and reactions to them.

The Arab Congresses

With Faysal away on diplomatic missions abroad seeking to salvage whatever he could, the Syrians sought to reinforce their representative's bargaining position by actively and explicitly outlining their demands. In an age of conferences where, under the guise of "international law," the world's future destiny was being decided by the victors of the Great War and their thirst for spoils, the means the Syrians themselves resorted to, in an attempt to endow their own demands with an air of legitimacy, were to convene conferences of their own. Perhaps placing far too much faith in the Allies' inter-war promises, Wilson's Fourteen Points (specifically, the right of nations to self-determination), and, ultimately, in the Allies' sense of reason and justice, they might have naively hoped that by unequivocally demonstrating what their "legitimate" goals and aspirations were, the Allies, and indeed the world at large, would not begrudge them those rights.

On the internal level, the congresses and their resolutions served as a definitive formal step towards the forging of a Syrian national discourse. By furnishing an explicit and unambiguous set of notions and demands to a population that, while vehemently rejecting foreign occupation and Zionism as a concept, still had no unique, independent experience of nationalism or nationhood, these endeavors evince a clear element of national soul-searching. Through providing them a coherent set of demands that gave clear form to their aspirations, the congresses offered the incipient nation direction for their immediate goals, amid the tumult of the immediate postwar era.

Four main congresses convened during this period dealt directly with the issue of Southern Syria, rendering them particularly relevant and therefore deserving of special attention. These were the First Palestinian Congress (January-February 1919), the first General Syrian Congress (July 1919), the Second Palestinian Congress (February 1919), and finally, the second General Syrian Congress (March 1920); they will be examined in chronological order.

The First Palestinian Congress

One of the first Arab congresses to be convened after the war, the First Palestinian Congress was held in Jerusalem between January 27 and February 9, 1919; representatives from all over Palestine attended it and ʿArif al-Dajani, head of the Muslim-Christian Association in Jerusalem, presided over it. After almost two weeks of deliberation, the conference finally issued a statement, addressed to the Paris Peace Conference, entitled: "Resolution presented by the representatives of all the regions of Southern Syria also known as Palestine meeting in Jerusalem to the Peace Conference held in Paris—Historical and Political Resolution."

The "Resolution" started by providing an exact definition of the area in question:

> Southern Syria, which has been called by the name 'Palestine' and is composed of three *mutasarrifiya*s: Nablus, Acre and Jerusalem...[1]

The delegates began by stating how *they* wanted the region to be defined—"Southern Syria"—and then proceeded to furnish all other possible names and definitions of the area, for the sake of dispelling any possible ambiguity. They then provided an explicit declaration of their desires and intentions regarding the future of their country with regard to its being a part of the region of Syria. The crux of the "Resolution," however, centered on rejecting Zionism and all Zionist claims to Southern Syria/Palestine, and it went to great lengths to argue these points.[2]

Following its "Resolution," the Congress issued a "Memorandum to the Paris Peace Conference" on February 3, 1919, containing the following petition intended for presentation at the Conference in Paris. This petition is worth quoting at length, because it provides a definitive illustration of the Palestinian delegates' understanding of the situation, and their feelings regarding the future of their country and its status as a province of Syria, stated in clear, unequivocal terms:

> The principles declared by President Wilson...have compelled us, the representatives of Southern Syria, also known as Palestine, to decide in our Congress, held in Jerusalem, to pass this resolution in the name of the Arab inhabitants of this country, both Muslim and Christian, numbering around a million people, to make clear our desires and wishes for the future of our country and its destiny, fully confident in the fairness of this great Conference in seeing the justness of our cause and granting us our wishes and desires.

---

[1]Mudhakkirat al-Muʾtamar al-ʿArabī al-Filasṭīnī al-Awwal ilá Muʾtamar al-Ṣulḥ fī Bārīs. "ʿArīḍah turfaʿ ilá Muʾtamar al-Silm al-munʿaqid fī Bārīz min qibal jamīʿ mandūbī anḥāʾ Filasṭīn ayy Sūrīyā al-Janūbīyah." Text in *Wathāʾiq al-Ḥarakah al-Waṭanīyah al-Filasṭīnīyah, 1918-1939: Min Awrāq Akram Zuʿaytir*, edited by Bayān Nuwayhiḍ al-Ḥūt (Beirut, 1979), 14.

[2]For an examination of these arguments, see ibid., 14-16.

> Firstly: We do not consider Palestine to be anything but a region of the [many] regions of Arab Syria, never were [we] separated from her at any stage in the stages [of her history], and we share with her national, religious, linguistic, moral, economic and geographic ties
>
> Secondly: Monsieur Pichon's—France's foreign minister—speech in which he claimed that France has rights in our country based on the wishes of its inhabitants and their desires has no basis in fact, and we do not consent to any of his statements given in this speech of December 29, 1918. We have no aspirations other than Arab unity and complete independence.
>
> Third: Based on these considerations, we wish that this, our region, Southern Syria, or Palestine, not be separated from the independent Arab Syrian government that is committed to Arab unity, free from all foreign influence and protection.
>
> Fourth: According to the framework laid down by President Wilson and agreed upon by most of the leaders of the Great Powers, we do not recognize all [previous] promises and treaties [affecting] that concern our country and its future, considering them all to be null and void.
>
> Fifth: The nation's government seeks the assistance of her friend Great Britain, when necessary, in matters of construction, on the condition that this [relationship] will in no way compromise her independence or her [dedication to the principles of] Arab unity, while ensuring good relations with all the allied nations.
>
> These are the wishes of the people which we represent, these are their desires that we present to you oh great men that have taken upon yourselves to be the impartial judge, basing your decisions on the foundations of human rights and happiness, we are fully confident that we will attain our goals and that our hopes and desires will be respected.[3]

The statement was signed by 26 representatives from various regions of Palestine.[4] Two official delegations were then scheduled to travel to Damascus

---

[3]Ibid., 16-17.

[4]These were: al-Ḥājj Saʿīd al-Shawwā and Aḥmad al-Ṣūrānī from Gaza; Aḥmad Sayf al-Dīn al-Ḥusaynī from Lydd and Ramlah; Muḥammad Baydas, Yūsuf al-ʿĪsá, and Aḥmad Abū al-Suʿūd al-Dajānī from Jaffa; Kamāl al-Dīn ʿArafāt and Muḥammad ʿIzzat Darwazah from Jamaʿin; Saʿīd al-Karmī and Muḥammad Tawfīq al-Ṭībī from Tulkarem; Nāfiʿ al-ʿAbbūshī and Ḥaydar ʿAbd al-Hādī from Jenin; ʿAbd al-Ḥamīd Abū Ghawsh and Shukrī Kārmī from Jerusalem; Rāmiz al-Nimr and Ibrāhīm ʿAbd al-Hādī from Nablus;

and Paris to deliver the resolutions of the Congress in person. The British authorities, however, did not approve and prevented the delegation from traveling, thus forcing them to resort to sending their resolutions by mail.

Initially, the Palestinian Congress' confirmation of Palestine's national identity as Southern Syria might seem somewhat surprising, particularly because the Palestinian community was generally conservative and reticent towards the Arab movement in the late Ottoman period. Indeed, according to a British report in the final months before the end of the war:

> Until the advent of the recent recruiting campaign conducted by one of the Sherif Faisal's officers, the Moslem population of Judea took little or no interest in the Arab national movement. Even now the Effendi class, and particularly the educated Moslem-Levantine population of Jaffa, evince a feeling somewhat akin to hostility toward the Arab movement very similar to the feeling so prevalent in Cairo and Alexandria.[5]

But it is nevertheless clear from the text of the "Resolution" that Zionism and the Palestinian community's fears of it were their primary concern and motivation. In their wartime promises, Faysal's recruitment officers had assured the population that Palestine would be included in the liberated independent Arab state established after the war. Faysal's victorious march into Damascus in October and his proclamation (within five days of his arrival) of the establishment of a "completely independent constitutional government" with "Damascus as the Arabs' eternal capital,"[6] further reinforced his image and standing among Palestinians, rendering him the only hope in their eyes. With the Ottomans decisively out of the picture, the Palestinians were now

---

Ilyās Qaʿwār, Maḥmūd Ḥusayn, and Maḥmūd Ṭabarī from Tiberias; Jubrān Iskandar Kazmā and Ḥusayn al-Zuʿbī from Nazareth; Muḥyī al-Dīn ʿĪsá and Ṣalāḥ al-Dīn al-Ḥājj Yūsuf from Safad; ʿAbd al-Laṭīf Abū Hanṭash from al-Shaʿrawiyah; Rashīd al-Ḥājj Ibrāhīm and Iskandar Mansī from Haifa; ibid., 17.

[5]"Report on the existing Political Situation in Palestine and Contiguous Areas by the Political Officer in charge of the Zionists' Commission," by W. Ormsby-Gore, 22 August 1918 [147225], in *British Documents on Foreign Affairs: Reports and Papers from the Foreign Office Confidential Print, Part II: From the First to the Second World War; Series B: Turkey, Iran and the Middle East, 1918-1939. Vol. 1: The End of the War, 1918-1920.* General Editors: Kenneth Bourne and D. Cameron Watt, Volume Editor: Robin Bidwell ([Frederick, Maryland] 1985), 1.

[6]Muḥammad ʿIzzat Darwazah, *Ḥawl al-Ḥarakah al-ʿArabīyah al-Ḥadīthah: Tārīkh, wa-Mudhakkirāt,wa-Taʿlīqāt,* Sidon, 1950, 1: 71. For the full text of Faysal's proclamation of an independent Arab state in Syria on October 2, 1918, see *al-Sharīf Fayṣal yuʿlin taʾsīs al-dawlah al-ʿArabīyah fī Sūrīyah bi-ism "al-Sulṭān" Ḥusayn,* in Qarqūṭ, *al-Mashriq al-ʿArabī,* 17.

faced with the reality of a British occupation whose declared official policy was the creation of a Jewish "national home" in their lands; turning to Faysal's "Arab state" became the only viable option.

From a different standpoint, however, with this new process of modern "nation-building" underway in the region, the belief that the geographical area known as Palestine should be included as part of the new state based and founded on the notion of "Syria" was clearly not alien to either community. Indeed, it was justifiable on both Arab and "greater Syrian" nationalist grounds. Certain events did nonetheless hasten to demonstrate to the Palestinians their need for the Faysali state and consequently strengthened their pro-Syrian convictions.

On November 2, 1918, the first anniversary of the Balfour declaration, the Palestinian community was outraged by the parade held by the Zionist Commission in Jerusalem. During this event, "Jewish flags"[7] were flagrantly displayed, accompanied by zealous festivities and celebrations among the resident Jewish community.[8] Meanwhile, prominent Zionists, including the movement's leader, Chaim Weizmann, became ever bolder in their public statements regarding Palestine. The Zionists portrayed Palestine as their "country," graciously "liberated" by the British forces. On the aforementioned occasion of the first anniversary of the Balfour declaration, Chaim Weizmann stated in a speech to the Zionist Conference in London:

> We should be wanting in our duty if at this solemn moment we did not remember the victorious British Army under the leadership of a great General and a great statesman, General Allenby, who has liberated our fair country. The whole of Eretz Israel is at present free, and there is great scope for our future activities.[9]

The underlying theme in Weizmann's speeches that the Jews "do not arrive, but return"[10] confirmed the Palestinians' worst fears regarding the Zionists'

---

[7]"Mudhakkirah min al-Jamᶜīyah al-Islāmīyah al-Masīḥīyah fī Yāfā ilá al-Jinīrāl Klāytūn Iḥtijājan ᶜalá Taṣrīḥāt Ṣahyūnīyah wa-Barīṭānīyah, 2/11/1918" in *Wathā᾽iq al-Ḥarakah al-Waṭanīyah al-Filasṭīnīyah, 1918-1939*, 4.

[8]Porath, *Emergence of the Palestinian-Arab National Movement, 1918-1929,* 32.

[9]"The Zionist Commission at Work," London, 2 November, 1918, in *The Letters and Papers of Chaim Weizmann*, edited by Barnet Litvinoff (Jerusalem, 1983), Vol. 1, Series B, August 1898-July 1931, p. 196. Weizmann was also quick to point out wherever possible that: "I think it is perhaps right also to remember on this occasion that in this last victorious conquest of Palestine participated also a fair number of Jewish troops." See ibid.

[10]Of the many things protested by the Palestinians were Weizmann's speeches in which he reportedly stated that the Jews "do not arrive in Palestine, but return." "Mudhakkirah min al-Jamᶜīyah al-Islāmīyah al-Masīḥīyah fī Yāfā 2/11/1918" in *Wathā᾽iq al-Ḥarakah*

plans for the establishment of a "Jewish Kingdom" on their own lands and distressed the Palestinian community everywhere. Subsequently, a delegation composed of the heads of the various Muslim and Christian communities, with the Mayor of Jerusalem, Musa Kazim al-Husayni, at its head, delivered a petition protesting Zionism and Zionist policy to the Military Governor of Jerusalem, Sir Ronald Storrs. The local Muslim-Christian Association delivered a similar note to the Military Governor of Jaffa.[11] General Clayton sought to mollify them with a conciliatory response, two days later, urging them "not to be concerned at all with this matter",[12] claiming that the Jews would only display their flags in their synagogues and giving assurances that the "Military Governor was beholden to the entire Muslim and Christian communities to ensure that their rights would never be impinged upon."[13]

THE ANGLO-FRENCH DECLARATION OF 1918

Perhaps alarmed at the Arab reaction, Sir Ronald Storrs made certain that the Anglo-French Declaration of November 7, 1918, was well-publicized in Jerusalem and copies of it were displayed everywhere.[14] Issued as a *communiqué* by the General Headquarters, Egyptian Expeditionary Force, the primary purpose of this Anglo-French Declaration was to appease the Arabs and allay their fears and apprehensions. Accordingly, states Antonius:

> copies of it were posted on the public notice-boards in all towns and a great many villages in the Arab territories then occupied by the Allied forces, that is to say throughout the length and breadth of Palestine, Syria and Iraq.[15]

Officially, the "declaration" was an ostensible statement of the Allies' "war aims" in the East; hence, it proclaimed:

> The goal envisaged by France and Great Britain in prosecuting in the East the War set in train by German ambition is the complete and final liberation of the peoples who have for so long been oppressed by the Turks, and the setting up of national governments and administrations that shall derive

---

al-Waṭanīyah al-Filasṭīnīyah, 4.

[11]For text, see *Wathāʾiq al-Ḥarakah al-Waṭanīyah al-Filasṭīnīyah,* 4-5. Interestingly enough, at this point, the protest notes referred to the area as "Palestine"—*Filasṭīn*—not as "Southern Syria."

[12]"Iḥtijāj min al-Jamʿīyah al-Islāmīyah al-Masīḥīyah fī Yāfā ilá al-Ḥākim al-ʿAskarī ʿalá rafʿ al-Yahūd li-Aʿlāmihim: al-Taṣrīḥāt al-Wāridah bi-Tārīkh 4/11/1918 min al-Ḥākim al-ʿAskarī," text in *Wathāʾiq al-Ḥarakah al-Waṭanīyah al-Filasṭīnīyah,* 5.

[13]Ibid.

[14]Porath, *Emergence of the Palestinian-Arab National Movement, 1918-1929,* 71.

[15]George Antonius, *The Arab Awakening,* 435.

> their authority from the free exercise of the initiative and choice of the indigenous populations.
>
> In pursuit of those intentions, France and Great Britain agree to further and assist in the setting up of indigenous governments in Syria and Mesopotamia which have already been liberated by the Allies as well as in those territories which they are endeavouring to liberate, and to recognize them as soon as they are actually set up.[16]

Nevertheless, it was clear from the outset that the declaration was intended primarily for public consumption and did not convey the Allies' true intentions for the region. The French almost immediately sought to safeguard their interests by pointing out, somewhat discreetly, that the terms of this declaration were open to interpretation. Commenting on it in the French Chamber on December 29, 1918, Pichon "very properly"[17] stated:

> Of course, we admit the complete freedom of the Conference, and its right to give these agreements their proper conclusions, but these agreements are binding upon England and upon us.[18]

The French diplomatically claimed that the Paris Peace Conference, or indeed the world at large, was "free" to interpret this declaration to mean whatever it pleased them to believe. Nevertheless the onus of translating its words into concrete policy fell upon the British and French, the powers upon whom the "agreements are binding." The actual meaning of what was being promised, therefore, should be left to the discretion of those promising it—Britain and France.

The Syrians and Palestinians had their own apprehensions regarding the actual wording of the declaration. Essentially, the name "Palestine" was not specifically mentioned in the text, thus causing the Palestinians, who had just protested the Balfour Declaration, further distress and alarm. Whether this exclusion had been intentional on the part of the Allies or whether "Palestine" was simply being included as part of the *geographic* region of "Syria"[19] certainly required clarification. If the latter interpretation were true, then the Palestinians, as Syrians, could look forward to being part of an independent Syria and playing a role in choosing their government. If, however, the Allies' intention had been to exclude them from the process of setting up an

---

[16]Full text in ibid., 435-6.

[17]*Papers Relating to the Foreign Relations of the United States,* 12: 784.

[18]Ibid.

[19]According to Antonius, "In official parlance, 'Syria' was still used to denote the whole of geographical Syria, from the Taurus range to the Egyptian frontier." Antonius, *Arab Awakening, 436,* n. 1.

independent government based on the wishes of their people, then why was the declaration even sent to them?

The Muslim-Christian Associations decided to interpret the declaration in a positive light. Accordingly, they made sure that copies of this document were distributed widely "to all, in order that they become aware of their situation."[20] Moreover, a delegation of Muslims and Christians met with the Governor to "offer their thanks"[21] on behalf of their community to the government of Britain for its declaration. The Governor, in turn, thanked the delegation for their gratitude and promised to relay their sentiments to his government assuring them that the "people of Palestine (which is a part of Syria) will have maximum freedom in choosing the type of government they desire."[22]

A varying interpretation of the exact sequence of events, however, has been offered. According to the scholar Yehoshua Porath, the heads of the Arab community in Jerusalem, having noticed the exclusion of "Palestine" from the declaration, immediately requested that the Governor clarify these points. After the Governor answered, somewhat unsatisfactorily, in "general terms",[23] the next day "the heads of the Muslim and Christian communities assembled and decided to demand a government headed by the *Sharīf* of Mecca; the Muslims requested the Mufti to make mention of the *Sharīf*'s name, as Caliph in the Friday prayers."[24]

The outcome was nevertheless the same. By the end of the year, many Palestinians believed that unity with Syria was their only path to salvation. At the time the conference convened therefore, the "Southern Syria" notion was firmly established and gained a sense of urgency, particularly since the Palestinians wished to be included amongst the "liberated peoples" clamoring for independence. The belief was justified on the basis that both Syria and Palestine had been united in their past and shared a common vision for their future; it was only natural therefore that they should now become unified as one independent nation.

A few weeks after the First Palestinian Congress was convened the mayors, representatives, and notables of the towns of Nablus, Jenin, and Nazareth signed three petitions, albeit using the same text, in which they protested the British policy regarding the establishment of a Jewish national home in Palestine and demanded that Palestine not be separated from Syria. The original petition

---

[20] "Nashr al-Jamʿīyāt al-Islāmīyah al-Masīḥīyah li-Iʿlān al-Ḥākim al-ʿAskarī al-Mutʿalliq bi-Ahdāf al-Ḥulafāʾ min al-Ḥarb al-Kubrá, 7/11/1918" in *Wathāʾiq al-Ḥarakah al-Waṭanīyah al-Filasṭīnīyah,* 6.

[21] Ibid.

[22] Ibid.

[23] Porath, *Emergence of the Palestinian-Arab National Movement, 1918-1929,* 72.

[24] Ibid.

signed on February 27, 1919[25] by notables, political representatives, and the mayor of Nablus ʿUmar Zuʿaytir[26] began by expressing its support for the resolutions of the Palestinian congress "approved by the representatives from all the districts of our region of Southern Syria known as Palestine."[27] It went on to strongly condemn British policies regarding Zionism, Jewish immigration, and the establishment of a Jewish national home, attempting to refute all Jewish claims to Palestine and attacking Zionist schemes. It concluded:

> We once again raise our strongest objections to any agreement, negotiation, treaty, promise, or contract that would endow the Jews...with the rights to immigration, residence, or nationality [in our country]...we shall preserve our country and our rights therein by every means possible, and we shall never, under any circumstances, accept that our country be separated from Arab Syria, we want our fate to be one, in which our Arab independence and unity is immediately guaranteed.[28]

According to the memoirs of Khalil al-Sakakini—the founder of Madrasat al-Najah and noted Palestinian intellectual—(writing on January 20, 1919):

> The notion of uniting Palestine with Syria has begun to circulate and gain popularity. It is said that Palestine and Syria are as two sisters that have shared the burden of numerous calamities in the past and are united in their vision for freedom and independence, it is therefore imperative that they now share their future destiny together, and it is no way justifiable that one should be severed from the other, no matter what that destiny might hold...[29]

This opinion was repeated a few months later from Beirut by Rafiq al-Tamimi, who, in a letter to ʿAwni ʿAbd al-Hadi (Faysal's personal secretary) in Paris in mid-May, reports:

---

[25] The first petition was signed in Nablus on that date; the other two were signed a few days later in early March.

[26] For full list of signatories from Nablus, see "Thalāth ʿArāʾiḍ min al-Wujahāʾ wa-al-Makhātīr fī Nāblus wa-Jinīn wa-al-Nāṣirah yaḥtajūn fīhā ʿalá siyāsat al-waṭan al-qawmī wa-yuṭālibūn bi-ʿadam faṣl Filasṭīn ʿan Sūrīyah, 27/2/1919 [ʿArīḍat Wujahāʾ wa-Makhātīr Nāblus]," in *Wathāʾiq al-Ḥarakah al-Waṭanīyah al-Filasṭīnīyah,* 19-20. For the signatories from Jenin and Nazareth, see 20-21.

[27] Ibid., 19.

[28] Ibid.

[29] Khalīl al-Sakākīnī, *Kadhā Anā Yā Dunyā: Yawmāyāt* (Jerusalem, 1955), 161.

> Palestinian opinion is leaning toward one word, 'unity' with Syria from the economic and political perspectives, coupled with demands for complete and unqualified independence.[30]

Another clear illustration of the tenor of the political mood in Palestine during this period was demonstrated by the name given to the first new Palestinian newspaper to be established after the war: *Sūrīyah al-Janūbīyah* (Southern Syria). Published in Jerusalem by Muhammad Hasan al-Budayri and edited by ʿArif al-ʿArif, the paper clearly conveyed the nationalist perspective in Palestine on Syrian unity and was closely associated with the famous "Arab Club," known for its unflinching Arab nationalist line. Although it lasted only from September 1919 until the British authorities closed it down permanently in April 1920, "it appears to have been the most influential organ of opinion during its short lifetime; it was highly political and intensely nationalist; and its articles were extremely vividly written."[31]

Nor was this vehement "Syrian nationalist" sentiment in Palestine lost on the British, despite attempts by the Zionists and their supporters to downplay it. In a letter to Earl Curzon, the private secretary of the foreign office, written in August 1919, for example, Colonel French reports:

> Dr. Weizmann in a letter to Sir L. Mallet...wrote of 'artificial agitation' in Palestine. It is considered the opinion of the British officers who know Palestine well that the opposition to Zionism, which is based to a certain extent on the national sentiment of its inhabitants, has grown stronger during the past months, and it is believed that this is well known to the Commission, which has an efficient 'intelligence' service. It may be an oversight on his part, but Dr. Weizmann invariably refers in his letter to the non-Jewish inhabitants of Palestine as 'Arabs'. He no doubt realizes that these 'Arabs' consider themselves primarily as 'Syrians' and form the greater part of the population, and that it is among the Moslem and Christian Syrians that the idea of nationalism is strongest.[32]

THE GENERAL SYRIAN CONGRESS (JULY, 1919)

On July 2, 1919, some five months following the convening of the First

[30] *ʿAwnī ʿAbd al-Hādī: Awrāq Khāṣṣah*, edited by Khayrīyah Qāsimīyah, Beirut, 1974, 33.

[31] Rashid Khalidi, *Palestinian Identity,* 162. For a detailed discussion of the newspaper and its articles, see ibid., 162-170.

[32] *Colonel French (Cairo) to Earl Curzon (Received September 17) No. C.P.O. 311 [130392/2117/44A] Cairo, August 30, 1919* in *Documents on British Foreign Policy,* 4: 369.

Palestinian Congress, the first General Syrian Congress was held in Damascus with representatives hailing from all major centers of "Geographic Syria," including Lebanon and Palestine.[33] While Palestine was not the primary focus of the congress, it figured prominently in its resolutions, being explicitly mentioned in four of the Congress' eleven demands. Among the resolutions adopted, the ones formally embracing the notion of "Southern Syria" in Damascus were:

> 1. We request complete political independence for Syria within these boundaries: the Taurus system on the North; Rafah and a line running from Al Jauf to the south of the Syrian and the Hejazian line to Akaba on the south; the Euphrates and Khabur rivers and a line extending east of Abu Kamal to the east of Al Jauf on the east; and the Mediterranean on the west.
>
> 7. We oppose the pretensions of the Zionists to create a Jewish commonwealth in the southern part of Syria, known as Palestine, and oppose Zionist migration to any part of our country; for we do not acknowledge their claims and consider them a grave peril to our people from the national, economical, and political points of view. Our Jewish compatriots shall enjoy our common rights and assume the common responsibilities.
>
> 8. We ask that there should be no separation of the southern part of Syria, known as Palestine, nor of the littoral western zone, which includes Lebanon, from the Syrian homeland. We desire that the unity of the country be guaranteed against partition under any circumstances.
>
> 10. The fundamental principles laid down by President Wilson in condemnation of secret treaties impel us to protest most emphatically against any treaty that stipulates the partition of our Syrian nation and against any private engagement aiming at the establishment of Zionism in the southern part of Syria; we therefore ask for the complete annulment of these conventions and agreements …[34]

[33] Among those representatives were fifteen Palestinians: ʿIzzat Darwazah, Amīn al-Tamīmī, Rafīq al-Tamīmī, ʿAdil Zuʿaytir, Ibrāhīm ʿAbd al-Hādī, Aḥmad Qadrī, Muʿīn al-Māḍī, Ṣalāḥ al-Dīn al-Ḥājj Yūsuf, Salīm ʿAbd al-Raḥmān, Yūsuf al-ʿĪsá, ʿAbd al-Raḥmān al-Naḥawī, Ibrāhīm al-ʿAlī, Rashīd al-Ḥājj Ibrāhīm, ʿAlī al-Mahdī, and Ḥusayn al-Zuʿbī. al-Hakim, *Suriyah wa-al-ʿAhd al-Faysali,* 93-94. For a complete list of representatives, see ibid., 91-94.

[34] Resolutions of the General Syrian Congress at Damascus, 2 July 1919, in Hurewitz, *Diplomacy in the Near and Middle East*, 2: 63-4. For a full detailed list of the resolutions,

These were among the first resolutions to give the notion of Palestine as Southern Syria direct and official sanction as the formal public demands tendered by an allegedly representative Syrian body. Unlike Iraq, which was recognized as a separate "Arab" region deserving independence in its own right and with whom an optional economic union of sorts should be made attainable,[35] Palestine, while acknowledged as a distinct region, was clearly seen as an intrinsic part of the "*Syrian* whole." Palestine was thus at the heart of the very notion of "*Syrianness*," while Zionism and its goals were perceived as both an injustice and a threat directed immediately at Syria and its territorial integrity.

It is nevertheless important to consider the degree to which this congress and its decisions were indicative of Syrian popular opinion and indeed, to what extent this congressional process was truly representative or even "constitutional." The participants themselves were mostly either young, educated Arab nationalists eager to take charge of the changing times, or older notables who had played a political role under the Ottomans with a stake in maintaining their standing and respectability under the new regime. In other words, they fit the profile of the class and category of citizens that were most likely going to play the leading role in the political process under the circumstances.

Still, there were some criticisms regarding the process by which the participants were selected and the degree to which the Congress and its resolutions accurately represented the Syrian population. The American King-Crane report, for example, states:

> The Congress was not elected directly by the people, or by a fresh appeal to the people, the reason given being that time was lacking to revise the voting lists and carry through a new scheme. At the last Turkish election, before the war, electors were chosen to select deputies for the Turkish parliament. The survivors of these electors chose the members of the Damascus Congress. Criticisms were made against the plan of choice to the effect that it was unconstitutional and extra-constitutional, that the electors had mostly belonged to the Party of Union and Progress, and that the members of the Congress were not distributed in proportion to the population. Sixty-nine members attended, and about 20 others from the west and north had been elected but had not arrived. Much

---

see ibid.

[35] According to the Congressional Resolution no. 9: "We ask for complete independence for emancipated Mesopotamia and that there should be no economical barriers between the two countries." See ibid., 64.

> evidence goes to show that the program represents well the wishes of the people of Syria.[36]

Despite the criticisms that these congresses did not strictly adhere to the most stringent rules and regulations of democratic representation, they did provide an unmistakable illustration of the trend in both Syria and Palestine towards unity and independence. Since the Congress took place right before the arrival of the American Commission in August, its delegates did have a vested political interest in demonstrating their views regarding Palestine, Syrian unity, and the threat of Zionism, with added zeal. Nonetheless, the Congress and its resolutions do appear to have faithfully conveyed the Syrian populace's nationalist aspirations and its convictions regarding their future.

The Second Palestine Congress

On February 27, 1920, a second General Palestinian Congress was held in Damascus in which Syrian unity was reaffirmed by fiery speeches, and Palestine's status as "Southern Syria" was even more vigorously upheld. The congress, which convened at the Arab Club building, was attended by:

> The representatives of the National Defense Committee—many members of the Syrian Congress—and the representatives of the political parties, viz., the Arab Independence Party, the Syrian Union, the Syrian Covenant, the Irak Covenant, the Syrian National Arab Club, the princes of the Arab tribes of Hauran, El Soukhour, El Fadle, El Kerak, the Circassians, the notables of Kus, the clergymen, the lawyers, the doctors, the journalists, the chief merchants and a big number of students of high schools of all sects and creeds.[37]

During the course of its discussions, some participants, such as Muhammad ʿIzzat Darwazah, (a Palestinian member of the Syrian parliament) went so far as to request that the very appellation "Palestine" be altogether dropped in favor of the more encompassing term *al-Bilād al-Shāmīyah* ("Syrian regions") for all of Syria.[38]

Another speaker, Yusuf al-ʿIsa, drew the parallel between Syria's relationship to Palestine and that of France to Alsace-Lorraine. He continued that the very notion of a "national government" in Palestine was a mere ruse

---

[36] "The Program of the Syrian Congress," The King-Crane Report, in *Papers Relating to the Foreign Relations of the United States*, 12: 780.

[37] *The Palestine Congress* [E 2915/2/44] in *British Documents on Foreign Affairs*, Part II, Vol. 1, Doc.173, 297.

[38] "Muqarrarāt al-Muʾtamar al-Filasṭīnī al-ʿĀmm fī Dimashq, Shubāṭ (February) 1920," text in *Wathāʾiq al-Ḥarakah al-Waṭanīyah al-Filasṭīnīyah, 1918-1939,* 35.

by the colonialists through which they attempted to lure the population by claiming that independence from Syria would benefit them by providing them with better jobs. Zionism was also declared not only a danger to the "Syrian interior" but to Lebanon as well.[39]

When the issue of a Jewish national homeland was being discussed, it was maintained that Jews, since their arrival in Palestine, were permitted to vote and voice their opinions, while the Muslims and Christians, who arrived there from neighboring countries, were accorded no such rights and were not allowed to voice a political opinion.[40]

Yusuf al-ᶜIsa then asserted:

> The people of Palestine should not be deceived by claims and promises of a national government. It is not the land of Palestine that will be ultimately betrayed by this independence from Syria, but its people, for the land will continue to yield its fruits, but it is Syria whose land and people will be betrayed, economically and politically.[41]

"Only the insane," he concluded, "would refuse independence, and we take pride in refusing independence and separation from Syria."[42]

When the issue of accepting a Palestinian national government independent of Syria was finally put to vote, the majority chose to refuse it. The Congress then issued four main resolutions overwhelmingly confirming the Palestinian people's resolve to be united with Syria, thereby providing an unequivocal declaration of the "Syrianness" of Palestine; these were as follows:

> The inhabitants of northern and coastal Syria have never at any time considered southern Syria (or Palestine) to be a region apart from Syria as they have affirmed in the resolutions of their Syrian Congress. They now, once again, confirm this decision.
>
> The inhabitants of northern and coastal Syria have always firmly believed Zionism to be a dangerous threat, which, were it to become entrenched in Palestine, would eventually overwhelm and destroy their entire political existence over time. They have thus openly opposed Zionist immigration before the American Commission, and continue to stand behind their decision and refusal to allow Palestine to be converted into a national homeland for the Jews. Furthermore, they petition their Arab government to officially denounce

---

[39] Ibid.

[40] Ibid.

[41] Ibid., 35-36.

[42] Ibid., 36.

> this promise, even if it has been approved by the rest of the Allies, and call for an economic boycott from all three Syrian zones.
>
> The inhabitants of northern and coastal Syria refuse the formation of any form of national government in Palestine before the occupying government recognizes the demands of the Palestinians that were presented before the American Commission, namely that first, they not be separated from Syria, and second, that Zionist immigration be prohibited. They also reject any [contradictory] decision taken at a meeting hosted by the occupying power, since such a decision would be deemed to have been forced under pressure and by the threat of the power of bayonets.
>
> In conclusion, since the existent nationalist movement in this land (Palestine)[43] that advocates the independence of the Syrian nation within its natural boundaries, still makes the distinction between "Palestine" and "Syria" in all its statements and publications as a means of manipulating public opinion, the inhabitants of northern and coastal Syria, in order to clarify any uncertainty that may arise regarding the [true] goals of their own political labors, declare that this movement, in its current orientation, aims at ousting the representatives from the coastal regions as well as Palestine.[44]

Clearly, the main objective of the second Palestinian Congress was the bold reaffirmation of Palestine's place as the southern region of Syria. Once again, several factors may have given the Palestinian congressional representatives the added impetus to express their wishes resolutely to the Allies, the world at large, and indeed their own constituents, for a second time barely a year later. Faysal's return from Europe practically empty-handed certainly may have served to rekindle their doubts and fears about the Allies' intentions for their future, thus reviving their pro-Syrian convictions and prompting them to renew their calls for unity and independence.

From the nationalists' standpoint, Faysal's failure to achieve any tangible results abroad and the perseverance of foreign agents working for the interests of the European powers in the region, whose express purpose was to sow dissent, no doubt tremendously threatened the unity of their movement. The nationalists legitimately feared that, in this atmosphere of uncertainty, the Allies and their agents would succeed in coaxing various segments of

---

[43] My parentheses.

[44] Ibid., 36; cf. *The Palestine Congress* [E 2915/2/44] in *British Documents on Foreign Affairs*, Part II, Vol. 1, Doc. 173, p. 297.

the population into separate negotiations with them, thereby dividing Syria under the pretext that this indeed was the will of its inhabitants. It was of crucial importance therefore for the nationalists to "guide" the population by reaffirming and clearly underlining their "true" goals, aspirations, obligations, and policies, openly condemning all that should be deemed "reprehensible," before they could be pressured or manipulated by "destructive influences"—in other words the separatist tendencies the nationalists believed were being fostered and encouraged by the Allies.

Second, the arrival of high-ranking Allied officials in the region at this particular juncture may have also played a part in confirming the nationalists' fears and apprehensions, thereby determining the timing of the congress. The appointment of a new French High Commissioner in Syria and Lebanon and Commander-in-Chief of the Army of the Levant to the region, for example, was one factor to consider. Whether resulting from direct manipulation by French agents as the British had maintained and suspected, or due to their own concerns and suspicions about the future, the arrival of General Gouraud in Beirut on November 19 played a part in further inflaming Palestinian and Syrian nationalist fervor.

Third, the arrival of an official British representative in Palestine, whose specific mission was to report on the "financial and administrative conditions there, and to advise concerning the line of policy to be followed in the future in these respects, should the mandate fall to Great Britain,"[45] may have also been a factor influencing the Congress. Moreover, Sir Herbert Samuel's presence provided the Palestinians and Syrians with the opportunity and extra incentive to demonstrate their wishes directly to His Majesty's Government with added zeal.

The Congress subsequently took place amid nationwide demonstrations and protests in most major centers of the country. The British, directly in control of Palestine, were not only fully aware of the local population's demands, and the various fears and pressures influencing their actions, but also suspected that these events were taking place with French support and encouragement. This was so much the case that there appears to have been a body of British officials who advocated immediately reproaching the French government and formally demanding that it desist from further incitement of the Arab population before it could significantly jeopardize British interests.

As Colonel Meinertzhagen described the situation:

> Demonstrations organized by the Moslem Christian League took place at Jerusalem and other centres in Palestine on

[45] *Letter from Mr. Samuel to Earl Curzon, April 2, 1920, [E 3109/131/4]* in *Documents on British Foreign Policy, 1919-1939*, 13: 242, n. 1. For his own account of this mission see Viscount Samuel, *Memoirs*, London, 1945, 148-150. Samuel would later become the first High Commissioner for the British Mandate of Palestine.

> February 27th. They passed off quietly. Their object was to protest against Zionism and to demand unity of Syria. Mention was made of complete independence.
>
> These demonstrations though taking advantage of presence of Mr. Samuel in Palestine undoubtedly owe their origin to French instigation and guidance. I have satisfied myself from documentary evidence that French propaganda has greatly increased in Palestine during the last two months and is now working against Zionism and for a French Palestine in a Unified Syria. Evidence is naturally based on agents' reports solely, but it is frequently confirmed by facts and is of such growing volume that one is compelled to credit it. The French representative at Jerusalem appears to be the source of the propaganda in Palestine and is spending much money to attain his object. Some months ago, at our request, French activity in Palestine ceased and it is only since General Gouraud's arrival[46] and Feisal's return that recrudescence has been noted. Changed conditions make it difficult for us to approach the French on the subject. You will realize how easy it will be to wreck at its outset our administration and policy of His Majesty's Government. I am of the opinion that the French aim at nothing less and if you could make a strong protest to French Government before more harm is done, it will be of great assistance to our Palestine Administration and will put a stop to what amounts to most dishonourable conduct on the part of an Ally.
>
> The Chief administrator concurs in above.[47]

The General Syrian Congress (March, 1920)

A few days later, on March 7, 1920, another Congress was held in Damascus that built upon the same decisions of the previous Syrian congress and was attended by many of the same members, in addition to a number of new participants.[48] In sum, it declared:

> Complete and absolute independence of our Syrian nation—including Palestine—within its natural borders, an

[46] General Gouraud, appointed French High Commissioner in Syria and Lebanon and Commander-in-Chief of the Army of the Levant in October 1919, had arrived in Beirut on November 19.

[47] *Colonel Meinertzhagen (Cairo) to Earl Curzon (Received March 3, 12.50 p.m.)* No.15 Telegraphic [E 920/920/44] *Cairo, March, 2, 1920* in *Documents on British Foreign Policy,* 13: 219-220.

[48] For a discussion of this Congress see Mārī Almāz Shahrastān, *al-Muʾtamar al-Sūrī al-ʿĀmm, 1919-1920* (Beirut, 2000).

> independence built upon a civil, representative framework safeguarding the rights of minorities, while rejecting the Zionists' pretensions to turn Palestine into a Jewish national homeland or into a place to which they could [freely] immigrate.[49]

It then went on to crown Faysal as the constitutional monarch of Syria, giving the official date of the *bayʿah* (or "oath of allegiance") as March 8, 1920, at 3:00 p.m., and proclaimed his brother ʿAbdullah as King of Iraq. Finally, it declared the termination of the Allied military administrations from the occupied Syrian territories and Iraq.

The Arabs were, once again, characteristically consistent in informing their allies of precisely what took place, laboriously explaining the exact reasons behind their actions, and subsequently going to great lengths to make their position unequivocally clear. On March 15, ʿAli Rida al-Rikabi, the first prime minister of Faysal's new government as King of Syria, immediately presented the Allies with his government's official stance on the new developments. First, he explained the Arabs' rationale by restating their reasons for initially joining the Allied war effort:

> The Arab people ventured to join the Allies, confident in the authenticity of their proclamations regarding their war aims, and, accordingly, bore a heavy burden, sacrificing lives and possessions, during the course of their joint struggle. The Allied Commanders have, on more than one occasion, officially acknowledged the value of this Arab support.
>
> During this period, the Allied heads of state were unceasing in their promises to the Arabs regarding the realization of their natural aspirations and regaining the rights of which they were deprived by the Turks. These promises added impetus to the Arabs' valor in the battlefield and intensified their dedication to the Allied cause to the greatest extent.
>
> Then came the Peace Conference, in the age of the League of Nations, presenting them with renewed promises of independence and self-rule.[50]

Rikabi thus began with the cogent argument that would become the crux of Arab nationalist discourse for decades to come, namely that it was only because of their own desire for unity and independence that the Arabs had

---

[49] al-Ḥakīm, *Suriyah wa-al-ʿAhd al-Faysali,* 140.

[50] *Mudhdhakirat Ḥukūmat ʿAlī Riḍā al-Rikābī ilá Duwal al-Ḥulafāʾ, al-ʿĀṣimah, al-ʿadad 109, 3/15/1920* in *al-Bayānāt al-Wizārīyah al-Sūrīyah wa-Munāqashātuhā fī al-Majlis al-Niyābī, 1918-1958*, edited by Yūsuf Ḥusayn Ibīsh and Yūsuf Quzmā Khūrī (Beirut, 2000), 2.

joined the war effort against the Ottomans and their camp, fought honorably, and borne their share of heavy burdens like everyone else. Nor were these aspirations or their desire to attain these goals ever kept secret or deemed unrealistic and unacceptable by anyone. On the contrary, according to their understanding, the Arabs had repeatedly been promised independence and unity by the Allies, both before and during the course of the war and, initially, by the Peace Conference itself, and were assured of their attainment once the war ended.

Rikabi then proceeded to point out all the disappointments that the Arabs had undergone in the aftermath of the war, largely as a direct result of Allied policies and actions, underlining the dangerously volatile situation that ensued.

> Many months have passed, however, and none of these promises has reached the stage of implementation, and the Arabs have not achieved any of their demands regarding the rights for which they paid dearly in terms of men and possessions. Syria is now divided into three regions each governed by a separate military administration, creating circumstances lacking any semblance of administrative or economic order. As a result, the nation has been reduced to a lamentable state at a time when its greatest need is organizing its resources in order to counter the all the damages resulting from the war.
>
> The people viewed with apprehension the postponement of the realization of their aspirations, which they had promised on numerous occasions, and began to fear for the unity of their country and its future status. Consequently, they became drawn, through the prevalent dysfunctional economic and administrative situation, to actions that are the result of despair and resentment; political conspiracies and rumors began developing in numerous areas and spreading at an alarming rate.[51]

The "nation," after undergoing the devastating effects of war, was being further destabilized by division, insecurity, and administrative and economic chaos, resulting in seething discontent among its inhabitants, and rendering it fertile ground for conspiracies and rash, destructive actions. Such a situation was naturally detrimental to everyone's interests. Something, therefore, needed to be done, Rikabi explained and it was imperative to take action. Consequently:

---

[51] Ibid.

> The enlightened sector of the population was of the opinion that, under these circumstances, it was its duty to try to salvage the situation before it became untenable. It was for this purpose, that the Syrian Congress convened, composed of officially elected representatives from all the Syrian regions. After an in-depth study and analysis of the situation, the Congress issued a resolution on March 8, 1920 declaring the full independence of Syria, in all its three regions, and the election of His Majesty, Amir Faysal to the Syrian throne.[52]

In this manner, the new Syrian government sought to legitimize its position by indicating that the burden of responsibility fell upon the "enlightened sector of the population" that now had to take charge of the desperate situation. The means it had chosen was democratic action: convening a representative congress that would carefully analyze and discuss the situation and ostensibly come to acceptable and reasonable conclusions on how to resolve the problem. In other words, the Syrians were attempting to demonstrate that they were fully capable of dealing with their own problems and governing themselves in an enlightened and civilized manner. The present regime, hence, was presented as the direct outcome of this civilized democratic process, and therefore an expression of the true desires of the Syrian people.

In order to strengthen its position further, the Syrian government pointed to the degree of approval with which the Arabs, the people fundamentally at issue, received the resolutions:

> This resolution has been met with great celebrations everywhere and the vast majority sees it as the means to ending the crisis from which they are suffering, and a guarantee of their legitimate rights to independence and self-determination, those natural rights, which were supported and backed by the Allies on numerous occasions.[53]

Rikabi then sought to allay any fears the Allies might have regarding the new government and its future intentions. Accordingly, he was careful to present them with an outline of its future agenda; summarized as follows:

> The plan of this government, which has been approved by His Majesty, includes the following:
>
> 1. The support and maintenance of the independence that has been declared.
>
> 2. The maintenance and development of general security in every Syrian region, equal justice for all without regard

[52] Ibid.

[53] Ibid.

> to race or creed, protecting the rights of minorities, and the protection of the interests of our allied nations and their citizens.
>
> 3. The creation of good relations between Syria and foreign nations.
>
> 4. Endeavoring to organize the nation in a manner that will guarantee the most effective utilization of its natural resources and the advancement of its culture.
>
> 5. Loyally assisting the Allies in maintaining general peace in the East.[54]

Rikabi assumed that he had made an abundantly coherent and irrefutable case. Nevertheless, he concluded his statement by going to painful lengths to reassure the Allies. Neither the Congress, its resolutions, nor indeed the regime subsequently established by them, he pleaded, meant to offend the Allies or challenge their position. The new status quo, he assured them, did not threaten their future interests in the region in any way, provided they did not conflict with Syria's independence and unity. The new government, moreover, fully recognized of the value of the Allies' friendship, acknowledged their status, and planned to base its policies on full cooperation with them.

> I am thus sending you a faithful translation of the original resolution of the Syrian Congress, confident that your government will take into consideration the factors that have resulted in the Congress' action and to recognize that it was forced to submit to necessities that could not be ignored, and to support what is essentially a sacred right.
>
> As you can see, the plan, which I am honored to present to you, leaves no room for doubt regarding our staunch determination to establish friendly relations which guarantee the mutual interests shared between the Allies and ourselves, particularly with your great nation which has provided us with valuable support in accomplishing our national aspirations.
>
> With this, I hope that we will continue to gain your government's confidence and its valuable aid and support, as in the past, in order to help us accomplish our mission. Your Excellency can rest assured that we will spare no effort in continuing to ensure the continuation of the friendly relations that our two countries presently enjoy.[55]

---

[54] Ibid., 2-3.

[55] Ibid., 3.

Once again, the new government's stance with regard to Palestine can be plainly inferred from Rikabi's statement. Palestine is simply alluded to as one of Syria's "three regions" that had been created by the Allies in the wake of the war. Its inclusion within the boundaries of the united Syrian state is presumed to be a foregone conclusion, particularly since there was no question of the government compromising on the integrity of Syrian unity and independence.

Rikabi, true to his word, promptly sent a translation of his statement to the British government; attached was a letter from Faysal and a statement of policy by the Syrian Congress. The purpose of the latter two documents, again, was to demonstrate the Arabs' willingness to maintain friendly relations with the Allies, to confirm that Allied interests would be safe, and also to express the Arabs' resolve to declare independence on their own terms. In this way, the new regime hoped to force the Allies into recognizing their newly declared independence as the best possible solution to the developing problem. After all, the new regime, in the final analysis, was more than willing to cooperate and no one presumably wanted to deal with armed revolt, which, they claimed, was the only other alternative outcome.

In his attached letter, Faysal concludes:

> I sincerely hope that in answer to this letter you will announce recognition of principle of independence and United[56] Syria which will allow me to come at once to Europe to thank His Majesty's Government and to enlighten the Supreme Council as to conditions existing in this country.
>
> I affirm also that Syrian people are always ready to come to an agreement with British and French Governments on matters relating to safeguarding of their interests in Syria, Palestine and Irak.[57]

Furthermore, in their statement of policy, the Syrian Congress declared:

> We undertake to respect friends[58] of our Allies as well as their foreign interests and we trust that Allies will agree to our (? proposals)[59] and [with]draw their forces from Western and

---

[56] *Field Marshal Viscount Allenby (Cairo) to Earl Curzon (Received March15, 9:30 a.m.) No. EA 3023 Telegraphic [E 1599/2/44], Cairo, March 14, 1920* in *Documents on British Foreign Policy,* 13: 229-230. The original letter here read: "la reconnaissance du principe de l'Indépendance et de l'Unité de la Syrie," ibid., n. 1.

[57] Ibid., 230.

[58] In the text of this statement received later under cover of despatch No.33 of March 16 (not printed) received March 29, this word read 'friendship,' ibid., n. 2.

[59] The text received later read: 'our independence,' ibid., n. 3.

> Northern zone[s] as security and order will be maintained by our national troops.[60]

Once he received the statements sent by the new regime and its ruler, Lord Curzon's answer was nevertheless characteristically brief and dismissive: "No response."[61]

While this Congress and its resolutions were perceived as nothing short of a "coup d'état"[62] by the outraged Allies, the reactions it generated and its repercussions were quite telling. Strictly speaking, the Congress and its objectives certainly did not take the Allies the least bit by surprise; they plainly understood the political mood in the country and its population's inclinations. After all, the Arabs in Syria and Palestine had consistently made their wishes obvious. Furthermore, the Allies had very precise information of when the Congress was going to be held, and what kind of decisions it would take. Faysal himself had been quite diligent in keeping the British, in particular, apprised of the volatile situation with which he had had to contend prior to its convening. The numerous active agents the Allies had operating in the region, moreover, not only provided them with the latest reports on all developments, but were also playing a direct role in manipulating events.

The Allies' official response to the Congress and its resolutions was therefore largely predictable. The legitimacy of the Congress as being truly representative of the Syrian people was brought into question, the practical viability of its decisions were ridiculed, and the whole affair was generally dismissed as being inconsequential.

Even before receiving any formal instructions regarding his government's official reaction, the British Civil Commissioner in Baghdad, for example, upon hearing of the crowning of Faysal as King of Syria and his brother as King of Iraq, immediately telegrammed the acting British political agents and representatives in "Bushire, Koweit, Maskat, and Bahrain"[63] with the following:

> Information has been received that Sherif Feisal was crowned King of Syria at Damascus on March 8th by an assembly at that place who also declared that Sharif Abdullah was King of Mesopotamia. I am as yet without official information as to the attitude which will be adopted in this connection

[60] Ibid., 230.

[61] Ibid., n. 7.

[62] The British report actually refers to it as such; see 'Notes on the Middle East', No.3, 1 April 1920 [*IOR:L/P&S/10/658*] in *Records of the Hashemite Dynasties*, 10: 323.

[63] *Civil Commissioner, Baghdad to Political Agent, Bahrain, 15 March 1920* [FO 371/5062] in *Records of the Hashemite Dynasties,* 10: 322. The political agent in Bahrain was also supposed to relay this message by mail to Ibn Saud in Najd.

> but it may be assumed that neither H.M.G. nor the French Government will find themselves able to recognize as valid any acts or declarations of this self constituted assembly. Syria, Palestine, Mosul and Mesopotamia were conquered by the Allied Forces from the Turks and their future can be decided only by the Allied Powers acting in concert. It may also be taken for granted that H.M.G. under no circumstances can admit the right of anyone in Damascus to decide the future of Mesopotamia.[64]

In their efforts to diminish the significance of the Congress and its resolutions, the British sought to give them as little credence as possible by portraying the event as an elitist gathering of a few foolhardy zealots with unrealistic goals which, once made public, would be immediately disavowed by a significant majority of the Syrian population. In addition, the British also resorted to accusations directly implicating France in engineering the whole affair. They sought to undermine the authority and credibility of the congress even further by implying that its goals were more in accord with France's future designs on the region, rather than a true reflection of Arab aspirations. In this manner, they also hoped to thwart any potential circumstantial advantage the French could derive from these events as they unfolded.

Herbert Samuel, who had been observing the situation in Palestine over the past two months, expressed characteristic disdain for the power, authority, and effectiveness of the Syrian Congress, its resolutions, and its elected leader. In his own private correspondence with Lord Curzon, he stated:

> I feel convinced that no-one would have been more surprised than Faisal himself and his chief supporters had he been recognized by the Powers, no matter under what conditions, as King of Palestine—unless indeed it were [the] population of Palestine itself. Such a prospect has not yet, I believe, been regarded by them as within the bounds of serious consideration. Faisal, I am told, has never even set foot in Palestine. It is universally known, and not denied, by the Arab Nationalist leaders that the Syrian Congress was quite unrepresentative of the populations both of Palestine and of Mesopotamia.[65]

Aside from being simply "unrepresentative," he claimed that the Congress and its decisions divided Palestinian society, rather than uniting it:

---

[64] Ibid.

[65] *Letter from Mr. Samuel to Earl Curzon, April 2, 1920, [E 3109/131/4]* in *Documents on British Foreign Policy,* 13: 243.

> The declarations of the Syrian Congress are said to have disturbed the Christian elements which had combined with the Moslems to oppose Zionism. The Christians of Palestine would not at all welcome the prospect of being the subjects of an independent Moslem King, and it is reported that the unity of the Christian and Moslem Society is being impaired as the result of the policy announced at Damascus.[66]

A similar analysis was given by the Arab Bureau in Cairo, which also stressed France's involvement in the affair:

> There appears to have been a touch of the "Arabian Nights" about the affair, and numerous protests are said to have been sent in from different parts of Syria. They come, however, from the sources which one would expect, and there is little doubt that the Congress was supported by the vast majority of the Moslems. Some of the people thought that Feisal had made a secret agreement with the French, and it was stated in some quarters that the Emir's life was not at all safe.[67]

Further, by implying that Faysal himself was in danger and therefore perhaps a victim of French duplicity, the British attempted to control the potential damage that this "incident" could unleash on their future plans for the region. Accordingly, they sought to absolve at least two of their leading Hashemite clients from direct responsibility—namely the Sharif Husayn and Amir ʿAbdullah, Faysal's father and brother respectively.

> There are no indications that King Hussein or Emir Abdullah took any part in arranging the coup d'état, but it is highly probable that both of them knew the Congress was to assemble.[68]

Britain's obsession with France and its connection to the Congress was nevertheless not without foundation. In many ways, the Congress had played directly into France's hands by placing the British somewhat on the defensive. Hypothetically speaking, Britain had more to lose by being forced to take a clear, definitive stance on Syria than France did. With a foothold in Palestine, Iraq, and Egypt (not to mention Iran and the Gulf), it was evident to the French that Britain was getting the lion's share of the spoils in the region. Moreover, Britain's relationship with Faysal ensured that it would remain the dominant power in Syria should he retain control there. Time was therefore of essence to

[66] Ibid.

[67] 'Notes on the Middle East', No.3, Arab Bureau, Cairo, 1 April 1920 [*IOR:L/P&S/10/658*] in *Records of the Hashemite Dynasties*, 10: 323.

[68] Ibid.

Britain, in order to maneuver its way into granting Faysal control of as much of Syria as possible while maintaining its own grip on Palestine and Iraq.

France was fundamentally at odds with the Faysali regime, because it sought to establish a sovereign regime in all of Syria—the very area the French coveted as their own rightful domain. Thus, France could not afford to see Faysal's rule become firmly entrenched. Britain's growing power and influence in the region and their open support for Faysal and his regime had thus far prevented the French from taking any direct action against him. In attempting to reach a compromise solution with the British, however, France had already slowly been forced to concede more territories in Palestine and Iraq. The French, hence, only stood to lose more by inaction.

The Congress put Britain and France in an extremely difficult position. As an expression of the Arabs' mounting fears and frustrations, and their determination to take control of their own future, the Congress and its latest resolutions now compelled the Allies to respond. Neither of the Allies was willing to risk escalating the tensions with the other by taking opposing sides, which left them with two possible options. The first was the rejection of the new status quo outright, rendering military confrontation the only course of action. Thus, France would finally be free to unleash its superior army to occupy and forcefully impose its will upon Syria. Since, in such an eventuality, Britain would have declared itself opposed to the Congress and eager to prevent the implementation of its decisions, it could either join the French military effort against Faysal or remain neutral. France could therefore rest assured that, once it guaranteed that the integrity of the acknowledged British spheres of interest was preserved, there would be no pretence of any meaningful British protest to such a course of action.

The second option was one where the Allies, as the Arabs naively hoped, would seek to avoid confrontation, ultimately forcing them to acknowledge Arab demands. The Congress' demands were essentially simple: recognition of Syrian unity and independence under Faysal's crown. It was obvious that Faysal, a faithful British ally, would choose Britain as his primary source for political, military, economic, and technical support and supervision. This, in turn, would have presented Britain with an excellent opportunity to drive France out of the region. Unfortunately for the British and those hoping to court their support in the Arab camp, adhering to the demands of the Congress also meant recognizing full Syrian sovereignty and independence. Ideally, this would have implied that both powers should withdraw their respective military forces simultaneously from the region—that is, if they wished the other to comply with the terms. Complete military withdrawal nevertheless had very different implications for the two powers. For France, it meant withdrawing primarily from Syria—the goal both the Arabs and the British were driving towards—and perhaps from Lebanon, where it could easily be drawn back in by the will of substantial portions of the local population. Withdrawal for

Britain, however, under the terms of the Congress, meant losing Palestine and Iraq, something the French knew Britain was not prepared to do at any cost.

Aside from its own desire to maintain a foothold in Palestine, Britain's official and public pledges to Zionism and the Jewish national home in international circles were not something it could easily disavow. Even if it did manage to reach a compromise solution on the Zionist issue with Faysal's government,[69] Britain would never be willing to concede the independence of Iraq to anyone except on very specific terms and according to its own timetable.

The British certainly did not hide their disdain for the position the Congress had placed them in, while the French, equally suspicious of Britain's intentions and its agents' activities, were eager to ensure British cooperation. On March 13, Earl Curzon met with the French Ambassador to review the situation and discuss a joint strategy; in his briefing to the Earl of Derby, the British Ambassador at Paris, he stated:

> I informed the French Ambassador that we had heard yesterday evening that this self-constituted Congress, of the composition, authority, or credentials of which we knew nothing, had been held; had nominated the Emir Feisal, not only as King of Syria, but as King of Syria, Palestine and Mosul, and further, that it also appointed his brother, the Emir Abdullah, King of Mesopotamia.
>
> These operations, we agreed were an unwarranted and intolerable exercise of authority by this unknown body in Damascus, and they compelled the French and British to act in complete unison, as they had hitherto done, to repudiate the intentions of the Congress, and to reaffirm the position that the future of those territories could be determined only by the Allied Powers now assembled in London, in whose hands lay the construction of the Peace Treaty with Turkey, and the settlement of the future of the areas belonging to the old Turkish Empire, which it had been decided to sever therefrom.[70]

Curzon was also careful to clarify Britain's unwavering position regarding Iraq, a clear indication that compromise with the new regime would not be possible. In essence, the Congress had firmly sealed its own fate simply by

---

[69] Faysal's negotiations with the British and the Zionists regarding the future of Palestine are discussed in more detail in Chapter 5, below; also of interest with regard to Hashemite-Zionist negotiations is Avi Shlaim, *The Politics of Partition: King Abdullah, the Zionist Movement, and the Partition of Palestine*, New York, 1988.

[70] *Earl Curzon to the Earl of Derby (Paris), Foreign Office, March 13, 1920, [E 1595/2/44]* in *Documents on British Foreign Policy,* 13: 226-7.

including that region in its resolutions.

> I added that there was one special feature in the proceedings of the Damascus Congress which concerned the British Government even more than it did the French. It was that the Emir in addition to the inclusion of Palestine in the area of Syria, over which he had been proclaimed King, appeared to have actually incorporated Mosul as well while it seemed that his brother Abdullah had simultaneously been proclaimed King of Mesopotamia. His Majesty's Government could not possibly allow the fate of these regions to be determined in such a manner. Indeed, what a Congress of Syrians, of whatever element it was composed, could have to say to Mosul or Mesopotamia it was difficult to imagine.[71]

The Syrian Congress had therefore placed the Faysali government on a collision course with both the French and the British governments, a course from which it could not back down. France was eager to exploit this opportunity and pursue it to its fullest advantage with results that proved disastrous for Faysal and his fledgling regime.

CONCLUSION

In many ways, the Arab congresses signified an attempt by the politically active citizens of the Syrian region to express their wishes and demands for the future on behalf of the population. It is evident from their demands that those Palestinians, represented by their Congresses, were eager to impress upon the Paris Peace Conference and the world that they were a part of Syria and insisted on being regarded and treated as such. They sought to emphasize through their resolutions that they had no desire to be separated from Syria, nor associated with any power that they perceived as intending to implement such a plan.

Their policies were in concord with those of the Faysali regime in Damascus and they remained faithful to the Arab nationalist stance. Accordingly, they voiced their hostility towards France, whose designs they viewed as detrimental to their future, and hence wholly unacceptable. Similarly, they were willing to cooperate with Britain, albeit on the express condition that the latter be willing to grant them their unity with Syria and independence (in other words, if Britain agreed not to implement its Balfour declaration and further divide the area between itself and France). Unity was consequently their primary underlying concern, particularly since it incorporated a crucial safeguard against the creation of a separate Jewish homeland.

Because of the great lengths to which the Palestinian Congressional

---

[71] Ibid., 229.

resolutions went to refute any possible arguments that the Zionists and their British sponsors could muster in support of Jewish pretensions to statehood in Palestine, the Palestinian Congresses' adamant allegiance to Syria certainly appears to have been motivated by their fears of Zionism. Nevertheless, while the Zionist factor might have influenced the degree and timing of the Palestinians' commitment to their "Syrianness," it is doubtful that it was the sole incentive behind it.

The Syrian Congresses, on the other hand, attempted to legitimize Palestinian demands by affirming that Palestine constituted an indivisible part of the Syrian nation and therefore fell within the purview of Syrian unity and independence. Allegiance to Palestine nevertheless remained an Arab nationalist issue at its root, and its propagators were primarily Arab nationalists who called for complete Arab independence and unity. To those nationalists, a cohesive and undivided Syrian state was thus perceived as only the first step towards this ultimate goal. A localized and limited "Syrian" nationalism, even if it included Palestine, to the exclusion of the rest of the Arabs, would have been anathema to many of the more zealous among them. Syrian "nationalism," or rather Syrian political parties that focused exclusively on Syrian interests, as they would develop during the Faysali era, also paid allegiance to Palestine as "Southern Syria" not only as a political tactic, in order to outmaneuver the Arab nationalists who dominated the "nationalist" card, but because it was part of their own vision of what fundamentally constituted the Syrian nation.[72]

The last Syrian Congress thus signified a final attempt by the Arab nationalists in Faysal's regime to take matters into their own hands and force Syria's unity and independence on the Allies as a *fait accompli*. Despite the dismissive attitude which the Allies adopted towards the Arab congresses and their decisions in general (and the second Syrian Congress in particular), and their mutual suspicions and incriminations regarding each other's complicity in the events, they could not ultimately deny that the resolutions taken in Damascus and Jerusalem did, to a large extent, convey the true aspirations of the Palestinian and Syrian people to be united.

Samuel, whose opinion was hardly free from bias, after two months of observation, analyzed the Palestinian movement towards unity with Syria as follows:

> The movement in Palestine for its union with Syria springs from several sources.
>
> There is a natural patriotic sentiment among the small class of politically-conscious Arabs in favour of an independent Arabia, which should be as extensive and as important as possible.

[72] This issue will be discussed in further detail in Chapter 4, below.

> There is a feeling that to insert economic divisions between neighbouring countries which have hitherto been under a single government, would cause much inconvenience and would be a retrograde step. Commerce and travel between Palestine, the Hauran and Syria have hitherto been untrammeled by frontiers, and there is resistance to the economic inconveniences that would be likely to follow from political separation.
>
> There is an anti-Zionist movement, based largely upon the anticipation that a large Jewish immigration would lead to the reduction of the rest of the population to a lower status. A united and independent Syria is regarded as the only means of combating Zionism.
>
> There is the personal interest of the effendi class in Palestine which expects that the administrative posts under an independent government would be filled by its own members, to a far greater degree than under a British mandate, particularly if it were combined with a Zionist policy.
>
> There is also a social question in Palestine, the fellaheen and the effendis being in antagonism to one another. The latter fear the consequences of any government which they did not control being in a position to exact social legislation.
>
> All these motives combine to foster the movement. It is certain, nevertheless that it is not deep-seated. The mass of the population is not concerned with any question of general politics. Moreover, the fellaheen view with suspicion any movement which is organized by the effendis, simply for the reason that it is so organized.[73]

Although he cast doubts on how representative the movement was on the grass roots level, contending that the average Palestinian's allegiance to it was merely superficial, Samuel still could not deny:

> Besides, there is substance in part, at least, of the arguments that are advanced for a united Syria. It cannot be denied that the establishment of customs and other barriers between various parts of Syria would cause inconvenience to its inhabitants and would be detrimental to prosperity. It is true that it would be wrong to create an Arab state without access to the sea. It is true that the Arab patriotic sentiment,

[73] *Letter from Mr. Samuel to Earl Curzon, April 2, 1920, [E 3109/131/4]* in *Documents on British Foreign Policy,* 13: 241-2.

> to such extent as it exists, ought to be respected and, as far as possible, satisfied.[74]

"But," he maintains, "to meet these contentions by the recognition of Faisal as King of Palestine appears to me to be both objectionable and unnecessary."[75]

The Congress thereby presented France with the prime opportunity to move in and take control of events, an opportunity that it did not hesitate to utilize immediately. The fact that Arab demands had been clear, consistent, and justified did not ultimately factor into the equation; the Arab armies proved to be no match for France's superior military and France consequently imposed its will on Syria and ousted the Faysali regime. The division of Syria would soon begin to take its real and ultimately permanent form, but the Allies nonetheless sought to maintain the charade of legitimacy by continuing to work under the guise of the League of Nations and the Peace Conference. Did the Paris Peace Conference take any notice of the Arab Congresses and their demands, or did it systematically adopt the Allied stance that the Congresses and their resolutions were essentially unrepresentative of the wishes of the general population? Furthermore, before dismissing the Congresses as the efforts of a few foolhardy zealots with a distinct political agenda and rubberstamping the Allied plans for the region, did the Peace Conference make any concerted effort to find out what the real demands of the general Syrian population were? These are some of the questions that will be examined in the following chapter.

---

[74] Ibid., 243.

[75] Ibid.

CHAPTER THREE
THE KING-CRANE COMMISSION

The official position of politicized Syrians and Palestinians regarding the future of Syria, and Palestine's place within it, was quite unambiguous. The resolutions of the main congresses held in the region during this period made it perfectly clear that its inhabitants, insofar as they were represented by the congresses, demanded Syrian unity within borders that explicitly encompassed Palestine. Nevertheless, the Allies raised doubts regarding the degree to which the views expressed by the individuals attending the Congress and drafting its resolutions were in fact representative of the population as a whole. Furthermore, Britain and France questioned each other's involvement in the congresses and motives vis-à-vis their own interests in the region. Were the ardent beliefs in Syrian unity and independence underlined by the congresses something that the vast majority of the region's inhabitants adhered to as the congressional resolutions claimed? Or, were they the radical convictions of a handful of zealots, fanatics, and political opportunists in Faysal's pay, who engineered and dominated the Congresses to further their political programs, as the Allies maintained?

Since the parties involved—the British, French, and Faysal's Arab nationalists—each had their own distinct political agendas and designs for the region, it was not likely that any of them would make an honest, sincere, and impartial effort to discover what the general population really wanted. Indeed, if any one of those groups did conduct a survey of the population, the results would have been tailored and manipulated to suit that particular group's interests. This would have ordinarily rendered the true wishes of the Syrian population difficult—if not impossible—to gauge with any definitive authority. In this particular instance, however, not only was an effort made to survey the region in order to determine its population's real desires and aspirations, this effort was conducted by outside observers, with no real interests in the region or political agenda of their own. Moreover, it was carried out under the auspices of the Paris Peace Conference, with its official support and full backing and with the, albeit grudging, consent of all parties involved.

To the extent that the Paris Peace Conference was set up for the complex purpose of picking up the pieces and creating a viable global plan to rebuild the world in the wake of the Great War, it also served as an international forum where nations could play some role in determining their own future destiny. Primarily, it functioned as an effective platform for the victorious Allies to conduct negotiations amongst themselves in order to put their own predetermined post-war plans into effect. The Syrian Arabs, as represented by Faysal, were among those nations clamoring to present their case for unity and independence, only to find that the victors—the ultimate judge and jury at this conference—already had their own set designs for the region prefigured.

Included among the Allies, however, was the traditionally isolationist United States, which, having no clear-cut future imperial ambitions of its own in the region, provided the Arabs with at least one ostensibly impartial adjudicator in these proceedings. The fact that the United States did not have much stake in the Middle East also meant, unfortunately, that it would not be compelled to apply any consequential amount of pressure to ensure enforcement of a just solution. The presence of America's idealist president Woodrow Wilson, with his dedication to his fourteen points (which included the ideals of liberty and the nations' right to self-determination) and his League of Nations project, nevertheless ensured he would be sufficiently concerned with endowing the conference and its decisions with at least a semblance of fairness and integrity.

Insofar as Syria and the Palestinian question were concerned, perhaps the most salient outcome of American participation at the Paris Peace Conference was the King-Crane Commission.[1] Although ultimately ineffective in terms of outcome, this commission provided a clear demonstration of the general attitude of the population and their aspirations for their future. The fact that the Commission managed to conduct a survey of the Syrian region in its entirety enabled it to provide valuable insight into how deeply rooted the notion of Southern Syria was among the population and the extent of its importance in the development of Syrian national identity. The Commission, moreover, offered further evidence regarding the degree of influence that the British and French exerted in the region on many levels, the extent to which they manipulated its population, and their ruthless determination to institute their own schemes in complete disregard of the wishes of its inhabitants, and indeed in direct contradiction to their own professed war aims and policies.

The purpose of this chapter therefore is to provide a detailed examination of the King-Crane Commission, its background, methods, findings, and ultimate recommendations, in order to gain a clearer perspective on the development of the concept of Palestine as Southern Syria. It explores nationalism, nationalist notions, and future ambitions among the local peoples of the region, examines their views and understanding of such notions, and the evolving political trends and opinions dominating their society.

---

[1] See, for example, Harry Howard, *An American Inquiry in the Middle East: the King-Crane Commission* (Beirut, 1963).

BACKGROUND

The King-Crane Commission, its reports, and its final recommendations, shed substantial light on a number of complicated political processes already underway in the Middle East. The Commission's very conception, its difficult birth, and its subsequent findings demonstrated the tortuous political and diplomatic quagmire in which the recently "liberated" Syrian region had fallen. The Commission seemed an obvious measure made reasonably necessary by the Allies' professed intentions for the region. By examining the perspective of the local inhabitants, the Commission managed to provide a clear picture of public opinion in Syria and those inhabitants' hopes, aspirations, and concerns for their future. The Commission was able to provide particularly valuable evidence, if not a glaring demonstration, of their feelings towards the question of Palestine/"Southern Syria" and its centrality in their developing national discourse by offering a fairly impartial investigation of the indigenous population.

With regard to its true motivations, the King-Crane Commission immediately sought to dispel any doubts or suspicions surrounding the integrity of its purpose. The Americans were eager to point out that they, as a nation, had no territorial ambitions in the Middle East and their sole and express goal was to determine, once and for all, what the inhabitants of the region wanted for themselves. The United States consequently sought to clarify its position by publicly declaring its own intentions and objectives for the commission from the outset:

> The American Section of the projected International Commission of Mandates in Turkey, in order that their mission may be clearly understood, are furnishing to the press the following statement, which is intended to define as accurately as possible the nature of their task, as given to them by President Wilson.
>
> The American people—having no political ambitions in Europe or the Near East; preferring, if that were possible, to keep clear of all European, Asian or African entanglements; but nevertheless sincerely desiring that the most permanent peace and the largest results for humanity shall come out of this war—recognize that they cannot altogether avoid responsibility for just settlements among the nations following the war, and under the League of Nations. In that Spirit they approach the problems of the Near East.
>
> An International Commission was projected by the Council of Four of the Paris Peace Conference to study the conditions in the Turkish Empire with reference to possible mandates. The American section of that Commission is

> in the Near East simply and solely to get as accurate and definite information as possible concerning the conditions, the relations, and the desires of all the peoples and classes concerned; in order that President Wilson and the American people may act with full knowledge of the facts in any policy that they may be called upon hereafter to adopt concerning the problems of the Near East—whether in the Peace Conference, or in the later League of Nations.[2]

The Commission was predictably the brainchild of none other than President Wilson himself. A neutral participant at the Paris Peace Conference, Wilson had attempted to settle what seemed to him to be an unjust power struggle over what should have been "liberated territory"—the future procedural guidelines for which had supposedly already been decided by the Allies' publicly professed war aims. Therefore, he sensibly suggested the appointment of an Inter-Allied Commission of Enquiry to be sent to "certain portions of the Turkish Empire which are to be permanently separated from Turkey and put under the guidance of Governments acting as Mandatories for the League of Nations."[3]

The initiative for the project initially developed out of a heated debate that occurred between the British and French representatives at a private meeting of the chief conference delegates at Mr. Lloyd George's residence at 23 Rue Nitot.[4] Wilson became quite concerned with the escalating tensions, and he asserted that he would now "seek to establish his place in the Conference,"[5] adding that "up to the present he had none."[6]

After reviewing the situation up to its current stage of development, Wilson declared that, although he was "not indifferent to the understanding"[7] reached by the Britain and France, and "was interested to know about the undertakings to King Hussein and the 1916 agreement," he nevertheless wanted to point out that the 1916 agreement had included Russia, and since "Russia had now disappeared," it "seemed" that the "partnership of interest had been dissolved"[8] thus fundamentally altering "the basis of the agreement."[9]

---

[2] *Papers Relating to the Foreign Relations of the United States,* 12: 751.

[3] Ibid., 745.

[4] See Chapter One, above.

[5] *Notes of a Conference Held in the Prime Minister's Flat at 23 Rue Nitot, Paris, on Thursday, March 20, 1919, at 3 p.m.,* The Council of Four: Minutes of Meetings March 20 to May 24, 1919, in *Papers Relating to the Foreign Relations of the United States,* 5: 8.

[6] Ibid.

[7] Ibid., 9.

[8] Ibid.

[9] Ibid.

He continued:

> The point of view of the United States of America was, however, indifferent to the claims both of Great Britain and France over peoples unless those peoples wanted them. One of the fundamental principles to which the United States adhered was the consent of the governed. This was ingrained in the United States of America thought. Hence, the only idea from the United States of America point of view was as to whether France would be agreeable to the Syrians. The same applied as to whether Great Britain would be agreeable to the inhabitants of Mesopotamia. It might not be his business, but if the question were his business, owing to the fact that it was brought before the Conference, the only way to deal with it was to discover the desires of the populations of these regions.[10]

Wilson dryly commented that if his participation and that of Orlando of Italy "were recognized as a matter of right and not of courtesy," then:

> The question he wanted to know was whether the undertaking to King Hussein, and the 1916 agreement, provided an arrangement which would work. If not, and you asked his opinion, he would reply that we ought to ask what is the opinion of the people in the part of the world concerned.[11]

Wilson postulated that, according to what he had been told, "if France insisted on occupying Damascus and Aleppo, there would be an instant war."[12] He speculated that, based on Faysal's estimates, the latter could muster around 100,000 men at any given time. This meant that France should count on facing that many men and therefore be prepared to commit a large number of her own troops in the region to enforce her will. Consequently, he was quite concerned about this impending "fight between friends"[13] and the possibility of a "scrap" developing. It was patently clear, he sternly pointed out, that the very reason this whole question was being raised before the Council was because "it was one of interest to the peace of the world," and "not merely a question of agreement between France and Great Britain."[14]

He thereby posed the following question to Allenby: "If before we arrive at a permanent settlement under the League of Nations we invite France to

[10] Ibid.

[11] Ibid.

[12] Ibid.

[13] Ibid., 10.

[14] Ibid.

occupy the region of Syria, even as narrowly defined, what would the result be?"[15]

In response, Allenby was eager to assert that this would result in "the strongest possible opposition by the whole of the Moslems, and especially the Arabs." He went on to explain how, when he visited Beirut and other various places in the region, "deputations had come to protest against the French administration,"[16] which, he claimed, "had included various Christians, Orthodox and Protestants, as well as Mussulmans." Allenby professed that, up to this point, he had done his "utmost to make a *rapprochement* between the Arabs and the French, but without success. The French liaison officers did not get on well with the Arabs."[17]

> If the French were given a mandate in Syria, there would be serious trouble and probably war. If Feisal undertook the direction of operations there might be a huge war covering the whole area, and the Arabs of the Hedjaz would join. This would necessitate the employment of a very large force. This would probably involve Great Britain also if they were in Palestine. It might also involve them in Egypt, and the consequences might be incalculable.[18]

After listening to Allenby's alarming assessment of the situation, Wilson made the following suggestion:

> The fittest men that could be obtained should be selected to form an Inter-Allied Commission to go on to Syria, extending their enquiries if they led them, beyond the confines of Syria. Their object should be to elucidate the state of opinion and the soil to be worked on by any mandatory. They should be asked to come back and tell the Conference what they found with regard to these matters.[19]

Expounding on his reasoning behind the nature, composition and responsibility of this Commission, Wilson was quick to point out that it was not due to a lack of "confidence in the experts whose views he had heard, such as Dr. Howard Bliss and General Allenby," but rather because the latter "had been involved in some way with the population, with special projects either educational or military."

---

[15]Ibid.

[16]Ibid., 11.

[17]Ibid.

[18]Ibid.

[19]Ibid., 12.

> If we send a Commission of men with no previous contact with Syria, it would at any rate, convince the world that the Conference tried to do all it could to find the most scientific basis possible for a settlement. The Commission should be composed of an equal number of French, British, Italian and American representatives.[20]

He would send it, he added, "with carte blanche to tell the facts as they found them."[21]

Clemenceau perceived this project to be an affront to France and a direct attack on French interests. He responded that while he was willing to agree to the notion of a commission of inquiry, certain "guarantees" were necessary. For one, Clemenceau maintained that the inquiry should not "confine itself to Syria," but should be extended to "other parts of the Turkish Empire" where mandates were required, areas such as Palestine and Mesopotamia.[22] In other words, those places earmarked to become British spheres of interest. Second, Clemenceau contested that Syria was Arab, and requested that it be recorded that "many Syrians were not Arab, and that if the Syrians were put under the Arabs they would revolt."[23] Finally, he also expressed concern with the fact that Faysal "only represented one side of the Arab race," and was renowned to be "practically a soldier of England."[24]

Ultimately, Clemenceau claimed to agree to Wilson's proposal "in principle," but requested "twenty four hours of reflection before setting up the Commission," since it would be quite difficult to ascertain the "real feelings of the people" as "Orientals were so timid and afraid to say what was in the back of their minds." Therefore the "whole inquiry would be an extremely delicate one," and it was "very important" that it "should not be merely superficial."[25]

Lloyd George and Wilson both willingly conceded Clemenceau's request regarding the extension of the inquiry to the other "Turkish regions" such as Armenia, Mesopotamia, and Palestine. The only objection to France's requested "guarantees," in fact, came from Lord Balfour, who claimed he felt "these proposals might postpone the making of peace."[26] Notwithstanding these differences, an agreement was reached to send a commission and Wilson,

---

[20] Ibid.

[21] Ibid.

[22] Ibid.

[23] Ibid., 13. Clemenceau was speciously arguing that the ethnic minorities in Syria, such as the Turkomans, Kurds, and Assyrians for example, constituted a much larger percentage of the predominantly Arab population.

[24] Ibid.

[25] Ibid.

[26] Ibid.

at Lloyd George's request, "undertook to draft a Terms of Reference to the Commission."[27]

Diplomacy (and its impediments)

Just as Wilson's ambitious project of an impartial inter-Allied Commission of Inquiry appeared to be making headway, the European powers began to present diplomatic obstacles in an attempt to derail the entire project. France, in particular, was quick to waver in its position and delay the process. By May 21, 1919, Wilson, with no imperial interests at stake and eager to begin, was becoming noticeably impatient.

While discussing the future of Anatolia, during a meeting of the American, British, and French delegates at his home at the Place des Etats-Unis in Paris, Wilson adverted to the issue of the Commission stating that the men he had nominated[28] were "of such standing that he could not keep them waiting any longer in Paris, consequently he had instructed them to leave for Syria on Monday to await their colleagues on the Commission."[29] Lloyd George implied that the reasons for the delay lay squarely on France's shoulders, and concurred with Wilson, asserting that the same applied to the British delegates whom he "thought" he would instruct in the same manner.[30]

Alleging that "the promises made to him had not been kept," Clemenceau retorted that "in this case he must drop out."[31] When pressed by Lloyd George as to what he specifically meant by his statement, Clemenceau responded by airing out a long list of French grievances against Britain. Among the many complaints enumerated by Clemenceau, for example, were the following:

> In the Autumn of 1918 when he saw how the British were acting in Syria, he had come to London and had asked Mr. Lloyd George to say exactly what he wanted. Mr. Lloyd George had said Mosul and Palestine. He had returned to Paris, and in spite of the objections of M. Pichon and the Quai d'Orsay, he had conceded it. Then Mr. Lloyd George had said that France and Britain would get along all right. Nevertheless they had not succeeded in getting along all right. Early in the year the proposal had been made for the evacuation of Syria by British troops and the substitution of French troops. Lord Milner had asked him to put this aside

[27] Ibid., 14.

[28] Namely, Charles R. Crane and H. C. King.

[29] "Notes of a Meeting Held in President Wilson's House, Place des Etats-Unis, Paris, on Wednesday, May 21, at 11 a.m.," in *Papers Relating to the Foreign Relations of the United States*, 5: 760.

[30] Ibid.

[31] Ibid.

> for the moment and had undertaken to discuss it with him. He had never done so. Then Lord Milner had promised to help M. Clemenceau with Emir Feisal. He had never carried out his promise.[32]

In the course of his response to Clemenceau's "observations" regarding the charge of "bad faith," Lloyd George resorted to all possible excuses to justify his government's position and attempted to demonstrate that France was overreacting, if not altogether at fault:

> In London, it had been agreed that Syria should go to France and Mesopotamia to Great Britain. In his statement, M. Clemenceau had entirely ignored the article of his scheme which gave the Mandate for Syria to France. This was clearly stated in the document. Was this a case of bad faith?[33]

Lloyd George then attacked France's position by stating that "President Wilson had proposed the Commission on Syria. The United States and Great Britain and Italy had their Delegates all ready. It was France who had never appointed their Delegates."[34]

> This was a formal document and had been signed by all of them. M. Clemenceau had not carried out his part of the bargain. He did not say that M. Clemenceau had not kept faith, but he certainly had not carried out the bargain.[35]

Wilson tried to ameliorate matters by asserting that he had instructed his colleagues that "he thought other processes of advice might come from the French government."[36] He then diplomatically pointed out that he believed:

> M. Clemenceau had misunderstood his proposal that the United States Delegates on the Syrian Commission should proceed to Syria to await their colleagues. At any rate they were men of such standing that he could not afford to keep them waiting in Paris. If they did not go to Syria, then they must go back to the United States.[37]

Lloyd George responded that it was his opinion that "they ought to go to

---

[32] Ibid.

[33] Ibid., 763.

[34] Ibid.

[35] Ibid.

[36] Ibid., 766.

[37] Ibid.

Syria."[38] Clemenceau, on the other hand, still waffled. While claiming, "he was ready for the French representatives to go,"[39] he made it contingent on the replacement of British troops in Syria by French.

The next day, May 22, the discussions resumed at the meeting held at Lloyd George's residence in Paris. Clemenceau claimed he would "confine himself to questions of fact,"[40] and began a new round of circular arguments regarding spheres of interest in the region. He asserted that:

> The Sykes-Picot Agreement detailed spheres in Syria, both of sovereignty and of influence. When he had gone to London, he wanted to settle the question once and for all. There had been a good deal of friction which he wanted to get rid of. Mr. Lloyd George then said he had wanted Mosul. He replied that he would do his best, but that he must consult the Quai d'Orsay. He had promised, however to defend Mr. Lloyd George's case and he had done so.[41]

Regarding the issue of Palestine, Clemenceau stated:

> He must recall at this point that Mr. Lloyd George had also spoken to him in London of Palestine, which, according to the Treaty of London was to be subjected to some kind of international rule. Mr. Lloyd George had asked for British rule, with arrangements for the sanctity of the Holy Places. He had replied that he had no objection, provided the sacred spots were protected.[42]

As the British and French continued to argue over spheres of interest, territorial boundaries, the status of France in Syria, and the future of the Arab state there, the French kept reverting to the Sykes-Picot Agreement, in face of Britain's indignant retorts that this agreement was "only invoked when it was desired to gain something from Great Britain."[43] Finally, drained by this seemingly endless dispute, Wilson wearily inquired exactly "what part he was asked to play in this affair,"[44] professing that "he, himself, had never been

---

[38] Ibid.

[39] Ibid.

[40] "Notes of a Meeting Held at Mr. Lloyd George's Residence, 23 Rue Nitot, Paris, on Thursday, May 22, 1919, at 11 a.m." in ibid., 807.

[41] Ibid.

[42] Ibid., 807-8.

[43] Ibid., 808.

[44] Ibid., 811.

able to see by what right France and Great Britain gave this country away to anyone."[45]

To this, Lloyd George replied that he was "quite willing to abide by the decisions of the inhabitants as interpreted by the Commission."[46] Wilson then asserted that this was "necessarily his own point of view,"[47] since:

> He had no other means on which to form to judgment. He did not think these peoples could be left entirely to themselves. They required guidance and some intimate superintendence, but this should be conducted in their interests and not in the interests of the mandatory.[48]

Lloyd George still insisted "he could not send Commissioners if the French would not send any, but," he agreed, "the American Commissioners could go alone."[49] Wilson quickly assured everyone that his Commissioners were "absolutely disinterested"[50] implying that they were perfectly capable of objectively carrying out the task on their own.

News of the Commission's impending arrival served to calm the mounting tensions in the region and was met with both great anticipation and some apprehension as events began to unfold. Almost inevitably, however, all manner of rumors began circulating pertaining to its viability, essential usefulness, the scope of its power and authority, and its underlying political agenda.

The British and French, while unsure of the ultimate outcome, were at odds regarding the Commission's purpose and effectiveness from the outset. Moreover, that which was being decided upon at the upper echelons of government was not necessarily being passed down faithfully to the succeeding tiers of command, thereby creating fertile ground for speculation and conspiracy theories.

Only a few days before the Commission's arrival, for example, General Clayton met with Georges Picot and was informed by the latter of the following developments, causing him to complain thus to his superiors in Cairo:

> Have seen Picot today. He tells me Syria is being divided without reference to Feisal and that American Commission is only coming out to keep Feisal in the dark while partition of Syria is arranged. This Picot professes to know for certain from French official sources. He and I agree that if true, this is a dangerous game to play. If Feisal finds that the fate of

---

[45] Ibid.

[46] Ibid.

[47] Ibid.

[48] Ibid., 811-812.

[49] Ibid., 812.

[50] Ibid.

> Syria has been decided without his knowledge and before Commission has made its report he will undoubtedly take hostile action.
>
> M. Picot also tells me while he was in Paris it was decided not to send an international Commission to Syria and Palestine. If this is true I would suggest that I ought to have been informed by you.[51]

Meanwhile, Faysal's sources appear to have provided him with analogous reports, which subsequently caused a great deal of panic in his own camp. Faysal was understandably concerned that, by secretly conceding to award France the Arab lands they had promised him, his British allies already decided the Arabs' future and had thus abandoned him to his own fate. Unsure of his options and the viable alternatives available to him under these circumstances, he demanded an immediate meeting with the resident British authorities.

According to the British report:

> At 1 o'clock on Thursday, the 29th May, Colonel Cornwallis and Colonel Joyce were sent for urgently by Emir Feisal. Arrived there they found him in a state of almost distress. He proceeded to read out a telegram which he had received from Rustum Haidar, the Hedjaz delegate at the Peace Conference. The gist of the telegram was that the Conference was now engaged in Turkish questions, that all British troops in Syria were going to be withdrawn, and that the Commission to Palestine and Syria had been stopped. This Feisal interpreted as meaning that we were going to abandon the country to the French without any attempt being made to ascertain the wishes of the people. This he said would inevitably cause bloodshed. It would mean war between the French and the Arabs. The Arabs would attack the French, and since in that case the British might be expected to come to the assistance of the French in the country, it would mean war with us as well. He made it fairly evident what part he would play in such a contingency. He did not even hint at trying to prevent trouble, and it is clear that he meant that he would identify himself with the movement, and place himself at the head of it. He stated that if our troops were withdrawn, and any French troops were left, even if only in the coastal sector, he would regard it as a hostile act.[52]

---

[51] "General Clayton (Cairo) to Earl Curzon," No. E.A. 2491 Telegraphic [82973/2117/44] Cairo, June 1, 1919 in *Documents on British Foreign Policy,* vol. IV, no. 181, p. 263.

[52] "Brigadier General Clayton to Earl Curzon, June 23, 1919" [98129] in *British*

The clear threat in his tone notwithstanding, Faysal seems to have been confused as to the course of action he deemed most desirable and did not appear to have a coherent alternative plan of his own. On the one hand, he wanted an independent Arab state in all of Syria under his rule, without any mandatory super-power rule or supervision, and certainly without French influence. On the other hand, however, he remained quite hesitant to terminate his reliance upon the British and their forces prematurely by requesting that they depart from the region. In other words, the British had him exactly where they wanted him, adamantly opposed to France and hopelessly dependent upon them.

> On being asked if he wanted all troops, British and French to be withdrawn, he hedged, and hinted that he would consider it an unfriendly act if the British troops were withdrawn under any circumstances. His point of view in this is rather hard to follow, as it is surely what would happen if he attained the objects of his programme and was granted complete independence without any mandatory Power.[53]

Hence, the British were able to justify their present position and reluctance to leave—if not determination to stay—on the premise that they were confused by Faysal's conflicting demands and their genuine growing concern at what might transpire if they did in fact decide to withdraw. Faysal narrowed his options, and finally decided to send the British Commander in Chief in Cairo a telegram with his demands, to which he requested an answer in twenty-four hours. These demands were as follows:

> 1. That no British should be withdrawn unless all French troops were withdrawn.
> 2. That the Commission should come out.[54]

It was clear that Faysal and his supporters naively placed a great deal of faith in the Commission and its ability to have an actual impact on the outcome of the decisions to be made in Paris. He evidently felt confident that the Commission's findings would help his case tremendously, so much so that he incorporated in his dispatch his demands for an independent Syria.

> He was very insistent about the Commission coming out, and scouts the idea that any arrangements acceptable to him might possibly have been arrived at in Paris. He is still unwilling to accept any compromise as regards an independent Syria.

Documents on Foreign Affairs, Part II, Series B, Vol. 1, Doc. 33, Appendix (A), p. 67.

[53]Ibid.

[54]Ibid.

> Although at one time he said he did not mind about the Lebanon being French, he afterwards hedged, and said that by the Lebanon he meant the mountains only without any portion of the coast, not even Beirut. He also showed himself very mistrustful of our Zionist aims, although he declared that he was only presenting the point of view of the people of the country to us.[55]

A problem which seems to have plagued Faysal from the outset was the issue of Palestine. From an ideological perspective, France could easily be portrayed as the common enemy and his Arab constituents could be rallied to reject all its offers and demands accordingly. But facing France militarily was naturally another question altogether; nevertheless if a diplomatic resolution involving the entire international community was sought, then perhaps such a confrontation could be avoided. Even reaching an agreement with the French regarding its control over Lebanon appeared, under the circumstances, to be a relatively attainable objective. The Mutasarrifiyah of Mount Lebanon, thanks to French sponsorship and intervention, had enjoyed a unique autonomous status under the Ottomans for some decades and many of its inhabitants genuinely desired separate independence from the Syrian "motherland" under French tutelage. An internationally administered arrangement therefore, which safeguarded his own rule in Syria and French control over those areas where the majority of the inhabitants did in fact request France's presence and supervision in Lebanon, seemed quite feasible.

The question of Palestine, however, was a different story. The inhabitants of Palestine desired to be a part of Syria and appeared to view themselves as such, perhaps as much, if not more so, than many of the Syrians themselves. They did not enjoy any special independent status previously, nor did they ultimately desire independence from the prospective Syrian state; moreover, many of its political elite seemed willing to look to Faysal for leadership. Britain, on the other hand, had promised the Zionists a national home in Palestine, in complete disregard of the wishes of its people. Although Faysal was not in principal opposed to such a scheme himself, the people he was about to govern certainly were, thus placing him in a precarious position.[56]

If military confrontation with France became a serious threat, Faysal knew he was going to need all the international support he could muster and, in this respect, British aid and backing were critical. Britain was the only power with any vested interest in Faysal, and the only nation with the necessary power, influence and incentives to restrain French ambitions in the region. Hence, while Faysal may have thought himself able to oppose France and its plans

[55] Ibid.

[56] Faysal's position on the Palestine Question will be discussed in more detail in Chapter 5, below.

for the region, he certainly could not afford such a stance with Britain, even though the latter's future intentions for Palestine were just as unpalatable to his Arab nationalist retinue, albeit less threatening to him personally.

The following day, Faysal regained his composure, but maintained his unyielding and confrontational posture:

> On Friday morning he was not quite so excited, but announced his intention unless he received a satisfactory answer to his telegram to the Commander-in-Chief of executing a *coup d'état* by proclaiming the independence of Syria, including the coastal sector, and sending troops to occupy the latter.[57]

Faysal was still uncertain of the full implications such a stance would ultimately have for Palestine. If pushed to carry out his threat, the reaction this would generate in the region was bound to have immediate repercussions in Palestine and would therefore definitely have a direct impact on the British presence there. Consequently, he needed to determine what Britain's reaction would be in case of such an eventuality.

> He asked what would be our attitude, having in view the fact that the Arabs in Palestine would probably rise. He was informed that such an act would finally and irreparably destroy all friendship between us, as it would probably entail the loss of British lives. He agreed that this would be the probable result, but asked what he could do.[58]

Fortunately for Faysal, both of his demands—that the British forces remain so long as those of France were present, and that the Commission be sent—were met, allowing him, for a time at least, to escape this test of his authority.

THE COMMISSION DISPATCHED

Wilson and the Americans, unencumbered by imperial interests and considerations, had been making the necessary preparations to send their commissioners from the project's very conception. By March 25, Wilson had completed the Commission's instructions from the Peace Conference. First, the Americans outlined the Conference's objectives in a manner that was satisfactory to all the powers involved:

> It is the purpose of the Conference to separate from the Turkish Empire certain areas comprising, for example, Palestine, Syria, the Arab countries to the east of Palestine

---

[57] "Brigadier General Clayton to Earl Curzon, June 23, 1919" [98129] in *British Documents on Foreign Affairs*, Part II, Series B, Vol. 1, Doc. 33, Appendix (A), p. 67.

[58] Ibid.

> and Syria, Mesopotamia, Armenia, Cilicia, and perhaps additional areas in Asia Minor, and to put the development of their people under the guidance of the Governments which are to act as Mandatories of the League of Nations...[59]

Then, they gave specific instructions to the commissioners, concerning their purpose, duties, and responsibilities in that regard:

> The Conference therefore feels obliged to acquaint itself as intimately as possible with the sentiments of the people of these regions with regard to the future administration of their affairs. You are requested, accordingly, to visit these regions to acquaint yourselves as fully as possible with the state of opinion there with regard to these matters, with the social, racial, and economic conditions, a knowledge of which might serve to guide the judgment of the Conference, and to form as definite an opinion as the circumstances and the time at your disposal will permit, of the divisions of territory and assignment of mandates which will be most likely to promote the order, peace, and development of those people and countries.[60]

About a week later, on April 2, the U.S. Secretary of State, Robert Lansing, sent Wilson a letter informing him that he had selected H. C. King[61] and Charles Crane[62] to send to those "certain portions of the Turkish Empire which are to be permanently separated from Turkey,"[63] and requested his authorization, thereby officially designating them as the "two American Commissioners."[64]

In his reply, dated April 15, Wilson explained that his tardiness in response had been "because the other Powers involved seem to have withdrawn from their agreement to send commissioners to Syria."[65] Unperturbed and determined to proceed with his project, Wilson nevertheless did give his authorization for the commissioners "in case we alone send them."[66]

---

[59]"The American Section of the International Commission on Mandates in Turkey (The King-Crane Commission)" in *Papers Relating to the Foreign Relations of the United States*, 12: 745.

[60]Ibid., 747.

[61]H. C. King was the President of Oberlin College, Ohio.

[62]Charles Crane was the Treasurer of the American Committee for Armenian and Syrian Relief.

[63]"The Secretary of State to President Wilson" in *Papers Relating to the Foreign Relations of the United States*, 12: 747-8.

[64]Ibid., 748; for full text of the letter see ibid., 747-8.

[65]"President Wilson to the Secretary of State" in ibid., 748.

[66]Ibid.

The much-anticipated Commission, accompanied by numerous advisers, experts, and assistants in various capacities,[67] finally arrived in Jaffa on June 10, 1919. They continued to travel, survey, and investigate the region until July 21, when they set sail from Mersina to Constantinople.[68] During its inquiry, the Commission visited thirty-six of the most important towns in Syria, and heard delegations from "other important centers,"[69] not to mention delegations from over 1520 villages that were not included in the list of the official report.[70] The towns visited were scattered all over the three different divisions of the Occupied Enemy Territory Administrations (Arab, British, and French).[71]

Arriving in Palestine—or O.E.T.A. (South)—one of the primary issues the Commission had to face was Zionism and the population's feelings regarding the prospect of a Jewish state. Indeed, one of the first communications received by President Wilson from King and Crane was dispatched from Jerusalem on June 20, in which they declared:

> Probably at no time has race feeling been so sensitive as just now...Here older population both Moslem and Christian take united and most hostile attitude towards any effort to establish Jewish sovereignty over them. We doubt if any British Government or American official here believes that it is possible to carry out Zionist program except through support of large army.[72]

By July 10, the Commission appeared to have covered considerable ground and become more familiar with the situation. Moreover, they began recognizing the advantages of having sent a Commission that was purely American in its composition as opposed to an Inter-Allied one. Reporting from Beirut, King and Crane stated:

---

[67]These were: Dr. Albert H. Lybyer, Dr. George Montgomery, and Captain William Yale (of the United States Army) as advisors; Captain Donald Brodie (of the United States Army) as secretary and treasurer; Dr. Sami Haddad, an instructor in the School of Medicine at the Syrian Protestant College of Beirut, as physician and interpreter; Laurence S. Moore as business manager; and Sergeant Major Paul O. Toren as stenographer. *Report of the American Section of the International Commission on Mandates in Turkey, Section One: The Report upon Syria*, in *Papers Relating to the Foreign Relations of the United States,* 12: 752.

[68]For a detailed itinerary see ibid., 753-4.

[69]Ibid., 753.

[70]Ibid. For a complete list of the towns visited see ibid., 753-755.

[71]It is perhaps noteworthy that the Commission briefly included Cilicia in the Syrian inquiry, since it was a disputed territory between the Arabs and the Turks. See ibid., 753.

[72]"Mr. C. R. Crane and H. C. King to the Commission to Negotiate Peace, Jerusalem, June 20, 1919," in ibid., 748.

> Commission has now covered strategic point[s] from Beersheba to Baalbek and from Mediterranean Sea to Amman. Every facility has been given Commission by various military governors, though inevitable some steering. Heartily welcomed everywhere. No doubt of great interest of people, some Bedouin delegates riding 30 hours to meet Commission. Gratitude to you and Americans constantly and warmly expressed. Popular program developed [*developing*] in range and definiteness showing considering [*considerable*] political insight. Much to indicate our inquiries greatly worthwhile and freer expression of opinion to American section than could have been to mixed commission.[73]

Up to this point, they claimed, their findings indicated that "certain points are unmistakable."[74] Specifically, that of the:

> Intense desire for unity of all Syria and Palestine and for as early independence as possible. Unexpected[ly] strong expressions of national feeling. Singular[ly] determined repulsion to becoming a mere colony of any power and against any kind of French mandate. Only marked exceptions to this statement are found in strong parties of Lebanese who demand complete separation of Lebanon with French collaboration. In our judgment, proclamation of a French mandate would precipitate warfare between Arabs and French, and force Great Britain to dangerous alternative.[75]

Further, King and Crane proposed that the majority of the British and French officers stationed in the region—in other words, those immediately involved—were already aware of the situation and the desires of its inhabitants.

> Both British Government and French officers share conviction that unity of whole of Syria and Palestine is most desirable. They feel that constant friction and danger to peace are otherwise inevitable between British subjects, French and Arabs. But there is little clear evidence that either British Government or French Government are willing entirely to withdraw.[76]

---

[73]"Mr. C. R. Crane and Mr. H. C. King to the Commission to Negotiate Peace, Beirut, July 10, 1919," in ibid., 749.

[74]Ibid.

[75]Ibid.

[76]Ibid.

They added, moreover, "subsequent experience only confirms earlier dispatch concerning Zionism."[77]

King and Crane then informed Wilson about the recently held General Syrian Congress,[78] describing its composition, the extent to which it was representative of the population, and its demands and decisions.

> Syria National Congress composed of 69 regularly elected representatives Moslem[s] and Christians from Syria including Palestine and Lebanon met at Damascus July 2nd. Formulated program acceptable to all Moslem[s] and many Christians, except that Christians preferring strong mandatary power for their protection. Congress asks immediate complete political independence for united Syria. Government a civil, constitutionalist, federal monarchy, safely guarding right of minority under Prince Feisal as king. Affirm Article 22 of Covenant does not apply to Syria. Mandate interpreted to mean economy and technical assistance limited in time. Asking this earnestly from America. Should America refuse then England. Deny all rights and refuse all assistance of France. Vigorously oppose Zionistic plan and Jewish immigration. Asking complete independence of Mesopotamia. Protesting against Sykes-Picot Agreement and Balfour Declaration. Concluding request that political rights be not stood [*less than*] under Turkey.[79]

In this private report to Wilson, King and Crane declared that the "whole situation here involves elements of world-wide importance,"[80] and came to the seemingly unavoidable conclusion that the "solution proposed in Paris putting Syria under France would not strengthen friendly relations of France with England but the contrary. Arabs would certainly resist by every means." There was, however, a possible way out of this quagmire in their opinion; the remedy suggested was Faysal:

> Emir Feisal despite limitation of education has become unique outstanding figure capable of rendering greatest service for world peace. He is heart of Moslem world, with enormous prestige and popularity, confirmed believer in Anglo-Saxon race; real[ly] great lover of Christians [*Christianity*]. Could do more than any other to reconcile Christians [*Christianity*] and Islam and longs to do so. Even

---

[77] Ibid.

[78] See Chapter 2 above.

[79] Ibid., 749-50.

[80] Ibid., 750.

> talks seriously [of] American college for women at Mecca. Most important Feisal be encouraged, support[ed] and given opportunity to work out his plan. Given proper sympathy and surroundings no danger of his getting adrift or taking big step without Anglo-Saxon approval. Every doctrine and policy concerning Syria[n] state should take this intimate [*into*] consideration.[81]

King and Crane assured Wilson that the veracity of these observations would be further confirmed by facts the Commission had gathered and would duly present to the Paris Peace Conference: "We are sending by courier important documents," King and Crane asserted, "showing general conviction of people."[82] Accordingly, the Commission completed their investigations and set sail for Constantinople on July 21, 1919.

Commenting on the Commission, Colonel French—the Chief Political Officer of the Egyptian Expeditionary Force—would report upon its departure:

> While it is impossible to tell what may have been the conclusions they reached, there is good reason to believe that their report will be a document of considerable interest and material assistance, in that it is drawn up by men with keen and unprejudiced minds who had opportunities of discussing the political situation and future of Syria with representative and intelligent men of every section of the community.[83]

Findings of the Commission

The final report, submitted to the Paris Peace Conference on August 28, 1919,[84] began by explaining the Commission's approach and the shortcomings inherent therein:

> The method of the Commission, in its inquiry in Syria, was to meet in conference individuals and delegations who should represent all the significant groups in the various

---

[81] Ibid.

[82] Ibid.

[83] *Colonel French to Earl Curzon*, [130392] in *British Documents on Foreign Affairs*, Part II, Vol. 1, Doc. 51, p. 92.

[84] The report itself was divided into three sections: Report on Syria; Report on Mesopotamia; Report on the non-Arabic-Speaking Portions of the Former Ottoman Empire. For the complete report see *Report of the American Section of the International Commission on Mandates in Turkey* in *Papers Relating to the Foreign Relations of the United States,* 12: 751-863.

> communities, and so obtain as far as possible the opinions and the desires of the whole people...We were not blind to the fact that there was considerable propaganda; that often much pressure was put upon individuals and groups; that sometimes delegations were prevented from reaching the Commission; and that the representative authorities of many petitions was questionable. But the Commission believes that these anomalous elements in the petitions tend to cancel one another when the whole country is taken into account, and that, as in the composite photograph, certain great, common emphases are unmistakable.[85]

The fact that the Commission was purely American was not, however, without its advantages. The Commissioners themselves commented on how they were "struck" by "the large degree of frankness with which opinions were expressed to them, even where there was an evident fear of consequences." They were also quick to point out how "in this respect, the American section had an evident advantage, which could not have held for a mixed Commission."[86]

According to its findings, in its inquiry of O.E.T.A. (South)—Palestine, out of a total of 260 petitions received, 221 (85 percent) were in favor of a united Syria, as opposed to 24 (9.2 percent) which preferred an autonomous Palestine within a Syrian State, and 3 (1.1 percent) which favored a separate Palestinian entity. The majority, 174 (67 percent) preferred absolute independence for Syria, but when given the choice of a mandate power,[87] 48 (18.4 percent) were in favor of a British mandate as a first choice; 17 (6.5 percent) preferred the French, and 8 (3.0 percent) chose the Americans. With regard to Zionism, 222 (85.3 percent) were opposed to the Zionist program; while 7 (2.7 percent) were in favor of the "complete Zionist program (Jewish State and Immigration)"[88] and 8 (3 percent) were in favor of a "modified Zionist program."[89]

In the O.E.T.A. (West)—Lebanon, the Commission received a total of 446 petitions: 187 (41.9 percent) were for a united Syria; 1 (0.22 percent) was for

---

[85]*Report of the American Section of the International Commission on Mandates in Turkey; Section One: The Report on Syria,* in *Papers Relating to the Foreign Relations of the United States,* 12: 752.

[86]Ibid.

[87]It is noteworthy that the Commission used three different criteria to arrive at the final "Total First Choice" for Mandate number: first, they calculated the number of petitions in favor of the various countries for viable mandate choices (e.g., Britain, France, and America); then, the number that favored each of these countries were their mandate made obligatory; and finally, they calculated the number that were in favor of receiving primary assistance from each of these countries. See ibid., 758-762.

[88]Ibid., 758.

[89]Ibid.

a separate Palestine; and 196 (43.9 percent) were for an independent Greater Lebanon (as opposed to 108 (24.2 percent) against an independent Greater Lebanon); and 33 (7.4 percent) were for an autonomous Lebanon within a Syrian State.[90] Regarding independence and choice of mandates, 130 (29.1 percent) chose absolute independence, whereas the majority 215 (48.1 percent) preferred a French mandate as a first choice, as opposed to 8 (1.8 percent) for Britain and 125 (28 percent) for America. With regard to the Zionist program, 88 (19.7 percent) were against it, and 2 (0.45 percent) supported its complete implementation.[91]

In its survey of O.E.T.A. (East)—Syria, out of 1157 petitions received, 1022 (94.3 percent) were for a united Syria, while 2 (0.17 percent) were for a separate Palestine. Regarding independence and choice of mandates, 1066 (92.2 percent) wanted absolute independence; if they had to have a mandatory power, 14 (1.2 percent) preferred a British mandate as a first choice, 42 (3.6 percent) chose France, and 996 (86.1 percent) chose the United States. With regard to the Zionist program, 1040 (90 percent) were opposed to it, while 2 (0.18 percent) were in favor of its complete implementation.[92]

Summing up its findings for all of Syria, the Commission stated that out of a total of 1863 petitions received, 1500 (80.4 percent) wanted a united Syria, 6 (0.32 percent) preferred a separate Palestine, and 24 (1.29 percent) preferred an autonomous Palestine within the Syrian state. Regarding independence and first choice for mandate power, 1370 (73.5 percent) were in favor of absolute independence, 70 (3.75 percent) preferred a British mandate, 274 (14.68 percent) chose France, and 1129 (60.5 percent) chose America. Insofar as the Zionist program was concerned, 1350 (72.3 percent) were opposed to it, 11 (0.59 percent) supported its full implementation, and 8 (0.4 percent) supported its implementation with modification.[93]

In evaluating the petitions they received, the Commission recognized "at least five unavoidable difficulties which have qualified their accuracy."[94] These can be summarized as follows:

> 1. The number of petitions received from the various sections of Syria was not "proportional to their respective

---

[90]While these percentages total over 100%, they are copied verbatim from the Commission's findings; see ibid., 759. It is not unreasonable to assume, however, that the some of the numbers overlap. For example, some of those who opposed an independent Greater Lebanon also supported a united Syria, and some of those who supported an autonomous Lebanon under Syria also supported a united Syria and opposed an independent Greater Lebanon.

[91]Ibid., 759-760.

[92]Ibid., 760-761.

[93]Ibid., 761-62.

[94]Ibid., 763.

populations."[95]

2. The number of petitions received from the various religious organizations was not "proportional to the numerical strength of the religious faiths."[96]

3. The clear influence, demonstrated in a number of petitions presented to the Commission, of organized propaganda (both external and internal) in an effort to shape their character and opinions.[97]

4. In addition to this issue of "general propaganda"—which the Commissioners describe as "entirely legitimate as well as natural and inevitable"[98]—there was also the problem of an, albeit small, number of petitions being "fraudulently secured."[99]

5. Finally, was the issue of the individual petitions' value being commensurate with the number of signatures, "although," they add, "mere numbers cannot be taken as the only criterion."[100]

---

[95] Ibid. The Commissioners cite the examples of O.E.T.A. (South) where they visited 13 cities and interviewed delegations which presented them with only 260 petitions, and O.E.T.A. (East) where they visited 8 cities and interviewed delegations which presented them with 1157 petitions. They also add, "As the Commission progressed northward the petitions became more numerous, due to the increased time afforded for the knowledge of the Commission's coming, for the preparation of petitions, for the activities of propaganda agents, and for the natural crystallization of pubic opinion." See ibid.

[96] Ibid. The Commissioners cite the example of 53 delegations of Christian organizations received in O.E.T.A. (South) versus 18 delegations of Muslims, "whereas the Moslem population is fully eight times as large as that of the Christian." See ibid.

[97] Ibid. The Commissioners cite such evidence as "numerous similarities of phrasing," "many identical wordings," and "few instances in which printed forms, obviously intended as models for written documents, have been signed and given to the Commission." In addition, the Commissioners claimed that there were "many external indications of systematic efforts to influence the character of the petitions." They cite the example of "the same Arab Agent" being "observed in four cities of Palestine assisting in the preparation of petitions. Similar activities on the part of French sympathizers were observed in Beirut." See ibid.

[98] Ibid.

[99] Ibid. The Commissioners cite, for example, two cases in which the signatures had the same handwriting; three cases of "repeater" signatures being discovered; and the discovery that the seals of certain new organizations alleging to be Trade Unions of Beirut were all ordered by the same "propaganda agent" within a few days of the Commission's arrival. See ibid., 763-4.

[100] Ibid., 764. The Commissioners go on to claim that "some petitions signed by only a small Municipal Council may represent a larger public opinion than a petition signed by

These "qualifications" notwithstanding, the Commission believed that its efforts were not in vain and that the "petitions as summarized present a fairly accurate analysis of political opinion in Syria," concluding that, on the whole, "the petitions are certainly representative."[101]

Based on its findings, the Commission was able to outline several distinct programs that dominated the Syrian political environment and a number of clear demands on which they were founded. Overall, the Commissioners presented "six distinct political programs that were clearly revealed in the petitions, and that in some instances were developed during the investigation of the Commission."[102] From a total of 1863 petitions received for Syria, 1364 are described as being "exact copies" of these programs, while many others have "close resemblances." These six programs were: the Independence Program; the "Damascus" program; the Lebanon programs; and the Zionist program. Each of them will be examined in turn.

The Commission encountered petitions for the "Independence Program" first, and describe this program as having "three planks in its platform,"[103] namely:

> 1. The political unity of Syria, including Cilicia on the north, the Syrian Desert on the east, and Palestine, extending as far as Rafah on the South.
> 2. Absolute Independence for Syria.
> 3. Opposition to a Zionist State and Zionist Immigration.[104]

This seemed to be the dominant trend in O.E.T.A. (South), Palestine, where 83 of the 260 petitions presented (32 percent) were "simply the Independence Program, while many others closely resembled it."[105]

The "Damascus" Program was an expanded and modified version of the Independence Program, which took place following the General Syrian Congress at Damascus on July 2. In addition to the three main "planks" of the Independence program, the new program was modified by requesting "assistance" from the United States, or Great Britain as a second choice; and expanded by adding six more points to its program:

---

a thousand villagers." See ibid.

[101] Ibid.

[102] Ibid., 764.

[103] Ibid., 765.

[104] Ibid.

[105] Ibid.

1. The rejection of Article 22 of the League Covenant.[106]

2. The rejection of all French claims to Syria.

3. Rejection of all secret treaties and agreements (namely the Balfour Declaration and Sykes-Picot).

4. Rejection of the independence of Greater Lebanon.

5. Demanding a federal, democratic government under Faysal.

6. Demanding the freedom and independence of Iraq.[107]

Initially, the Commission received three petitions that contained the entire Damascus program, prior to its adoption by the Syrian Congress. Once the Congress officially endorsed the program as its own, however, it was embraced in 1047 out of 1473 petitions received by the Commission; 964 of which "were

[106] Article 22 basically created the Mandate system, thus endowing the Allies with the required official sanction to enforce the system where they would maintain control and supervision of those areas which they deemed incapable of self-government until such time as they saw fit, but allowed them a certain leeway in determining who ruled which area. The only caveat was that the inhabitants allegedly had to have the principal say in the selection of the Mandatory power. The Article itself states:

> To those colonies and territories which as a consequence of the late war have ceased to be under the sovereignty of the States which formerly governed them and which are inhabited by peoples not yet able to stand by themselves under the strenuous conditions of the modern world, there should be applied the principle that the well-being and development of such peoples form a sacred trust of civilization and that securities for the performance of this trust should be embodied in this Covenant.
>
> The best method of giving practical effect to this principle is that the tutelage of such people should be entrusted to advanced nations who by reason of their resources, their experience or their geographical position, can best undertake this responsibility, and who are willing to accept it, and that this tutelage that should be exercised by them as Mandatories on behalf of the League.
>
> The character of the Mandate must differ according to the stage of the development of the people, the geographical situation of the territory, its economic conditions and other similar circumstances.
>
> Certain communities formerly belonging to the Turkish Empire have reached a stage of development where their existence as independent nations can be provisionally recognized subject to the rendering of administrative advice and assistance by a Mandatory until such time as they are able to stand alone. The wishes of these communities must be a principal consideration in the selection of the Mandatory.

Text in *Official Documents, Pledges, and Resolutions on Palestine*, The Palestine Arab Refugee Office (New York, [1959]), 16.

[107] *Report of the American Section of the International Commission on Mandates in Turkey; Section One: The Report on Syria* in *Papers Relating to the Foreign Relations of the United States,* 12: 765.

on printed blanks of which there were seven distinct 'forms' with the program printed in full."[108]

The Lebanon programs can be divided into three distinct programs: a) the French Independent Greater Lebanon program, which demanded complete independence of "Greater Lebanon" from Syria and requested France as the mandatory power; b) the Independent Lebanon program, which had the same demands as the former, with the exception of requesting independence without the French mandate; and c) the Autonomous Lebanon Program, which demanded Greater Lebanon to be an autonomous province within a larger united Syrian state.[109]

Finally, there was the Zionist program, whose ardent supporters sent eleven petitions to the Commission demanding the establishment of a Jewish state and the facilitation of extensive Jewish immigration into Palestine. Quite predictably, all of these petitions were sent by Jewish delegations. On the other hand, eight additional petitions were sent to the Commission, which supported and approved of the "Zionist colonies" in Palestine without endorsing the Zionist program; four of these were supposedly sent by Arab peasants who were on "good terms with the Jewish colonies."

The Commissioners listed a number of definitive "requests" that became clear from the various petitions. The number one demand, which received the "largest percentage for any one request"—1500 petitions (80.4 percent)—was for a "United Syria, including Cilicia, the Syrian Desert and Palestine."[110]

"The boundaries of this area," the report indicates, "are usually defined as:

> The Taurus Mountains on the north; the Euphrates and the Khabur Rivers, and the line extending east of Abu Kamal to the east of Al Jauf on the east; Rafah and the line running from Al Jauf to the South Akaba on south; and the Mediterranean Sea on the West.[111]

Furthermore, the report adds that, aside from being the "first plank" on the Damascus program, the concept of a United Syria "received strong support from many Christians in all the O.E.T.A.'s, as the number of petitions indicates."

Nevertheless, the demand for a United Syria was not unanimous. Six out of the nineteen pro-Zionist petitions demanded a separate Palestine and this demand is "presumably implied"[112] in the others. Moreover, two

---

[108] Ibid.

[109] Ibid., 766.

[110] Ibid.

[111] Ibid.

[112] Ibid.

Christian groups in Palestine requested a separate Palestine under the British as opposed to a United Syria under France. Other Christian sources in O.E.T.A. South (Palestine) requested an autonomous Palestine within a Syrian State (24 petitions), while "this was doubtless implied in the general request for independence and non-centralized government"[113] by many other delegations.

The demand with "the second largest percentage of all"—1370 petitions (73.5 percent)—was for "absolute independence."[114] This was the second "plank" in the Damascus program and had the general support of all the Muslim delegations.

Opposition to Zionism and Zionist claims and purposes was the third largest point—1350 petitions (72.3 percent)—and represented "a more widespread general opinion among both Moslems and Christians than any other."[115] The anti-Zionist sentiment was notably strong in Palestine where 222 out of 260 petitions (85.3 percent) declared themselves openly opposed to the Zionist program. "This," stated the Commissioners, "is the largest percentage in the district for any one point."[116] Indeed, even when the inhabitants of a particular of region in Palestine could not agree on a coherent program for the future, they were united on their position towards Zionism. This was the case, for example, when the Commission conducted its initial inquiries in Jaffa:

> The first petitions received by the Commission, those at Jaffa on June 11, except in the case of the Zionist statements, do not give evidence of any agreed and elaborated policy for the future of Syria. The petitions varied greatly in content and wording.[117]

Other requests included the demand for the establishment of a "democratic, non-centralized, constitutional kingdom"[118] with Faysal as its king. Another one of the "planks" of the Damascus program, it received 1107 petitions (59.3 percent), most of which came from O.E.T.A. East, where Faysal had his strongest base of support.[119] In fact, it appears that this particular part of the Damascus program had not been fully accepted in Palestine, at least not at the time of the arrival of the Commission, since, out of 260 petitions

---

[113] Ibid., 767.

[114] Ibid.

[115] Ibid., 769.

[116] Ibid.

[117] Ibid., 765.

[118] Ibid., 768.

[119] 1005 out of 1157 petitions from O.E.T.A. East requested a kingdom with Faysal as its monarch. See ibid.

from O.E.T.A. South, only five requested a kingdom, and only two of those mentioned Faysal.[120]

Insofar as their choice for a mandatory was concerned, the majority of groups indicated that they preferred "assistance" and foreign aid to the tutelage of a mandatory power, while a few others gave their preference "under protest"—"if a mandatary is obligatory."[121] Nevertheless, when faced with having to make a choice, Britain received 66 petitions (3.5 percent) for first choice (and 1073 or 57.5 percent for second choice, if America declined.) France, on the other hand, received 274 petitions (14.68 percent) for first choice, almost all from Lebanon,[122] (and a total of three for second choice). Finally, the United States received 1129 petitions (60.5 percent) requesting it as the first choice (and a total of eleven for second choice).[123]

Recommendations

After surveying the population and studying their petitions, the Commission then proceeded to give a series of multi-part recommendations (six in total) for the "treatment of Syria."[124] In its first recommendation, the Commission made several suggestions regarding the Mandate system, the guidelines it should abide by, and the nature of its mission. The Mandatory power, it claimed "should come in, not at all as a colonizing Power in the old sense of that term, but as a Mandatary under the League of Nations, with the clear consciousness that "the well-being and development" of the Syrian people form for it a "sacred trust."[125]

The second recommendation, more importantly, concerned Syrian unity. Here, the Commission recommended that "the unity of Syria be preserved, in accordance with the earnest petition of the great majority of the people of Syria."[126]

> The territory concerned is too limited, the population too small, and the economic, geographic, racial and language unity too manifest, to make up the setting up of independent states within its boundaries desirable, if such a division can possibly be avoided. The country is very largely Arab in language, culture, traditions, and customs.[127]

---

[120] Ibid.

[121] Ibid., 769.

[122] In fact, all but 59 were from the Lebanon District. See ibid., 769.

[123] Ibid.

[124] Ibid., 787; for a full text of the recommendations, see ibid., 787-799.

[125] Ibid.

[126] Ibid., 789.

[127] Ibid.

The Commission did not include Cilicia within the boundaries of Syria, whose "precise boundaries," they suggested, "should be determined by a special commission on boundaries after the Syrian territory has been in general allotted."[128] They also made special accommodations for Lebanon due to its unique history and its predominant Christian population. Nevertheless, no special status was deemed necessary for Palestine in their estimation, since it appeared to fit naturally within the scope of Syrian national unity.

Thirdly, the Commission recommended that all of Syria be placed under a single Mandatory power as "the natural way to secure real and efficient unity."[129] As a fourth point, the Commission recommended that Faysal be made "head of the new united Syrian State."[130] The Commissioners gave several reasons for this latter recommendation, not least among which was: "The insight and breadth of sympathy revealed by Emir Feisal make him peculiarly well fitted, also, for the headship of a State involving both Oriental and Occidental elements."[131]

Fifth, and perhaps most important with regard to the question of Palestine/Southern Syria, were the Commission's recommendations concerning Zionism. The Commissioners claimed they "began their study of Zionism with minds predisposed in its favor;"[132] nevertheless, they asserted, their recommendations derived from "the actual facts in Palestine, coupled with the force of the general principles proclaimed by the Allies and accepted by the Syrians."[133]

The Commissioners acknowledged that they had been supplied with abundant material regarding Zionism, were aware of the support the Zionists received from the Allies, and had personally witnessed some of their achievements. Accordingly, they analyzed Lord Balfour's much cited declaration,[134] pointing out that if the Zionist program were carried out in its present form (with unlimited immigration) it certainly would "prejudice the civil and religious rights of existing non-Jewish communities in Palestine,"

---

[128] Ibid.

[129] Ibid., 790.

[130] Ibid., 791.

[131] Ibid., 786.

[132] Ibid., 792.

[133] Ibid.

[134] The Balfour Declaration, issued as a letter to Lord Rothschild on November 2, 1917, states:

"His Majesty's Government view with favour the establishment in Palestine of a national home for the Jewish people, and will use its best endeavours to facilitate the achievement of this object, it being clearly understood that nothing shall be done which may prejudice the civil and religious rights of existing non-Jewish communities in Palestine, or the rights and political status enjoyed by Jews in any other country." Quoted in *Official Documents, Pledges and Resolutions on Palestine*, 12.

and would thereby conflict with Balfour's alleged original intentions.

They went on to further analyze the distinction between a "national home for the Jewish people" and a "Jewish State," pointing out that the latter objective could not be accomplished without the "gravest trespass upon the civil and religious rights"[135] of those non-Jewish communities. "The fact came out repeatedly," they added, "in the Commission's conference with Jewish representatives, that the Zionists looked forward to a practically complete dispossession of the present non-Jewish inhabitants of Palestine by various forms of purchase."[136]

The Commissioners stated that if they were to abide by Wilson's principle regarding the "settlement of every question...upon the basis of the free acceptance of...the people immediately concerned,"[137] then "the wishes of Palestine's population are to be decisive as to what is to be done with Palestine."[138]

> Then it is to be remembered that the non-Jewish population of Palestine—nearly nine tenths of the whole—are emphatically against the Zionist program. The tables show that there was no one thing upon which the population of Palestine were more agreed upon than this.[139]

Consequently, subjecting "a people so minded" to the Zionist program and unlimited Jewish immigration was deemed "a gross violation of the principle just quoted, and of the people's rights."[140]

After sternly recommending "serious modification of the extreme Zionist Program for Palestine of unlimited immigration of Jews, looking finally to making Palestine distinctly a Jewish State,"[141] the Commissioners further emphasized their point by warning that "the Peace Conference should not shut its eyes to the fact that the anti-Zionist feeling in Palestine and Syria is intense and not lightly to be flouted."[142]

---

[135] *Papers Relating to the Foreign Relations of the United States,* 12: 792.

[136] Ibid.

[137] The full text is: "The settlement of every question, whether of territory, of sovereignty, of economic arrangement, or of political relationship upon the basis of the free acceptance of that settlement by the people immediately concerned, and not upon the basis of the material interest or advantage of any other nation or people which may desire a different settlement for the sake of its own exterior influence or mastery." *Papers Relating to the Foreign Relations of the United States, 1918* (Washington D.C., 1947), supp. 1, vol. 1, p. 268.

[138] *Papers Relating to the Foreign Relations of the United States,* 12: 793.

[139] Ibid.

[140] Ibid.

[141] Ibid., 792.

[142] Ibid., 794.

The Commissioners were thus eager to point out to the Conference in Paris that this anti-Zionist sentiment was prevalent in all of Syria and not only in Palestine—the area the British had earmarked to become a "Jewish national home." Moreover, opposition to Zionism had become one of the fundamental tenets of the evolving Syrian nationalist discourse and hence demanded serious consideration.

> It is to be noted also that the feeling against the Zionist program is not confined to Palestine, but shared very generally by the people throughout Syria, as our conferences clearly showed. More than 72 per cent—1350 in all—of all the petitions in the whole of Syria were directed against the Zionist program. Only two requests—those for a united Syria and for independence—had a larger support.[143]

Mindful of the nationalist sentiments of the Syrian and Palestinian inhabitants, their position towards Zionism, and the place of Palestine in the evolving Syrian nationalist discourse, the Commission consequently recommended:

> There would then be no reason why Palestine could not be included in a united Syrian State, just as other portions of the country, the holy places being cared for by an International and Inter-religious Commission, somewhat as at present, under the oversight and approval of the Mandatary and of the League of Nations. The Jews, of course, would have representation upon this Commission.[144]

The Commission's sixth and final recommendation was that a single Mandate be created for all of Syria, supervised by a solitary Mandatory power. The Commissioners then established numerous criteria for determining which power was most suited for this responsibility: these included the power being "freely desired by the people"; its willingness to "withdraw after a reasonable period and not seek selfishly to exploit the country"; its possessing a "passion for democracy" and the "development of the national spirit"; its having "unlimited sympathy and patience"; and enjoying "abundant resources in men and money."[145] After review, the Commission nominated the United States as its first choice for mandatory power. If the Americans were unable or unwilling to take on such a responsibility, then the Commission recommended Britain as a second choice. Insofar as France and its claims to Syria were concerned, the Commissioners felt that, under the circumstances, it was "impossible to

---

[143] Ibid., 793.

[144] Ibid., 795.

[145] For a complete list and discussion of the necessary qualifications, see ibid., 795-797.

recommend a single French Mandate for all Syria."[146]

Conclusion: The Commission's Assessments

In their evaluation of the situation in Syria, the Commission made a number of important observations, while reinforcing certain assumptions about the professed intentions of the Allies in the region, and how they were perceived and understood by the Syrians. The Commission indicated the degree of sincerity with which the inhabitants of the region took the promises and utterances made by the Allies regarding their future.

> Our survey made it clear that this Anglo French Declaration and similar utterances of the Paris Peace Conference, and President Wilson's Fourteen Points, had made a deep impression upon the Syrian people and lay in the background of all their demands.[147]

Consequently, the Commissioners felt it incumbent upon the Allies and the Paris Peace Conference to fulfill these former assurances and pledges.

> The promises involved cannot justly be ignored by the Peace Conference, but should be faithfully fulfilled. This is particularly true of the British-French Declaration; for it is completely in accord with the repeated statements of the aims of the Allies, and was expressly directed to the Arabic speaking portions of the Turkish Empire, especially Syria and Mesopotamia.[148]

The Commissioners established that the Allies' promises "were specific and unmistakable"; they then pointed out, "there is also probably no other region where the Allies are freer to decide their course in accordance with the principles they have professed." Accordingly, they declared:

> The sincerity of the professed aims of the Allies in the war, therefore, is peculiarly to be tested in the application of these aims in the treatment of the Arabic-speaking portions of the former Turkish Empire.[149]

Ultimately, the Commissioners saw no real obstacles to translating these promises into effective policy, since, in their opinion, a more "opportune" moment was not likely to be forthcoming:

---

[146] Ibid., 798.

[147] Ibid., 785.

[148] Ibid.

[149] Ibid.

> The war and the consequent breaking up of the Turkish Empire, moreover, give a great opportunity—not likely to return—to build now in Syria a Near East State on the modern basis of full religious liberty deliberately including various religious faiths, and especially guarding the rights of minorities. It is a matter of justice to the Arabs, the recognition of the Arab People and their desire for national expression, and of deep and lasting concern to the world, that an Arab State along modern political lines be formed.[150]

In essence, the commissioners felt that the Paris Peace Conference could finally resort to dividing the territory as initially planned by the Allies should the Commission's proposed unification plan prove to be a failure. Nevertheless, there was no reason to assume *a priori* that such a plan would definitely fail. Indeed, it was the Allies' policy—that of dividing Syria—which appeared to be fraught with unnecessary risk and danger.

> If the experiment finally failed, division of territory could still follow. But to begin with division of territory along religious lines is to invite increasing exclusiveness, misunderstanding and friction...And there is real danger in breaking up Syria up into meaningless fragments.
>
> Any policy adopted, therefore, for Syria should look to "the establishment of a national government and administration deriving their authority from the initiative and free choice of the native populations," and should treat it as far [as] possible in harmony with its natural geographic and economic unity.[151]

If one were to concede therefore that uniting Syria under a single government and/or a single mandatory power to supervise it was the natural or logical course of action to take, what then were the real factors that could now encumber Syrian unity? The Commissioners outlined them as follows:

> The practical obstacles to the unity of Syria are: the apparent unwillingness of either the British or the French to withdraw from Syria—the British from Palestine, or the French from Beirut and the Lebanon; the intense opposition of the Arabs and the Christians to the Zionist program; the common Lebanese demand for complete separate independence; the strong feeling of the Arabs of the East against any French control; the fear on the part of many Christians of Moslem

[150] Ibid., 786.

[151] Ibid., 786-7.

> domination; and the lack of as vigorous a Syrian national feeling as could be desired.[152]

In other words, the main hindrance to Syria's unity was the Allies and their meddling in the internal affairs of the Syrians. The Lebanese demand for "a complete separate independence" was neither unanimous nor indeed an insurmountable obstacle that could not be resolved through negotiations between the Syrians and Lebanese with or without great power supervision. The "fear" that "many" of the Christian inhabitants seemed to share concerning Muslim domination could be reduced through a number of safeguards inherent in a secular, constitutional government which could be internationally supervised until it became firmly entrenched in the system.

Finally, the "lack" of a "vigorous Syrian national feeling" was to be expected, given the circumstances, and could certainly be strengthened and reinforced with a wise and enlightened leadership and a liberal civil constitution—something the Commissioners believed Faysal was fully capable of providing. Accordingly, all the other "obstacles" potentially impeding Syrian unity were directly tied to the Allies' presence in the region and their own plans, interests, and subsequent activities. The next chapter will investigate the impact of the Palestine question and the notion of Southern Syria on national feeling in Syria through an examination of its role in the ideological discourse of the major political parties and its place in their party platforms.

[152] Ibid., 787.

Chapter Four

POLITICAL PARTIES: THE PALESTINE QUESTION IN SYRIAN POLITICS

The notion of Southern Syria, as has been demonstrated, was fast becoming entrenched in the evolving national discourse and thus an established characteristic of the incipient Syrian ideological landscape.The resolutions of the various Arab congresses representing the population asserted a clear consensus among the population on that issue. The findings of the American King-Crane Commission surveying the general populace in the Syrian region also appeared to support these claims. How much bearing then did this notion actually have on the nascent political scene in Syria, and what was the nature and extent of its impact on the development of Syrian political thinking?

During the Faysali era, Syria experienced a period of political effervescence during which a substantial number of political parties were established and many communities, both ethnic and religious, became more politicized. While the nation was still in its formative stages, each of its component groups sought to find a place within the emerging political framework in order to voice its wishes and establish its position. The purpose of this chapter therefore is to examine the place of the Palestine question in the demands and ideologies of the various political parties and communities extant in Syria during this period in an attempt to determine the role it played in their development, the extent of its importance, and the reasons behind it. Accordingly, this chapter will first provide an investigation of the major Syrian political parties under the Faysali regime in terms of their structure and political programs, with particular focus on their position regarding Palestine/southern Syria. It will then examine various political statements and declarations from a diverse number of groups and political parties and the place of Palestine/southern Syria therein.

Political Parties

Under Faysal's brief tenure from 1918-1920, Syria experienced a distinct upsurge in political activity. During that time, the country witnessed the manifestation and flourishing of a substantial number of political parties. Some of those parties had already been functioning since the late Ottoman period and had transformed themselves accordingly to suit the times; others, however, established themselves during the Faysali era and were thus imbued with its spirit.

The extent to which they played an actual determining role in the political decision-making process notwithstanding, these parties represented the dominant political trends in the region, thereby providing a clear illustration of the priorities that consumed the politicized urban public in Syria at this time. Since the parties generally sought to increase their membership and popular support, the tenets and goals they espoused were necessarily a reflection of the prevailing concerns and beliefs of the Syrian political community. Thus, the parties were the ones most likely to appeal directly to the populace and its desires and aspirations. Furthermore, many of these political parties called for establishing certain parameters and safeguards for themselves and others, regarding the future of the incipient nation. Consequently, even while certain parties remained guarded towards the prevalent Arab nationalist trend or indeed willing to make demands contradictory to its ultimate goals, there were certain boundaries that would not "officially" be crossed. By gently calibrating the public's moral patriotic compass regarding what could and could not be compromised, depending on the influence they wielded, the parties and the goals they professed played a crucial role in fundamentally shaping the national discourse. Several parties therefore deserve special attention.

Ḥizb al-ʿArabīyah al-Fatāt / Ḥizb al-Istiqlāl

Ḥizb al-ʿArabīyah al-Fatāt (the Young Arab Party) had been active since late Ottoman times and was one of the main "revolutionary" Arabist secret societies that agitated for the Arab cause and for Arab unity and independence. Following the installation of Faysal's administration in Damascus, al-Fatat managed to become firmly entrenched in Syrian politics, playing a prominent role in the decision-making process. Since it had established lasting ties with the young Amir at least as early as 1915, al-Fatat was in a sufficiently powerful position to play a prominent role in Faysal's government. The party was unflinchingly pan-Arab in its line and objectives and, as such, continued to retain its diverse Arab membership of Syrians, Lebanese, Palestinians, Jordanians, and Iraqis.[1]

Following Faysal's entry into Damascus, al-Fatat decided to reorganize itself in December 1918, but opted to remain a clandestine organization, thus allowing it to maintain its high standards for membership and jealously continuing to guard its secrecy. Indeed, "so secret was al-Fatat that T. E. Lawrence had heard nothing of it until January 1919, when Faysal disclosed its existence to several American delegates at Versailles."[2] The party experienced some important changes, such as the election of a new administrative committee to direct its affairs. This committee was composed of ʿAli Rida al-

[1]For a list of membership during Faysali period see Muḥammad ʿIzzat Darwazah, *Ḥawla al-Ḥarakah,* 1: 77-78.

[2]Malcolm B. Russell, *The First Modern Arab State,* 223, n. 8.

Rikabi, Yasin al-Hashimi, Dr. Ahmad Qadri, Nasib al-Bakri, Rafiq al-Tamimi (secretary general), and Tawfiq al-Natur (treasurer).[3] According to Amin al-Saʾid:

> [The committee] had full effective control over the government, akin to that of the Committee for Union and Progress over the Turkish Government, whereby no decision could be taken without its approval and nothing would be done without its consent.[4]

In early 1920, al-Fatat decided to expand its activities in the public sphere by forming an official political party with a wider membership, an executive committee, and a central committee. This party was named *Ḥizb al-Istiqlāl al-ʿArabī* (the Party of Arab Independence) and its official goal, as its name implies, was the independence and unity of the Arab lands and their liberation from all foreign influence. As a front organization for al-Fatat, Hizb al-Istiqlal essentially toed the party line in the political arena and disseminated al-Fatat's pan-Arab ideology to the public, thus allowing al-Fatat to actively participate in the political system while maintaining its cloak of secrecy. The party's first executive committee was composed of Saʿid Haydar, Asʿad Daghir, ʿIzzat Darwazah, Zaki al-Tamimi, Fawzi al-Bakri, ʿAbd al-Qadir al-ʿAzm, Salim ʿAbd al-Rahman and Fayiz al-Shihabi.[5]

Insofar as their stance on Palestine was concerned, both al-Fatat and its public proxy al-Istiqlal adopted the Arab nationalist ideological standpoint in its purest and most unflinching form. The ultimate goal from their perspective was all-Arab unity and independence; any adopted strategy had to be geared toward the attainment of that final objective. Palestine, like Syria, formed an indivisible part of the Arab whole. Consequently, there could be no compromise with Zionism, or any other divisive schemes or tendencies of any form, whether foreign or local.

AL-ʿAHD

Like al-Fatat, al-ʿAhd was one of the most prominent revolutionary Arabist secret societies active in the latter days of the empire and, as such, managed to maintain its activities up until the end of the war. Similarly, al-ʿAhd's initial focus was universal Arab unity and independence, particularly after the onset of the Arab revolt. Unlike al-Fatat, however, al-ʿAhd drew most of its membership primarily from military circles, many of whom fought

---

[3] Amīn al-Saʿīd, *al-Thawrah al-ʿArabīyah al-Kubrá,* 2: 35. This committee went through several reshuffles in its membership, first in May 1919, then again in March 1920. For list of members, see ibid., 36.

[4] Ibid., 36.

[5] Ibid., 37.

with Faysal's army during the Arab revolt and were among the troops who participated in the liberation of Damascus.

Once Syria had been "liberated" from Ottoman rule and Allied intentions towards the region had become more apparent, al-ʿAhd began undergoing an internal crisis. The founders subsequently called an organizational meeting during which the decision was made to split the party into two separate factions: an Iraqi branch and a Syrian one. Each of these factions now diverted its attention to its own affairs, focusing primarily on saving its own respective region, thereby weakening the party structure, and severely compromising the party's original goals. This, according to Muhammad ʿIzzat Darwazah, was:

> The first incident of a regional division within a hitherto synchronous national movement, thus exposing one aspect of the [many] weaknesses inherent in the national social structure.[6]

Although al-ʿAhd's original membership was drawn preponderantly from the ranks of the military—men who had either fought with Faysal or joined the movement after the Ottomans had been defeated—the composition of the Syrian branch of the party was not exclusive to the military and included a number of prominent civilian figures among its leadership; these included politicians such as Fuʾad al-Shihabi, Hasan al-Hakim and Husni al-Barazi.[7]

After the split, the Syrian ʿAhd's professed goal became the unity and independence of Syria—that is, Geographic Syria in its entirety, including Palestine. While its leadership may have felt that circumstances in the immediate aftermath of the war had rendered their initial objective of universal Arab unity and independence impractical, they nevertheless held fast to the goal of Syrian unity and were not willing to compromise on the issue of Zionism.[8] The goal of Arab unity was not relinquished altogether either, and the Syrian ʿAhd continued to maintain close ties with its sister Iraqi branch in the hope that a political or economic union between the two regions might be realized at a more opportune future date.[9] Due to the structural and ideological destabilization it suffered as a direct result of the split, and a combination of other factors, al-ʿAhd in Syria did not manage to survive long after the war, and certainly could not weather the fall of Faysal's regime in Damascus in 1920.

Ḥizb al-Ittiḥād al-Sūrī

Formed at the end of the war by a number of Syrian *émigrés* living in Egypt,

---

[6]Darwazah, *Ḥawla al-Ḥarakah*, 1: 88.

[7]al-Saʿīd, *al-Thawrah al-ʿArabīyah*, 2: 37.

[8]Ibid.

[9]Ibid.

Ḥizb al-Ittiḥād al-Sūrī, or the "Syrian Unity Party," was one of the more unique parties that emerged during the Faysali era. The Unity Party was distinct because in an era dominated by Arab nationalism, it chose to focus its orientation almost exclusively on Syria and Syrian goals. Although it made its appearance during the Faysali era, the Unity Party had been reconstituted from the remnants of the Ottoman Decentralization Party, which functioned during the latter years of the Ottoman Empire. Its forerunner—the Ottoman Decentralization Party—as the name suggests, advocated the institution of a federal (or "decentralized") system within the framework of the Ottoman state. This would have accordingly allowed the various provinces more autonomy in conducting their own affairs, and security from the trend towards national chauvinism that dominated the Ottoman government in its final years and the resultant policies of Turkification promoted by the Young Turks.

The freedom and liberalism advocated by the Decentralization party found a favorable response among many of the Empire's Arab subjects, becoming popular in the Arab provinces, and playing a substantial role in the early Arab movement. The party consequently suffered severe persecution under the notorious Jamal Pasha's iron-fisted rule in Syria: many of its members were executed, while those who managed to escape (primarily to Egypt, among other places) received death sentences in absentia.

Those members who fled to Egypt began opening communications with the resident British authorities—Sir Ronald Storrs, in particular—regarding the prospect of cooperation in a revolt against the Ottomans in return for Arab independence. These dealings never amounted to much, however, since the British-Hashemite axis was already underway and seemed far more promising and fruitful from the British perspective.[10]

Initially, this group of expatriates was amenable to the idea of a Hashemite-led Arab revolt and decided to initiate direct contact with the Hashemites after its official declaration. A delegation which included at least three of the party's future founders—Kamil al-Qassab, Khalid al-Hakim, and Dr. ʿAbd al-Rahman Shahbandar—was subsequently dispatched first to the Hijaz, to meet with the Sharif Husayn and discuss the situation, and then journeyed on to meet with his son Faysal at his headquarters on the outskirts of Damascus shortly after the onset of the revolt.[11] They soon returned to Egypt, however, disheartened with the movement, and disappointed with its Hashemite leadership for "refusing to take some of the suggestions and directions they had given."[12] As a result, within a year or so, most of the group's future members began gradually turning away from the Sharif Husayn and his Hashemite camp. Husayn's intransigent attitude and his disdain for their counsel and opinions were nevertheless not

[10] Gelvin, *Divided Loyalties*, 57.

[11] Darwazah, *Hawla al-Harakah*, 1: 90.

[12] Ibid.

the only factors that drove this group away from the Hashemite fold.

By the spring of 1918, the terms of both the Sykes-Picot Agreement and the Balfour Declaration had been made public, to the shock and dismay of many Arabs in Syria, Palestine, and elsewhere. A number of the Syrians domiciled in Egypt, "all of them men of standing and influence, who had been made privy to the terms of the Husain-McMahon compact at that time and had worked with zeal ever since on the furtherance of the Revolt,"[13] promptly decided it was time they took matters into their own hands and embarked on direct negotiations with Britain.

In early 1918, as the Great War still raged, the group held a meeting and elected a committee composed of seven members: Rafiq al-ʿAzm, Dr. ʿAbd al-Rahman Shahbandar, Fawzi al-Bakri, Shaykh Kamil al-Qassab, Khalid al-Hakim, Mukhtar al-Sulh, and Hasan Hamadah.[14] For the next two to three months, this committee diligently "gathered and translated the documents of the Arab societies, the writings of the Arab martyrs and revolutionaries and their goals."[15] These were then compiled and integrated into a memorandum, which was signed and presented to the British Minister of War, Lord Milner, by way of the Arab Bureau in Cairo.

In this memorandum, the committee described the prevailing concerns in the Arab lands, and requested that Britain offer a clear, unequivocal statement of its war aims in the region and an elaboration of its position on the post-war settlement. Could the Arabs be fully assured, they inquired, of Britain's commitment to Arab independence and of its friendship, support, and assistance once the war was over? The committee was also anxious to discover the nature and style of government that would be installed in Syria after the war. Was Britain going to differentiate between the various Arab regions and hence support a federal-style government (such as that of the United States, for example), thus permitting each region to manage its internal affairs somewhat independently in correspondence with its own unique cultural characteristics and traditions? Or, alternatively, was the entire region going to be treated as a unitary whole and hence governed uniformly based on a centralized system of government? The committee expressed its own concerns in this regard, alluding to its apprehensions about the Sharif Husayn's personal agenda and plans for the "liberated" areas, insofar as creating his own "states" in the region, to be ruled individually by his sons, rendering them all ultimately responsible to his central authority in Mecca.[16]

The British response, commonly known as the "Declaration to the Seven," was orally transmitted to the committee at a special meeting, held specifically

---

[13] Antonius, *Arab Awakening,* 270.

[14] al-Saʿīd, *al-Thawrah al-ʿArabīyah*, 2: 38.

[15] Ibid.

[16] For a detailed list of their demands, see ibid., 38-40.

for that purpose, at Army Headquarters in Cairo on June 16, 1918. This declaration has been described as

> By far the most important statement of policy publicly made by Great Britain in connexion with the Arab revolt; and yet, strangely enough, it has remained one of the least known outside the Arab world.[17]

This is particularly so since it confirmed Britain's previous pledges to the Arabs "in plainer language than in any former public utterance, and, more valuable still, provides an authoritative enunciation of the principles on which those pledges rested."[18]

In their response, the British divided the region into four categories:

> (i) Territories which were free and independent before the outbreak of the War;
>
> (ii) Territories liberated from Turkish rule by the action of the Arabs themselves;
>
> (iii) Territories liberated from Turkish rule by the action of the Allied armies;
>
> (iv) Territories still under Turkish rule.[19]

"Palestine" (defined at that point from the Egyptian frontier to a line north of Jerusalem and Jaffa) was placed in the category of "Territories liberated from Turkish rule by the action of the Allied armies" and it was clearly stated that Britain's policy was "that the future government of those territories should be based upon the principle of the consent of the governed,"[20] indeed, that "this policy will always be that of His Majesty's Government."[21]

As for the rest of Syria, it fell under the category of "Territories still under Turkish rule" and it was the "desire of His Majesty's Government that the oppressed peoples in those territories should obtain their freedom and

---

[17] Antonius, *Arab Awakening,* 271.

[18] Ibid., 271-2. For a full text of the Declaration see ibid., 433-4. The declaration as previously mentioned was originally read out in English; an Arabic translation was then provided by one of those present for the benefit of the others who did not understand English. Antonius provides his own English translation of the Arabic version, which was provided by one of the "seven" and according to him, this was "the first occasion on which the full text has appeared in an English rendering or in any other language other than Arabic." Ibid., 271.

[19] Ibid., 433-4.

[20] Ibid., 434.

[21] Ibid.

independence,"[22] and that His Majesty's Government would "continue to work for the achievement of that object."[23] Coming after Sykes-Picot and the Balfour Declaration, this latest "Declaration to the Seven" seemed to be the most reassuring statement the Arabs could hope for, based, as it appeared to be, on the Wilsonian principles of nations' right to self-determination.

Since the British Declaration was issued after Britain's occupation of Palestine, Faysal's entry into Damascus, and France's occupation of Lebanon and the coastal areas, these Syrian émigrés believed it pertinent to found their own formal party in order to establish their position politically, and give themselves a public platform from which to defend their beliefs and make their voice known.

In December of 1918, *Ḥizb al-Ittiḥād al-Sūrī*, or the Syrian Unity Party, came into being, the bulk of its membership, as previously mentioned, being drawn from among the Syrian political exiles living in Egypt, predominantly former members of the Ottoman Decentralization Party. The party was therefore federalist in its political orientation; its express goal was to establish a Syrian nation with national unity

> From the Taurus mountains to the Khabour and Euphrates [rivers] to the east, the Arabian desert to the towns of Saleh (*Madāʾin Ṣāliḥ*) in the south, the Red Sea up to the line between Aqabah, Rafah, and the Mediterranean sea in the West; Syria would be fully independent and its rights to independence would be guaranteed and preserved by the League of Nations and its fundamental laws; it would be governed by federal principles and a civil code of laws (with the exception of those laws pertaining to personal status)... and, acceptance of uniting with the united Arab Nation, if it forms as an independent state, on the condition that it is able to preserve its essential unity and form of government.[24]

With their vision focused almost exclusively on Syria and its future, the Unity Party set their political agenda correspondingly. Upholding Syria's cohesive unity and integral sovereignty as their principal objective, they believed that, in order for this unity to be ensured and preserved, compromise formulas needed to be adopted to accommodate the unique geographic circumstances of the different Syrian regions and the local cultural traditions of their inhabitants.

---

[22] Ibid.

[23] Ibid.

[24] For a complete detailed list of the party's "Fundamental Laws" see Parti du l'Union syrienne centrale-Égypte, *Les Lois fondamentales,* quoted in *British Documents on Foreign Affairs,* Part II, Series B, Vol. 1, pp. 70-71.

Accordingly, they proposed that the Syrian nation be divided into various "states" or *vilayets*, each with its own internal administration and laws in accordance with its own history and traditions, all of whom would be ultimately accountable to a central government with an elected parliament.[25] Like Aleppo, Damascus, Dayr al-Zawr, Hawran and Lebanon, Palestine was deemed part of this fundamental Syrian unity, and whereas special measures were to be taken to ensure Lebanon's acquiescence in this unity, Palestine was simply viewed as another Syrian region albeit with special "local considerations."[26]

The party's open dedication and devotion to Syria would also have a direct bearing on their position towards any projected future Arab unity schemes, which always remained reserved at best. Hence, while supporting the notion of joining the united Arab state *if* it were to emerge in principle, their support is made contingent upon Syria's ability to preserve its unity and unique system of government.[27] Although it is clear from the wording of their stipulation that they did not actually believe such a state would in fact materialize, by accepting Arab unity in principle, the party could nevertheless hope to appease the ardent pan-Arab spirit prevailing in Syria and therefore avoid losing credibility with the public. Furthermore, if such a hypothetical union were to emerge, the party, having paid the required verbal obeisance, guaranteed their ability to participate in its founding. This, in turn, would at least enable them to continue lobbying for a federal structure for the projected union that would safeguard Syria's national integrity and the preservation their own political program.

The party's first executive committee included: Rafiq al-ʿAzm, Khalid al-Hakim, Wahba al-ʿIsa, Michel Lutfallah, Kamil al-Qassab, Rashid Rida, Salim Sarkis, and ʿAbd al-Rahman Shahbandar; Michel Lutfallah was elected as president.[28] In line with its goals and philosophy, one of the party's first activities was to lodge a protest to Britain regarding its partition of the Syrian lands. Since they had been somewhat directly responsible for the "Declaration of the Seven," the party considered this a reneging on earlier agreements on the part of the British, and demanded Syrian unity. Lutfallah promptly dispatched a party delegation to Syria to work towards the achievement of these goals.[29]

The party was hence a new phenomenon among a majority of political groups who were predominantly pan-Arabist in their thinking, strove for the unity of all the Arab countries, and did not distinguish in principle between the Hijaz, Syria, and Iraq. Moreover, since it harbored a clear enmity towards the

---

[25] The capital would be in Damascus, except for the winter when it would be moved to Beirut, ibid., 71.

[26] Ibid., 70.

[27] Ibid.

[28] Darwazah, *Ḥawla al-Ḥarakah*, 1: 89.

[29] Ibid.

Hashemites and their plans for the region from an early date, it was maintained that the party's ultimate goal was to create a Syrian republic to be presided over by a "Syrian."[30] Its republican predilections aside, the party once again proved to be a political chameleon and quickly changed that aspect of its ideology to suit the spirit of the times. Recognizing Faysal's popularity and political power, they soon professed their willingness to consent to a monarchy under his crown. Notwithstanding this, the Syrian Unity party had little influence during the Faysali era and its role in attempting to take the lead in uniting the Syrian and Palestinian (and Lebanese) causes on an international level did not become prominent until after the fall of Faysal's Kingdom.[31]

al-Nādī al-ʿArabī

While not exactly a political party, *al-Nādī al-ʿArabī* or "the Arab Club" was one of the foremost political organizations in Syria and a primary forum for political discussion and the dissemination of Arab nationalist ideology. Chief among several "quasi-political" groups that began forming in Faysali Syria, this organization was influenced by an earlier group, *al-Muntadá al-Adabī* (the Literary Club) of late Ottoman times.[32] Professing neutrality in its politics, it espoused "social and scientific goals"[33] and plans "to work for general enlightenment."[34] Nevertheless, as one British official—G.W. Courtney—put it, it was not long before "all the young hotheads in Damascus"[35] joined the club. While it had branches in other cities, the Arab Club was based and headquartered in Damascus and included many of the city's local notables among its members. The club's honorary president was ʿAli Rida al-Rikabi, a prominent political figure, and a close friend and avid supporter of Faysal.

Despite its claims of neutrality, the Arab Club was a solid base of support for the Faysali regime and a platform for espousing the principles of Arab nationalism. Consequently, the Club frequently hosted meetings between club members, politicians, and nationalist youth from Damascus and other Arab regions. In line with its general political orientation, a Palestinian religious

---

[30] Ibid., 90.

[31] Ibid., 89-90. For more on the evolution of this party into the Syrian-Palestinian Congress, see Conclusion, below; also see Khoury, *Syria and the French Mandate,* 220-227; Najāḥ Muḥammad, *al-Ḥarakah al-Qawmīyah fī Sūriyah min khilāl tārikh tanẓīmatiha al-Siyāsīyah, (1948-1967),* pt. 1 (Damascus, 1987), 72-73; Asʿad Dāghir, *Mudhakkirāt ʿalá Hāmish al-Qaḍīyah al-Arabīyah* (Cairo, 1959), 155-163; and Ḥarb Farzat, *al-Ḥayāh al-Ḥizbīyah fī Sūrīyah* (Damascus, 1955), 86-87. For a more detailed account of their thought and activities, see *La Nation Arabe,* edited by Shakib Arslan, 4 vols. (Farnham Common, England, 1988).

[32] Darwazah, *Ḥawla al-Ḥarakah,* 1: 91.

[33] Russell, *The First Modern Arab State,* 76.

[34] Ibid.

[35] Quoted in Ibid.

leader, and avid anti-Zionist, ʿAbd al-Qadir al-Muzaffar, was soon elected as its head. Muzaffar, who had served as a religious official with the Ottoman Fourth Army during the war, was a powerful and emotional speaker. Under his leadership, the Arab Club became "the focal point for political discussion under the benevolent eye of the Arab administration."[36] Furthermore, the fact that illustrious foreign visitors such as Sir Mark Sykes, the French High Commissioner Georges Picot, General Allenby, and Gertrude Bell addressed its official meetings immensely increased the Arab Club's prestige and stature.[37]

Due to its growing reputation, the club soon became the center for all public political activity. Since it retained the membership of all the radicals in the country, however, it acquired some notoriety for its extreme nationalist views and actions. In one instance, for example, its young militant members apparently "interrupted a meeting at the Alliance Israelite school for girls because some statements did not conform to their doctrines."[38] Club members were also extremely active in organizing mass demonstrations, the circulation of petitions for signatures, and general public protests. One such example was the active role they played in protesting and petitioning against French Foreign Minister Pichon's speech, in which he reiterated France's claims to Syria by alleging that the Syrians themselves desired French rule.

Following his return from Paris in early May of 1919, Faysal began to feel the need to control the Arab Club. Whether unwilling, or indeed unable, to close it down permanently, the government decided to try monitoring it from within. Its leader, Shaykh ʿAbd al-Qadir Muzzaffar, was subsequently replaced by Salim ʿAbd al-Rahman (another Palestinian); moderates were placed on its committees, and its "propaganda excesses were toned down."[39] The government therefore continued to finance it, while the new moderate leadership now shifted focus to the less inflammatory goals of national organization. Consequently, the Deputy Chief Political Officer at Damascus—Lieutenant-Colonel Cornwallis—would soon report that:

> The Nadi-el-Arab has affixed a notice to its club-room stating that as the club is scientific and social, politics must not be discussed inside the building, and no more political meetings will be held.[40]

---

[36] Ibid.

[37] Ibid.

[38] Ibid.

[39] Ibid., 77.

[40] *Report by British Liaison Officer on Political Situation in Arabia*, Damascus, May 16, 1919, Enclosure 1 in No. 182, in *Documents on British Foreign Policy,* 4: 264. Cornwallis nonetheless also remarks that this was merely a "camouflage." Ibid.

Despite these attempts to restrain it, the Arab Club remained one of the principal supporters and advocates of the uncompromising Arab nationalist stance. Moreover, it organized and maintained paramilitary units, which sought to back its position through "pompous and rough behavior."[41] In reality, however, these units were intended primarily for public display, since they were far less effective than they appeared to be. Indeed, their principal achievement seems to have been the further alienation of the wealthy and notable classes from the nationalists and government.

The Arab Club's goals were nevertheless generally in accord with those of Faysal and his government, and many of the club members were Faysal's personal friends. Under different circumstances, the Club may have even served the government's purposes well with its popular appeal, vehement nationalism, and fiery slogans, not to mention its function as a valuable emotional outlet in the charged political climate. In the precarious situation of Syria at this time, however, the Arab Club proved to be more of a burden than an asset; its lack of willingness for compromise and moderation ultimately played a role in bringing about the downfall of Faysal and his government.

AL-ḤIZB AL-SŪRĪ AL-MUᶜTADIL

Another "Syrian nationalist" party founded in Egypt by a group of Syrian expatriates, the Moderate Syrian Party (*al-Ḥizb al-Suri al-Muᶜtadil*), like the Syrian Unity Party, had as its professed goal to preserve and ensure Syrian unity. Unlike the latter, however, the Moderate Party expressly and actively sought to bring Syria under the auspices of an American Mandate. Similarly, it drew its membership from amongst the more prominent, politically active Syrian community residing in Egypt. These included: Dr. Faris Nimr (the proprietor of the *al-Muqaṭṭam* newspaper), Dr. Yaᶜqub Sarruf, Michel Ayyub Pasha, Saᶜid Shuqayr Pasha, Antun Mashaqah Pasha, Khalil Khayyat Pasha, Sulayman Nasif, Nasim Subayᶜah, Amin Mirshaq, Niqula Diyab, Salim Haddad, and Ilyas ᶜIsawi, among others.[42]

The party was structured in such a way that it did not have a single president who served for any extended period, preferring instead to elect a different presiding member for every session. The office of secretary-general, however, was endowed with a more permanent status; this post remained in the hands of Sami al-Juraydini.[43]

When the American Commission arrived in Beirut in mid-1919, the party recognized this as a unique opportunity to establish its standing and decided to take immediate action. A delegation was instantly formed and promptly dispatched to meet with the Americans to discuss the situation with them in

[41] Russell, *The First Modern Arab State,* 78.

[42] al-Saᶜīd, *al-Thawrah al-ᶜArabīyah*, 2: 43.

[43] Ibid.

person. Included among the delegation's members were Dr. Faris Nimr, Khalil Pasha al-Khayyat, Antun Mashaqah Pasha, and Nasim Subayʿah.[44]

The delegation arrived on the morning of July 10 and Khayyat and Nimr were able to secure a private meeting with Charles Crane. During the course of their interview, they had the chance to explain their party's position and to present Crane with a list of their demands. These are summarized as follows:

> 1. That Syria would be one nation undivided from the "Taurus mountains in the north to the borders of the Sinai desert in the south, and from the Mediterranean Sea westwards to the Arabian Desert in the east."[45]
> 2. That the "Allied Conference" declare Syria's full independence and delegate a nation to assist its government until it becomes capable of maintaining its independence. The nation that the party believed to be best suited for this task was the United States, since it was not driven by its own colonial interests in that region nor was it fettered by previous treaties and agreements that obliged it to acquiesce in the division of Syria.
> 3. That the country should be divided into united states, each of which would be able to exercise independent judgment in its internal affairs but would ultimately fall under the control of a central, civilian, representative government.
> 4. That Arabic would be the only official language of the nation.
> 5. That there would be complete separation of church and state.[46]

Like its other Syrian counterpart based in Egypt, the Syrian Unity Party, the Moderate Syrian Party was clearly both republican and federalist in its political orientation and secularist in its outlook. Similarly, these Syrian expatriates shared the vision of a united Syrian homeland, and did not want to see Syria's integral unity or geographic cohesiveness compromised. They also believed that Palestine fell within the Syrian nation's borders, as is clear from the boundaries they delineated. Their own political proclivities and future agenda, coupled with their desire to ensure that the unity of their nation be maintained, were clear motivations for this party's openly pro-American policy. Of course, the party was not successful either in attaining any of its ultimate objectives or in building a substantial following.

---

[44] Ibid., 44.

[45] Quoted in ibid.

[46] Ibid.

AL-ḤIZB AL-WAṬANĪ AL-SŪRĪ

One of the later parties to be established in the Faysali era, *al-Ḥizb al-Waṭanī al-Sūrī*, or Syrian National Party, was formed on January 25, 1920, following Faysal's return from Europe after a series of unfruitful negotiations with the Allies, to face the fiery, uncompromising antagonism of his own Arab nationalist allies at home. In his apparent desperation for a more compromising ally, Faysal approached the conservative landowning Damascene notables, who at this point were "ripe for the wooing."[47]

An outsider to the local political scene, Faysal had originally sought to establish relations with the existing power brokers—the Syrian notables—upon his entry into Damascus. Nevertheless, his own base of support consisted almost entirely of what was referred to by the notables as *rijāl al-ghayb,*[48] or "men of the unknown" (an allusion to their lack of proper breeding since they did not hail from "known" circles and established families from which politicians and political leaders were traditionally selected), which rendered him and his followers suspect in these notables' eyes.

As can be surmised, the notables had much stake in the Ottoman state which, for centuries, bestowed upon them their privileged position and power; most of them would have naturally preferred to see Ottoman rule prevail. They were hence far less apt to join an Arab movement with questionable "credentials" bent on overthrowing the Ottoman state and altering the status quo. Furthermore, even those who were in favor of ousting the Ottomans or were at least resigned to its disappearance as fact, did not want to see what they perceived as a motley crew of rabid zealots from the outside suddenly take charge of what they deemed to be their "natural" sphere of interest.

Despite their lack of enthusiasm for the Hashemites and the Arab revolt, and their reserved attitude towards Faysal and his regime, the notables had nevertheless become quite concerned about the position and influence the young nationalists had attained in this government. The unflinching Arab nationalist ideals these zealots espoused, and, more importantly, their inexperience and impetuous actions, as the seasoned notables rightly cautioned, would result in embroiling the Amir and the nation in a disastrous war with the French. The notables were also understandably incensed about losing their former political power and traditional standing to Faysal's Arab nationalists, most of whom, as previously mentioned, belonged to a younger generation of "unknowns."

When presented with the opportunity therefore, the notables were consequently eager to patch their differences with Faysal and attempt some form of an alliance in order to salvage the situation. Indeed, even a rapprochement between Faysal and his long-time enemy (and former devoted supporter of the Ottomans and the C.U.P.) ʿAbd al-Rahman Pasha al-Yusuf was finally

---

[47] Khoury, *Urban Notables*, 90.

[48] ʿAẓm, *Mudhakkirāt,* 1: 94.

made possible. In turn, al-Yusuf soon managed to gather a number of similarly disaffected notables, landowners, and ex-Ottoman officials from Damascus, Aleppo, Homs, and Hama and formed a political party, namely the Syrian National Party. Among its leading members were: Sami Pasha Mardam-Bey, Muhammad ʿArif al-Quwwatli, Muhammad ʿAli Pasha al-Qudamani, Badiʾ Bey Muʾayyad al-ʿAzm, ʿAtaʾ al-ʿAjlani, ʿAtaʾ al-Ayyubi, and ʿAlaʾ al-Din al-Durubi, among others.[49]

In its program, the National Party advocated full independence for Syria within its natural boundaries (Syria, Palestine, and Lebanon) under a constitutional monarchy with Faysal at its head. In reality, however, this was no more than a façade, a political ruse to attract more followers and mollify the zealous nationalists' suspicions towards them. The notables adopted the more realistic approach that Syria was in no position to defy France militarily, and they were in effect more than willing to negotiate with the French. Accordingly, they sought a compromise solution closely based upon the as yet unsigned Faysal-Clemenceau Agreement, and strengthened their contacts with French agents in the region in case a French invasion did take place.[50]

With regard to the Palestine question, there appears to have been some controversy regarding the National Party's willingness to negotiate with the Zionists and recognize a Jewish national home in Palestine.[51] On March 26, 1920, several supposed members of this party concluded a treaty with the representative of the Zionist Organization in Palestine, Yehoshua Hankin.[52] Since the treaty and its terms were to remain secret and were negotiated by men who were minor, unknown figures in the party, however, it is difficult to gauge to what extent the signatories truly represented the Syrian National Party and its position.

According to the terms of this agreement, the signatories recognized both the independence of Palestine from Syria and the Zionist Organization's right to "build in it a National Home for the Jewish people by means of organizing mass immigration of Jews from all countries to Palestine and through achieving the necessary political and economic advantages for the peaceful and free development of the National Home."[53] In return, the Zionist Organization

[49] Khoury, *Urban Notables*, 90.

[50] Ibid. For details on the compromise agreements see al-ʿAẓm, *Mudhakkirāt*, 1: 101-3.

[51] Porath, *Emergence of the Palestinian-Arab National Movement, 1918-1929,* 328, n. 26.

[52] The signatories from al-Hizb al-Watani al-Suri were Najib Sufayr, Yusuf Muʾadhdhin, Dr. Rashid Karam, Najib Hashim, and Dr. Antun Shihadah, none of whom were members of the Syrian Congress nor of al-Fatat or al-ʿAhd.

[53] Porath, *Emergence of the Palestinian-Arab National Movement, 1918-1929,* 328. For full terms of treaty, a photocopy of it is reproduced by Eliezer Tauber, "Agreement between the Syrian National Party and the Zionist Movement, March 1920" in *Cathedra* (Sept. 2000): 152-3.

pledged "not to trespass the boundaries of Syria and Lebanon"[54] (to be agreed upon by both sides); "to honour the religious property and customs and not to interfere in the questions pertaining to the Holy Places of the Muslims and Christians in Palestine"[55]; and to "assist the governments of Syria and Lebanon to develop their countries and to lend them money according to conditions to be defined in due time."[56]

According to this agreement therefore, the "Syrian National Party" supposedly acknowledged Syria, Lebanon, and Palestine as constituting three distinct "countries" or "regions."[57] Palestine's independence from Syria was essentially recognized, but only as a prelude to the establishment of a Jewish national home there. The exact boundaries of Palestine were to be subsequently determined by a "commission" composed of delegates from "both" parties: one party consisting of representatives from Syria and Lebanon, and the other by representatives of the Zionist Organization.[58]

While there was never any question with regard to Palestine (or Lebanon for that matter) forming a part of the Syrian national entity in the treaty itself, the professed representatives of "Syrian National Party" did not see the apparent contradiction in their negotiating on Palestine's behalf without any formal sanction to do so by the Palestinians themselves. The signatories evidently felt completely justified in deciding Palestine's fate, acting as though they had the authority and jurisdiction over that area which, as they had just proclaimed, did not form a part of their constitution.

In terms of actual border negotiations, the provisions of the treaty are even more poignant. The determination of the exact boundaries of Palestine was not considered the responsibility of the Palestinian people. The negotiations were not to be conducted by a Palestinian-Zionist commission. Nor was it going to be a joint inter-Arab-Zionist effort. Instead, it was left to the discretion of the Lebanese and Syrians on the one hand, and the Zionists on the other, to decide where Zionist jurisdiction ended and where the borders of Syria and Lebanon began. Therefore, the exact wording of the treaty notwithstanding, the whole affair can be summarized as a certain body of Syrians willing to negotiate away some of *their* territories (or indeed those of others) in return for financial and political concessions under extenuating circumstances. Nevertheless, the demise of the Faysali regime and the fall of the rest of Syria under French control naturally altered the political equation thereby rendering the treaty obsolete.

---

[54] Ibid.

[55] Ibid.

[56] Ibid.

[57] *Pays* or *aqṭār*, Tauber, "Agreement between the Syrian National Party and the Zionist Movement, March 1920", 152-153.

[58] Ibid.

AL-JAMᶜĪYAH AL-ᶜARABĪYAH AL-FILASṬĪNĪYAH

During the Faysali era, there was a sizable Palestinian community living in Damascus, many of whom enjoyed considerable political power and influence. A substantial number of Palestinians held high-ranking political posts in the government and prominent positions in the press, and were generally influential in political circles as leading members of political parties and clubs. They accordingly began to form their own minor political organizations to "support and defend the Palestinian cause and make their voices heard."[59]

The first such organization was *Jamᶜīyat al-Nahḍah al- Filasṭīnīyah* ("Palestinian Renaissance Society"), but this was soon replaced by *al-Jamᶜīyah al-ᶜArabīyah al-Filasṭīnīyah* ("Palestinian Arab Association") at the beginning of June 1920. Their goal was to unite all the Palestinian groups and their cause under one single organization.[60] This latter group had an elected administrative committee composed of a number of prominent public figures, who included: Ibrahim al-Qasim ᶜAbd al-Hadi, Amin al-Husayni (later the Grand Mufti of Palestine), Salim ᶜAbd al-Rahman, Muᶜin al-Madi, ᶜIzzat Darwazah, and ᶜArif al-ᶜArif.[61]

The organization's primary goals were to promote the Palestinian cause by vehemently opposing Zionism and Zionist schemes in Palestine and seeking to put an end to all Jewish immigration to the region. Despite its name, the Palestinian Arab Organization was also pro-Syrian and, deeming Palestine to be a part of the Syrian nation, worked to bring about Palestinian and Syrian unity.[62]

DECLARATIONS, PROCLAMATIONS AND PUBLIC STATEMENTS

While there were numerous official political parties with formal platforms and publicized agendas, they were nevertheless not the only political actors in Syria who were eager to play a role in the incipient nation's destiny. Numerous groups, whether religiously or politically affiliated, sought to rally public opinion and express their position on various occasions, whether by distributing leaflets, anonymous proclamations, or public statements made by their representatives. At this stage in Syrian history, the predominant concern was Syria's uncertain future and its destiny. Issues such as the future boundaries of Syria, the possibility of foreign tutelage, Palestine, and Zionism, consistently inflamed public emotions. Whether following the line of one of the major political parties, affiliating themselves with the interests of a particular religious denomination, or pursuing some independent course of action, many groups believed it incumbent upon themselves to urge and encourage the

---

[59] al-Saᶜīd, *al-Thawrah al-ᶜArabīyah,* 2: 43.

[60] Ibid.

[61] Ibid.

[62] Ibid.

population to take a particular stance and voice certain opinions, particularly in light of the arrival of the American King-Crane Commission.

This section will therefore examine a number of public statements, party *communiqués*, nationalist proclamations, and leaflets issued during this period, with the purpose of determining the place of the Palestinian issue in the general Syrian political arena, and the extent to which it was central to Syrian political thinking. Below are some examples of different declarations issued in various forms from a variety of sources, which reflect the political tenor with regard to the question of Palestine:

Al-Istiqlāl aw al-Mawt

One proclamation, distinctly Arab nationalist in tone, published during the King-Crane Commission's visit in May 1919, was entitled *al-Istiqlāl aw al-Mawt* ("Independence or Death.")[63] Signed simply *(waṭanī) ʿArabī* ("an Arab (patriot)") under the slogan "religion for God and the nation for all,"[64] it urges all Arabs—Muslims, Christians, and Jews, whatever their occupation or faith—to take immediate action in order to save the nation from the clutches of colonialism. Accordingly, it states:

> All regions of Syria, its south, north and west, place its hopes upon you; and here is Palestine (southern Syria), the first [region] to be polled for its opinion by the Commission, which has demanded full independence without any partition of Syria and refused all forms of [foreign] defense, tutelage or colonialism. Undoubtedly the rest of Syria is no less patriotic than the inhabitants of Palestine, who have shocked the Commission with their unity and consensus of opinion, does it not behoove us then to be united in our opinions and our hearts...[65]

The proclamation then issued a set of four demands, including: complete independence for the "Syrian nation" and "all other liberated Arab nations such as Iraq"[66]; refusal of all forms of protection, guardianship, or colonialism; and

> Comprehensive unity between all regions of Syria from the Taurus mountains to the north, the Khabur and Euphrates [rivers] to the east, the Arabian desert to Madaʾin Salih in the south, and from the Red Sea to the line from ʿAqabah to Rafah

[63] *al-Istiqlāl aw al-Mawt*, (manshūr), original text reproduced in Dhūqān Qarqūṭ, *al-Mashriq al-ʿArabī*, 25-26.

[64] In the original it states: *wa-al-dīn lil-Lāh, wa-al-waṭan lil-jamīʿ*, ibid., 26.

[65] Ibid., 25.

[66] Ibid., 26.

> and the Mediterranean in the west, and we unconditionally refuse all Zionist immigration.[67]

Finally, while recognizing the need for "specialists in certain areas"[68] it demands that they be hired, as is "customary in most civilized nations."[69]

It is evident from the text of the proclamation that Palestine and its inhabitants were clearly considered to be a part of Syria, indeed, patriotic Syrians whose example should be followed. Though allegedly "Arab nationalist" in orientation and hence meaning to advocate total Arab unity, the author(s) of the proclamation differentiated between themselves as Syrians and other "Arab nations" such as Iraq whom they also believe to be fully deserving of their own independence. Palestine, however, is not regarded as another Arab nation, but rather as an essential component of the Syrian national landscape.

SŪRĪYĀ MUSTAQILLAH, LĀ TAWKĪL WA-LĀ WIṢĀYAH

Another proclamation was similarly issued during that same period by *Jamᶜīyat al-Istiqlāl al-Sūrī al-Markazīyah*, or the Central Organization for Syrian Independence, entitled *Sūrīyā Mustaqillah, lā tawkīl wa-lā wiṣāyah*—"an independent Syria, no tutelage and no supervision." [70] This proclamation, addressed to the "noble population of Syria,"[71] was primarily concerned with Syrian unity and independence. As avid supporters of Faysal, the organization called upon the Syrian populace to show their gratitude for all that Faysal had done for their country insofar as "liberating" them from the "Turks' tyranny" and representing them at the Peace Conference.[72] The declaration exhibited extraordinary optimism regarding the effectiveness of the Foreign Commission and the Allies' general good faith, and urged all Syrians to continue Faysal's work by appearing before the American Commission and presenting a united front with regard to their demands and aspirations:

> Be fully assured oh nationalist Syrian that this committee represents the greatest men in the world today, delegated by the most powerful nations, and motivated by the most honorable intentions: Orlando who is famous for his love

---

[67] Ibid.

[68] Ibid.

[69] Ibid.

[70] *Sūrīyā Mustaqillah, lā tawkīl wa-lā wiṣāyah (manshūr)* original text reproduced in ibid., 26-29.

[71] *Ilá al-shaᶜb al-Sūrī al-karīm*, ibid., 26.

[72] Ibid., 26-27. The statement appears unduly confident about Faysal's role in general and his achievements at the Peace Conference, whereby it states that thanks to Faysal, Syria's independence was secured and made official.

> of the freedom of humanity, Lloyd George the friend of the Arabs, the liberal Frenchman Clemenceau who battles against the principle of colonialism, and Wilson, America's man, the friend of small nations and champion of the human race and [upholder of] the rights from which they have long been deprived. Those are the men whom this commission represents and upon which they directly stake their honor. It is incumbent upon you therefore to be honest and forthright with [the commission's representatives], to let them know that these men's honor depends upon them, and that it is your belief that they did not come here for the purposes of trickery and deception, for these men of the conference are greater and more honorable than to say what is not in their hearts. Declare to them that the Muslim is the Christian and Israelite's brother in nationality, and that religion is for God and the nation is for its children.[73]

The proclamation then proceeded to make a case for Syrian independence, claiming that Syrians are among the most sophisticated and civilized of nations, and, despite their need for technical and financial assistance at this particular juncture, are nevertheless fully capable and worthy of complete independence. It warned Syrians against believing the deceptions of the colonialists who claim that Syria does not possess the necessary foundations on which to build a modern nation. It also warned against the evils and dangers of sectarianism, citing Faysal's policy as exemplary in that regard, and maintaining that the only loyalty worthy of a true Syrian Arab is towards his country and its unity and independence.[74]

Once more, the essence of the declaration and its demands are quite straightforward: the Syrian people should concentrate on their nation's unity and independence, and make their wishes patently clear to the world via the King-Crane Commission. Again, Palestine was implicitly included in this unity, since there was no difference between a Muslim, Christian, or Jew, and no foreign intervention, division, or supervision was deemed acceptable. Indeed, the declaration concluded with the following:

> Whosoever attempts to fill your mind with other than the facts that you have just now read is a paid traitor whose honor, life, and place in the society have been corrupted for the price of a few coins a common seller of radishes is able to earn without losing his dignity and patriotism.[75]

---

[73] Ibid., 27.

[74] Ibid., 27-28.

[75] Ibid., 29.

MUʾTAMAR AL-JAMʿĪYĀT

One announcement, whose purpose was to proclaim the holding of a conference on July 30, 1919, echoes similar sentiments, but with a more elaborate list of demands and more emphasis on the Palestinian question.[76] "During these trying times,"[77] the announcement declared, the conference sought to unify the efforts of all the parties, organizations, clubs, and unions "that are concerned with the future of the nation and work for its progress."[78] Those "concerned" parties had all sent delegates to the conference,[79] where preliminary meetings were held by a preparatory committee to set the wheels in motion.

The conference itself was accordingly scheduled for July 30, 1919, when "selected speakers"[80] planned to discuss what were deemed as the most pertinent topics at hand. These can be summarized in five main points: first, there was the issue of Syrian independence, an independence "unblemished by any protection, supervision, or mandate of any form." Furthermore, if the nation were to seek economic aid, it could not be encumbered by any restrictions regarding which nations it could approach for help. Second, there was the issue of Syrian unity, and the "prevention of the partition of our Syrian nation." Third, it protested Article 22 of the League of Nations which sought to institute the mandate system and called for "ending all foreign privileges." They also believed that it was very important that the Syrians be allowed to speak for themselves by sending an official "delegation to represent the liberated Syrian nation at the Peace Conference." Fourth, they demanded the "prohibition of all Zionist immigration to Palestine and the prevention of Palestine from becoming a national home for the Jews." Finally, the conference called for the independence of Iraq.[81]

---

[76] *Muʾtamar al-Jamʿīyāt*, orginal text reproduced in ibid., 30-31.

[77] Ibid., 30.

[78] Ibid.

[79] The parties and organizations that sent delegates to this conference were: al-Istiqlāl al-ʿArabī (Arab Independence), al-Nādī al-ʿArabī (Arab Club), Taʿāwun al-ʿIrāqīyīn (Iraqi Cooperation), al-ʿAhd (Covenant), Jamʿīyat al-Ṭalabah (Student Association), al-Nahḍah al-Adabīyah (Literary Renaissance), al-Nahḍah al-Filasṭīnīyah (Palestinian Renaissance), al-ʿAhd al-Sūrī (Syrian Covenant), al-Jamʿīyah al-Zirāʿīyah (Agricultural Association), al-Jamʿīyah al-Biqāʿīyah (Bekka Valley Association), al-Hiraf wa-al-Niqābāt (Trade Unions), al-Nahḍah al-Ṭibāʿiyah al-ʿArabīyah (Renaissance of Arab Publishing), al-Nādī al-Tijārī (Club of Commerce), Jamʿīyat al-Aṭṭibāʾ (Doctors' Association), Fityān al-Jazīrah (Youth of al-Jazirah), Jamʿīyat Khirījī al-Madāris al-ʿĀliyah (Association of Graduates of Higher Learning), al-Isʿāf al-Khayrī (Charitable Relief), Jamʿīyat Ṭalabat al-Madāris al-Ṭibbīyah (Association of Medical Students), Jamʿīyat al-Maqāsid al-Khayrīyah (Association of Charitable Objectives), and al-Taʿāwun al-Khayrī (Charitable Cooperation). See ibid.

[80] Ibid., 31.

[81] Ibid.

The conferees thus deemed the question of Palestine central among the pertinent issues facing the "nation." Unlike Iraq, however, there was never any discussion of Palestinian independence or the creation of a sovereign Palestinian state, even when the delegates included Palestinian organizations among their number.[82] The only remedies offered to this serious problem were the preservation of Syrian unity and independence and the denunciation of any scheme that threatened to partition the "Syrian nation" such as Zionist immigration, Zionist plans for founding a national home on "Syrian" soil, and rejection of the Mandate system. This provides further evidence of the adamant Syrian belief that Southern Syria/Palestine constituted part of its integral whole, and could only conceivably be treated from this standpoint.

Maṭālib Abnāʾ al-Sāḥil al-Mawjūdīn fī Dimashq

These fervent beliefs in Syrian geographic unity, independence, and Palestine's place therein are even more pronounced in the memorandum issued to the King-Crane Commission by *Abnāʾ al-Sāḥil al-Mawjudīn fī Dimashq*—"the Sons of the Coast Present in Damascus."[83] Having more to lose by the division of the Syrian region and the institution of the Mandate system, this group's position, stated quite plainly in the five main demands they listed to the King-Crane Commission, illustrates these convictions. These were as follows:[84]

> 1. Full independence for Syria within its "natural boundaries"[85] that lie "from the Taurus Mountains in the north, the Khabur and Euphrates rivers in the east, the line between ʿAqabah and Rafah in the south, and the Mediterranean in the west."[86]
>
> 2. Rejection of Article 22 of the covenant of the League of Nations as relates to the Mandate system.
>
> 3. Refusal to acknowledge any French rights in Syria "with all our power"[87] and all the secret treaties pertaining to Syria.
>
> 4. "We refuse Israeli Jewish immigration to our lands, and that Palestine—Southern Syria—which is an integral part of Syria, become a national homeland for the Jews."[88]
>
> 5. Reserving the right to select the country from whom they wish to enlist support after receiving official recognition for

[82] See n. 80, above.

[83] *ʿArīḍah marfūʿah ilá al-Lajnah al-Amrīkīyah, Maṭālib Abnāʾ al-Sāḥil al-Mawjūdīn fī Dimashq*; for full text see ibid., 31-32.

[84] Ibid.

[85] Ibid., 31.

[86] Ibid.

[87] Ibid., 32.

[88] Ibid.

their independence—their first preference was the United States, refusing any form of aid from France.

ṢAKK IʿTIMĀD MIN AFRĀD AL-ṬĀʾIFAH AL-KILDĀNĪYAH

The prevalence of the trend towards an all-inclusive Syrian unity can also be witnessed in the demands of some of the more vocal religious minority groups present in Syria. While those groups' wishes were generally predicated primarily on their loyalty towards their own confessional group and its individual interests, they still stressed Syrian unity, thereby demonstrating the extent to which this notion had already become entrenched in the Syrian worldview at this stage.[89] Once such example was the Chaldean sect's statement issued to the King-Crane Commission on June 6, 1919.

The Chaldean sect in Aleppo gave their official authorization to their designated delegates to speak on their behalf to the Americans and listed their demands, which were as follows: "preservation of Syrian unity within its natural borders, its independence, and choosing the mandate of the nation of France over all other nations."[90] In this statement, which was signed by 176 people, full Syrian unity is considered to be the paramount concern. While the exact national boundaries of Syria are not specified in the text, it seems that the standard definition had become sufficiently accepted not to warrant explication—particularly, since no variant definition appears to have been openly put forth by any public or official representative Syrian body. In this respect, their position on Palestine, which lay within Syria's "natural borders," was self-evident.

The fact that the Chaldean sect, like many other (specifically Christian) religious minorities, requested France as the most desired mandatory power was hardly uncharacteristic. Britain's ties to the Hashemites on the one hand, and its dedication to Zionism on the other, rendered France as the more appealing option. The French, for their part, had been traditionally eager to cultivate strong ties with the Christian minorities in the region, and champion their cause. More importantly, the French consistently sought to dissociate themselves from Zionism and the Jewish homeland, condemning it as a British scheme to divide and rule the area, while portraying themselves as the champions of Syrian unity and true guardians of Syria's interests under their direct guidance. Consequently, many Christian minorities in the region appealed directly to the French, whether they were immediately concerned with Syrian unity or not, in the belief that French rule would ultimately prove to be the most favorable to their interests in general. The Christians of Amman, for example, stressed their Arabism and their sovereignty as a united

---

[89] For a more detailed discussion on the various minority groups and their demands to the King-Crane Commission see Chapter 3, above.

[90] *Ṣakk Iʿtimād min Afrād al-Ṭāʾifah al-Kildānīyah bi-Ḥalab lil-tamthīl amām al-Lajnah al-Amrīkīyah*, full text in Qarqūṭ, *al-Mashriq al-ʿArabī,* 35.

Arab nation but focused primarily on their loyalty to France and their desire for French tutelage.[91] The "Organization for Orthodox Brotherhood"[92] and the "Catholic Literary Youth Organization"[93] of Jerusalem, on the other hand, in their own petition to the French High Commissioner, made no mention of Syria or Syrian unity and independence. Instead, while claiming to speak on behalf of "all of the people of Jerusalem and its provinces"[94] who, in turn, represent "all the Arab Palestinian people, Muslims and Christians,"[95] they focused primarily on protesting Zionism, Zionist claims to Palestine, and their plans for the creation of a prospective Jewish state. Implicit in their wish to plead their case specifically before the representative of the French government, however, is their desire for French tutelage and, by association, their support for French plans for the future of the region, namely control of united geographic Syria.

Iḥtijāj ʿalá Ghabtat Baṭrīk al-Ṭāʾifah al-Mārūnīyah al-dhāhib ilá Bārīs

The aforementioned religious minorities nevertheless had to maintain a distinct level of caution in their dealings with the French and be extremely prudent in the manner in which they chose to express their wishes. In other words, if the demands of the religious minority groups did not fall within the accepted parameters of recognized nationalist aspirations, they risked unleashing a furious response from the Arab nationalists. The Maronite Patriarch generated such a reaction when he spoke exclusively of Lebanon and Lebanese interests during a trip to Paris. Consequently, Hizb al-Istiqlal, one of the most vocal advocates of Arab nationalism in Syria, issued an immediate statement which reiterated the Arab nationalist position, thus providing an articulation of this stance while seeking to undermine the Maronite Patriarch's credibility.

In their statement of August 7, 1919, addressed to the "President of the Peace Conference", Hizb al-Istiqlal—"which speaks in the name of hundreds of thousands of its members and expresses the hopes of the entire Syrian populace"[96]—accordingly protested the Maronite Patriarch's departure to Paris

---

[91] *ʿArīḍah min Masīḥī ʿAmmān*, full text in ibid., 34. It is noteworthy that this petition supposedly represented all the Christian sects of the city of ʿAmman, "Catholic, Greek Orthodox, and Protestant," and was accordingly signed by representatives from the three groups. Ibid., 34.

[92] *Jamʿīyat al-Ikhāʾ al-Urthūdhuksī.*

[93] *Jamʿīyat al-Nāshiʾah al-Adabīyah al-Kāthūlīkīyah.*

[94] *Ilá Saʿādat Muʿtamad Hukūmat al-Jumhūrīyah al-Ifransīyah al-Fakhīmah al-Muḥtaram*, quoted in ibid., 36; for full text of the petition see ibid., 36-37.

[95] Ibid., 36.

[96] al-Kātib al-ʿĀmm, Ḥizb al-Istiqlāl al-ʿArabī fī Sūrīyah, *Ilá Ḥaḍrat Raʾīs Muʾtamar al-Silm al-Muḥtaram, "Iḥtijāj ʿalá Ghabṭat Baṭrīk al-Ṭāʾifah al-Mārūnīyah al-dhāhib ilá Bārīs",* original text reproduced in Qarqūṭ, *al-Mashriq al-ʿArabī,* 39.

to represent "Lebanon" and "Lebanese" interests, and reiterated the demands of the Syrian Congress presented to the American commission, asking that they be acknowledged as the "true expression of every Syrian Arab's feelings."[97]

These demands, which they asserted were the "true expression" of the feelings of the "entire Syrian populace," are summarized as follows:

1. Complete political independence for Syria
2. "Refusing the partitioning of Syria in any form and the recognition of its natural geographical boundaries as falling from the Taurus in the north to Rafah and ʿAqabah in the south, and the Arabian desert in the north to the Mediterranean in the west, and the formation of a united Syria within those political and economical boundaries."[98]
3. Rejection of French aid.
4. "Prohibition of Zionist immigration to southern Syria (Palestine) and refusal to acknowledge their claims and propaganda in which they assert that it is their rightful home, since the majority of its inhabitants are Arabs which share all the common bonds of language, history, race, culture, and regional unity with the rest of the citizens of Syria."[99]
5. "Rejecting the separation of any region of the Syrian nation from the political unity which we demand for all of Syria, since partition will be harmful to its political and economic welfare and will render it vulnerable to avaricious foreign plots and schemes."[100]
6. Protesting Article 22 of the League of Nations' Charter regarding the necessity of assigning a mandate for Syria, while requesting the "technical and economical"[101] assistance of the United States, so long as it does not interfere with Syrian independence, and in the event that the United States should refuse to grant Syria its assistance, then Britain would be approached in its stead.[102]

In an attempt to discredit his authority, the statement questioned how the Maronite Patriarch could claim to represent the entire population of Lebanon

---

[97] Ibid.

[98] Ibid., 38.

[99] Ibid.

[100] Ibid.

[101] Ibid.

[102] Ibid.

based solely on his delegation by an "inconsequential minority."[103] His position as a religious leader representing a small confessional minority, they claimed, did not sanction him to speak on behalf of the Muslims, Druze, and Greek Orthodox who formed the majority of the population, particularly since a great number of Maronites did not even agree with his views.[104]

ʿArīḍah ilá Muʾtamar al-Silm

In an effort to take a stand and establish their political position, the notables of Damascus sought to make their voice heard by issuing their own petition to the Peace Conference in late 1919.[105] Focusing almost exclusively on Syria, its cause and future interests, the notables spoke primarily of the "Syrian Arab nation,"[106] its rights, contributions, and the sacrifices it had to endure for the goal of liberty.

The petition began:

> The Syrian Arab nation, with its glorious history, did not rise against the Turks in enmity, nor did it actively seek their expulsion from these lands, except that it may live free in its political life, happy in its constructive social life, and to gain its right to live freely and independently, that it may be an active participant in this human community and to serve civilization...[107]

The notables stressed how the "Syrians' moral and material strength, mustered and faithfully contributed"[108] to the Allied war-effort was "not to be underestimated."[109] "Syria," they further pointed out "had not welcomed the Allied armies as tyrannical armies of occupation, but rather in their capacity as allies of the Arabs who had come to grant us our freedom and full independence."[110] They went on to express their disappointment with the way events unfolded.

> Throughout this period, we have waited, watching our country being divided into different zones of occupation,

[103] Ibid., 39.

[104] Ibid.

[105] The petition is dated 28 Tishrīn, 1919, hence it is not clear whether it is Tishrīn al-Awwal (October) or Tishrīn al-Thānī (November). *ʿArīḍah ilá Muʾtamar al-Silm,* original text reproduced ibid., 40-41.

[106] *al-Ummah al-ʿArabīyah al-Sūrīyah* referred to interchangeably as *al-Ummah al-Sūrīyah* ("the Syrian nation"); see ibid.

[107] Ibid., 40.

[108] Ibid.

[109] Ibid.

[110] Ibid.

> governed by various authorities; and we did not, at first, doubt the sincerity of the Allies' intentions...Nevertheless, we finally began to sense, from statements by the foreign press, that there are forces working towards the partition of these ill-fated lands under a variety of names and forms, in addition to acknowledging the Zionists' claims whose purpose is to squash us in our own country in a manner unprecedented since the darkest of colonial times...We, the Syrians, protest with all our might any government which has plans for protection or guardianship over Syria, or any part of it, or designs for its partition. We desire nothing except full independence, without partition, for this natural geographic whole; and we would like to remind the Allies that they should fulfill their promises and respect the Syrian Arab population..."[111]

The petition then evoked the Allied inter-war promises, their commitment to Wilson's fourteen points, and warned them of the great "disgrace" that would befall them if they should fall prey to the avarice of colonialism and its temptations, thus robbing "the Syrian nation of its wishes and sacred rights after they fought valiantly alongside the Allied armies."[112]

Statement of Shukri Ghanim

In his statement before the Supreme Council in Paris on February 13, 1919, Shukri Ghanim, the Chief Representative of the Central Syrian Committee (another Egyptian-based Syrian nationalist party), argued the Syrian nationalist stance towards the Palestine in a forceful, yet conciliatory manner. In his own words:

> May we say one word as regards Palestine—although the subject is said to be a thorny one?
>
> Palestine is incontestably the southern portion of our country. The Zionists claim it. We have suffered too much from suffering resembling theirs not to throw open wide to them the doors of Palestine. All those among them oppressed in certain retrograde countries are welcome. Let them settle in Palestine, but in an autonomous Palestine, connected with Syria by the sole bond of federation. Will not a Palestine enjoying wide internal autonomy be for them a sufficient guarantee?
>
> If they form the majority there, they will be the rulers.

[111] *ʿArīḍah ilá Muʾtamar al-Silm,* reproduced in Qarqūṭ, *al-Mashriq al-ʿArabī,* 40-41.

[112] Ibid., 41.

> If they are in the minority, they will be represented in the Government in proportion to their numbers.
>
> Is it necessary, in order to establish them to dismember Syria...and to constitute a State in the midst of a country which, as a consequence, would be hostile to them?[113]

Thus, on the one hand, Ghanim adopted an uncharacteristically compromising stance on Jewish immigration and on the Jewish presence in Palestine, going so far as to guarantee their future status in the projected Syrian "federation." On the other hand, Ghanim was nevertheless careful to express an adamant "Syrian" position on Palestine comprising its southern region, affirming its status as such, and pointing out the hazards inherent in separating it from Syria.

Resolution of Conference of the Syrian Nationalist Parties in Cairo

Even more evidence for the conception of Palestine as Southern Syria is provided by the stance of the Syrian nationalists based in Egypt. The Syrian nationalist parties located in Egypt, namely the Syrian Union Party, the Moderate Syrian Party, and the Central Syrian Committee, held a conference in Cairo towards the end of 1919 in which they reaffirmed their stance on Syrian unity. According to the British report:

> Delegates of the Syrian Union Committee, the Central Lebanese-Syrian Committee, and the Moderate Syrian Party assembled in Cairo on December 13, and passed a resolution to the effect that Syria, as included between the frontiers of the Taurus Mountains to the north, the Kingdom of the Hejaz to the south, Mesopotamia to the east, and the Mediterranean Sea with the line Rafa-Aqabah to the west, should be constituted as one indivisible political unity. They protested against all conventions and dispositions deigned to effect a partition of Syria or to create in Palestine a *foyer national Sioniste*. A copy of the proceedings was duly posted to the President of the Paris Peace Conference.[114]

As can be seen, the parties involved were eager to affirm Syria's political and national unity within what had become established as Syria's geographic boundaries in the existing nationalist discourse. They also sought to condemn

---

[113]Extract from a Statement by M. Chekri Ganem, Chief Representative of the Central Syrian Committee, before the Supreme Council in Paris on February 13, 1919 [E 1305/6/31] in *British Documents on Foreign Affairs,* Part II: Series B, Vol. 15, p. 503.

[114]"Notes on Middle East", Arab Bureau, Cairo, 30 January 1920, in *Records of the Hashemite Dynasties,* 10: 317.

any form of partition or division that threatened the integrity of the Syrian whole. Palestine, yet again, was viewed within the context of this Syrian national and geographic unity and any plans that involved dissociating it from the rest of the Syrian body were adamantly rejected.

CONCLUSION

This survey of the main political parties extant during the Faysali era shows that Syria was experiencing a period of vibrant political activity during which a number of different political parties with varying visions and goals regarding the future of their nation vied for power and influence. Thriving in a relatively free atmosphere, these parties openly advocated their positions on such fundamental topics as Syria's political orientation, the nature of its government, its future status, and its ultimate role in the international and inter-Arab arena. It is nonetheless clear that there were certain boundaries that could not be officially crossed and some compromises that could not be made palatable to the public. While each group, depending on its inclinations, could freely debate whether the incipient nation should focus on broader pan-Arab unity or Syrian nationalism, monarchy or republicanism, full independence or American, French, or British tutelage, issues such as Syria's geographic cohesiveness and unity, and especially their position towards Palestine and Zionism in that regard, were the subject of a broad consensus of views.

Parties with an Arab nationalist bent vehemently stressed the Arab character of Palestine and demanded its inclusion within their projected schemes for a united Arab state. Nevertheless it was consistently referred to as part of the Syrian nation, rather than a sister Arab region against whom they feared a grievous injustice was about to be committed. It was hence always presented as part of the Syrian cause, falling within the context of their demands for Syrian unity and independence, and their rejection of foreign imperialist ambitions to divide and colonize Syria. The very notion of separating it from the Syrian national body therefore, under any pretext, was denounced as a crime.

Considering the circumstances, Palestine was perhaps the one region that was in most need of independence in order to confirm its sovereignty and ward off any impending dangers to its future existence. More than Iraq, for whose independence the Arab nationalists were eagerly clamoring—albeit as a prelude to future unity with Syria—Palestine faced the immediate threat of colonization by a foreign minority that sought to establish their own permanent independent state. These colonists, moreover, staked their claims to the land not only on remote historical and religious precedent, but also on the assertion that Palestine was an uninhabited region with no real indigenous population of its own.[115] Perhaps it might have seemed more logical therefore for the Arab nationalists to demand its independence as a sovereign Arab nation, and

[115] As one popular Zionist slogan proclaimed: "A land without a people for a people without a land."

then advocate unity with Syria based on the wishes of its own inhabitants. The fact that they did not proceed in this direction, however, is a testament to the extent to which the notion of Southern Syria was deeply ingrained in the minds of the region's inhabitants and the degree to which the national map of Syria had become established.

The Syrian nationalist parties, while far less eager to emphasize the Arab nationalist orientation for their nation, echoed these same sentiments with regard to Palestine. Facing no dilemma with regard to Palestine falling under the scope of Syria's national sovereignty, they denounced Zionism and Zionist designs as constituting a mortal danger to the future of Syria in particular and the entire Arab world as a whole. This position, which acknowledged Palestine as forming an integral part of Syria, falling within its natural boundaries just like any other "Syrian" region, was supported by a general consensus of opinion among the population and by both Arab and Syrian nationalists alike. This point becomes abundantly clear from a number of the public statements, party *communiqués*, proclamations, and leaflets issued by various groups during that time.

The Syrian political parties therefore, in conjunction with the Arab Congresses, managed to establish a map of Syria in the public mind, a Syria that included Palestine within its borders. Consequently, regardless of political or religious affiliation, most, if not all, vocal Syrian groups demanded Syria's unity and independence within those "natural borders"—a Syria that would remain incomplete without any one of its component parts.

The next chapter examines the Palestine question and the concept of Southern Syria from the perspective of Syrian foreign policy, such that it existed, under Faysal. It examines Faysal's position on Palestine in international circles, his stance on the subject in his correspondence with the British, French, and American officials, his dealings with the Zionist Commission, and the place Palestine occupied in Syrian diplomacy under the Faysali regime.

Chapter Five

SOUTHERN SYRIA IN SYRIAN DIPLOMACY: FAYSAL AND THE PALESTINE QUESTION

The overwhelming general consensus among both Syrians and Palestinians, as has been shown, was to view Palestine as the intrinsic southern extension of Syria's "natural borders." Insofar as their dealings with the outside world were concerned, however, almost all of Syria's foreign and diplomatic relations and correspondence at this critical juncture in its history were primarily in the hands of its new champion and liberator, the Hijazi prince, Sharif Faysal ibn al-Husayn.

Acting as a representative of his father, the Sharif Husayn—self-proclaimed "King of the Arabs"—Faysal became the primary spokesman for the Syrian cause at the Peace Conference in Europe. Furthermore, Faysal was given a clear mandate by the Syrian people to represent them and their cause abroad on several occasions, including the Damascus Town Hall Meeting of May 9, 1919,[1] leading up to his eventual proclamation as the constitutional monarch of a united and independent Syria, which included Palestine, by the Syrian Congress of March 1920. Syrian "diplomacy" and "foreign policy," to the extent that they could be exercised, were thus largely Faysal's responsibility.

The purpose of this chapter therefore is to examine Faysal's stance in his capacity as Syria's primary representative and leader with regard to the Palestine question and Syrian unity on the international level, and his position towards the Zionists and their aspirations in Palestine, and to analyze the evolution of that stance during his reign in Syria, and the reasons behind it. This chapter does not examine any of Faysal's correspondences and negotiations regarding issues that do not pertain directly to the Palestine question, nor does it examine the Battle of Maysalun,[2] which resulted in the fall of the Faysali regime and its aftermath, deeming them to be beyond its scope.

---

[1] See Chapter 1, above.

[2] For an account of the battle of Maysalun, see Abū Khaldūn Sāṭiʿ al-Ḥuṣrī, *Yawm Maysalūn, ṣafḥah min tārīkh al-ʿArab al-ḥadīth, mudhakkirāt muṣawwarah bi-muqaddimah ʿan tanāzuʿ al-duwal ḥawla al-bilād al-ʿArabīyah wa-mudhayyalah bi-wathāʾiq wa-ṣuwar* (Beirut, [1965]); also of interest is Ghassān Kallās, *Yūsuf al-ʿAẓmah Shahīd Maysalūn al-Khālid: safaḥāt min adab Maysalūn* (Damascus, 2001).

Background: Faysal and the Arab Movement

Faysal ibn al-Husayn was born in Mecca on March 20, 1885, but, "in accordance with Hashemite custom,"[3] was sent to the village of Rihab to be raised by his grandfather, the Sharif Muhammad ibn ʿAwn, until the age of seven, after which he returned to Mecca.[4] In 1893, Faysal moved with his father—the Sharif Husayn—and the rest of his immediate family to Istanbul. The Ottoman Sultan ʿAbd al-Hamid, who was not averse to resorting to "criminal means"[5] when his authority was challenged, had received reports

> depicting young Husain as a willful and recalcitrant person whose views, on the rare occasions when he consented to express them, revealed a 'dangerous' capacity for independent thinking. The family's standing in the Moslem world was so high that the sultans of Turkey, in their dealings with its members, moved with circumspection and maintained an outward show of regard. Husain was courteously invited to bring his household and come and reside in Constantinople.[6]

Faysal remained in Istanbul with his family, where he was privately tutored, until the Young Turk revolution in 1908, when the C.U.P. formally appointed Husayn as the "Sharif and Amir of Mecca," despite Sultan ʿAbd al-Hamid's adamant opposition.[7] Consequently, the Sharif Husayn and his family returned once again to Mecca in 1908, after some fifteen years residence in Istanbul. The following year, 1909, Faysal was elected to the Ottoman parliament as the deputy for Jeddah, while his elder brother Abdullah was elected the deputy for Mecca.[8]

With the outbreak of the First World War and the Empire's imminent embroilment therein, the Hashemites were faced with two options: either to support the Empire in its war efforts in the hope of winning the favor of its ruling clique and its rewards for their loyalty; or to take up arms against it, thereby making a bid for independence. The latter option was made all the more enticing by British overtures during the war in addition to their assessment of

---

[3] *Mudhakkirāt al-Malik Fayṣal al-Awwal, Malik al-ʿIraq*, edited by Muḥammad Yūnis al-ʿAbbādī (Amman, 2002), 9. According to Sami Moubayyed, however, "Prince Faisal was born in Taiif [sic] some time between 1883 and 1885, the exact date of his birth has never been known due to poor records in the Bedouin tribes at the time. Growing up and studying in Istanbul, Faisal did not move to Mecca until his father was made defender of the Holy Shrines and Prince of Mecca in 1908." Sami M. Moubayyed, *The Politics of Damascus 1920-1946: Urban Notables and the French Mandate* (Damascus, 1999), 13.

[4] Ibid.

[5] Antonius, *Arab Awakening*, 71.

[6] Ibid., 72.

[7] Ibid., 103.

[8] *Mudhakkirāt al-Malik Fayṣal*, 9.

popular Arab sentiment and their relationship with the Arab secret societies in Damascus.[9]

ʿAbdullah, from early on, appears to have been wholly in favor of taking up arms against the Ottomans and seeking independence, while Faysal cautiously favored the other alternative:

> He was convinced that France had designs on Syria and England on the southern regions of Iraq, and Kitchener's offer contained no guarantee against those dangers; moreover he did not think that the Arabs were sufficiently prepared and feared that a revolt would misfire.[10]

The Sharif Husayn himself, however, was more inclined to explore the possibilities and potential of a Hashemite-led Arab revolt. Hence, for the next couple of years, while being pressed to commit himself and his troops to the war effort, he continued to play a game of "cat and mouse" with the Ottoman authorities, biding his time and weighing his options.

According to one of Faysal's biographers, Hadi Hasan ʿUlaywi, Faysal was eager to discover the Ottoman government's position on the Arab lands and their fate from the beginning of Empire's involvement in the war. He consequently contacted all the top officials in the Ottoman capital seeking to hear their views.[11] During his meeting with the Ottoman Minister of the Interior, Talʿat Pasha, Faysal states:

> My brother ʿAbdullah and I were both deputies in the parliament; it was therefore natural that we would want to find out from Talʿat the position of our country in the war. ʿAbdullah questioned Talʿat saying: "the country's revenues can only provide us with provisions to last us for two months." To which Talʿat replied candidly: "In all its existence, Turkey has never gained a thing from the Arab provinces, it does not concern us if the Allies occupy them,

[9]For more on this see Dawn, *From Ottomanism to Arabism*; T. E. Lawrence, *Seven Pillars of Wisdom*; Antonius, *Arab Awakening*.

[10]Antonius, *Arab Awakening*, 131-2. Antonius also adds that "T. E. Lawrence, in *Seven Pillars of Wisdom*, and other writers have stated that Faisal was already a member of a secret Arab society and won to the idea of a revolt. I have it on Faisal's own authority that he had not joined any such society before the War and that it was only when he went to Damascus in 1915 that he became converted to the idea of an Arab revolt." See ibid., 132.

[11]These included the Sadr-i Aʿzam (prime minister), minister of interior, the Shaykh al-Islam, the Speaker of the House of Representatives, and a number of high ranking officials. Hādī Ḥasan ʿUlaywī, *Fayṣal ibn al-Ḥusayn: muʾassis al-ḥukm al-ʿArabī fi Sūrīyah wa-al-ʿIrāq, 1883-1933* (Beirut, 2003), 34.

> once peace is secured for Turkey's allies, then we can [worry about] recovering them." [12]

Faysal then concludes that "it was in this manner that Turkey had excluded our country and the fate of its people from all its considerations." [13]

In the period leading up to the Arab revolt in June 1916, Faysal and ʿAbdullah traveled back and forth to Syria en route to Istanbul, ostensibly conducting official business in the capital. While there, they both maintained contact with the prominent Arab secret societies (al-Fatat and al-ʿAhd) and surveyed the situation for their father under the suspicious and vigilant watch of the Ottoman governor, Jamal Pasha.

During one such visit to Damascus on 26 March 1915, Faysal met with some of the leading figures of the nascent Arab movement, who would take him into their confidence and admit him to the membership of al-Fatat and al-ʿAhd soon thereafter. A few months before his arrival, the higher committee of al-Fatat had issued a resolution stating:

> In consequence of Turkey's entry into the War, the fate of the Arab provinces of the Ottoman Empire is seriously imperiled and every effort is to be made to secure their liberation and independence; it being also resolved that, in the event of European designs appearing to materialize, the society shall be bound to work on the side of Turkey in order to resist foreign penetration of whatever kind or form. [14]

A foundation of shared aspirations and reservations explicitly articulated thus helped build an understanding between Faysal and al-Fatat: Arab desire for independence held in check by a very real fear of imminent European designs on the region.

Ottoman reversals during the war, and the failure of the Egyptian campaign in particular, for which he appeared directly responsible, led Jamal to adopt a more brutal policy towards all forms of perceived treason and dissent amongst the Arab population under his control. Beginning with his public hanging of Yusuf Hayik, a Maronite priest, in Damascus on March 22, 1915, Jamal began by replacing Arab troops in Syria with Turkish ones. Then, based on reports culled from documents seized at the French consulates, he ordered the arrest of a large number of Arab civilians who were "brought before a military court of sinister fame at ʿAley in the Lebanon, interrogated, tortured and tried." [15] Subsequently, thirteen were executed, while forty-five others who

[12] Ibid.

[13] Ibid. It is noteworthy that ʿUlaywi does not offer any citation or source for this or the previous quote.

[14] Antonius, *Arab Awakening*, 153.

[15] Ibid., 186.

were abroad or had managed to escape received death sentences in absentia.[16] Eleven were publicly hanged at dawn on August 21, 1915, at Martyrs' Square in Beirut, while two had their sentences commuted to life imprisonment due to their advanced years;[17] others were hanged in Damascus.

When Faysal returned to Damascus, the following January, "he found conditions changed beyond recognition."[18]

> The last remaining Arab divisions had been transferred with most of his friends from al-ʿAhd, and their place taken by battalions manned by Turks. Prominent civilians had been deported by the hundred, to distant places in Anatolia. The famine which was afterwards to take an appalling toll of lives had already begun; and the population, impoverished by army requisitions, currency depreciation and shortage of food, were mainly pre-occupied with their fight against hunger. It added to the general apprehension that another and larger batch of Moslem and Christian notables had been arrested on charges of treason and were awaiting their trial at ʿAley. Among these were some of the best known and most influential names in Syria...[19]

This trial lasted for several months, during which the Sharif Husayn tried to intervene on behalf of the accused with telegrams to Jamal, the Grand Vizier, and even the Sultan himself, in the hope that even if found guilty, at least their lives would be spared by commuting the sentences to life imprisonment. Faysal, for his part, personally pleaded with Jamal; both attempts were in vain.

Beginning with Joseph Hani, who was publicly hanged in Beirut, April 5, within a month, twenty-one others were to meet the same fate, seven in Damascus, and fourteen in Beirut.[20] The morning of May 6, special free editions of the Arabic daily newspaper *al-Sharq* were distributed "in which the charges, the trials, the sentences and the executions were announced in the same breath."[21] The Ottoman authorities sent a clear message, and "a shudder shook the country."[22]

According to George Antonius' highly readable, albeit dramatized and

---

[16]Ibid., 187. Antonius adds that the convicted were "all of them men of standing, and some of them personalities famed throughout the Arab world."

[17]Ibid.

[18]Ibid., 188.

[19]Ibid.

[20]For a complete list of names see Antonius, *Arab Awakening,* 189.

[21]Ibid., 190.

[22]Ibid.

somewhat romanticized, account of events,[23] Faysal received news of the executions while having breakfast at the Bakri farmhouse where he was staying, some five miles away from Damascus. Once the news was read aloud

> Long minutes passed in silence broken only by a prayer uttered in a low voice or a sighed invocation for the repose of the dead. One of the company recited the opening verse of the Qurʾan. Then like one suddenly demented, Faisal leapt to his feet and, tearing his *kufiya* from his head, flung it down and trampled it savagely with a cry: '*Ṭāb al-mawt yā ʿArab*!'[24]

Thus, according to Antonius, was the Arab Revolt ultimately set in motion.

Faysal in Syria

Upon his triumphant entry into Damascus on October 3, 1918, the Syrians bestowed upon Faysal the mantle of champion of Arab nationalism, giving the young Arab "liberator" a reception worthy of a king.[25] After boldly proclaiming the foundation of a unified and independent state in all of Syria in the name of his father the Sharif Husayn, one day earlier on October 2,[26] it became Faysal's duty henceforth to represent the Arab cause and save the Arabs from the clutches of the colonialists.

From the outset, Faysal immediately faced external and internal challenges which set him against insurmountable obstacles. Externally, Faysal had

[23] I have relied primarily on Antonius for this brief background for several reasons which include: his direct access—in his capacity as a British civil servant in Palestine and later as an Arab delegate to the League of Nations—to the main political actors including Faysal himself; the fact that his book, *The Arab Awakening,* was a seminal work on which many of Faysal's biographers rely; the effect this work had in its Arabic translation (*Yaqaẓat al-ʿArab*) which developed a life and power of its own, and in many ways shaped the way people in that region would understand the roles and sequence of events for this period; in addition to the fact that he provides a thorough and highly readable, albeit romanticized, account of Faysal's role in the early Arab movement and revolt. For an account of the trials, see the Proceedings of the Aley Court Martial in *La Vérité sur la question syrienne* (Istanbul, 1916).

[24] Ibid., 191. With regard to Faysal's "cry", Antonius translates and expands on its meaning fairly accurately, by stating, somewhat dramatically: "A phrase which I find it beyond me to render adequately by mere translation. Literally, it is the equivalent to: 'Death has become sweet, O Arabs!" But the Arabic is much richer in meaning and amounts to an appeal to all Arabs to take up arms, at the risk of their lives, to avenge the executions in blood."

[25] al-Ḥakīm, *Sūriyah wa-al-ʿAhd al-Fayṣalī,* 23.

[26] See, for example, Faysal's proclamation of an independent Arab state in Syria in the name of his father, the "Sultan Husayn", on October 2, 1918, *al-Sharīf Fayṣal yuʿlin taʾsīs al-dawlah al-ʿArabīyah fī Sūrīyah bi-ism "al-Sulṭān" Ḥusayn,* full text in Qarqūṭ, *al-Mashriq al-ʿArabī*, 17.

to contend with formidable European foes, superior to him in every way, determined to implement their longstanding plans for the region under the guise of "international law," using their tortuously sophisticated diplomacy with which he was quite unfamiliar. At home, Faysal had to struggle with a complex Syrian political structure and cultural milieu, to which he remained essentially a stranger, and a people with cohesive nationalist demands that they expected him to fulfill, demands which naturally conflicted with those of his European enemies.

To the extent that he was hailed as the great liberator, Faysal would now be held accountable for the future of the region and the outcome of the revolt. Moreover, Faysal had to endure the prejudices incumbent upon the outsider, particularly one seeking to rule and represent a society fairly distinct from his own. Some of these Levantine cultural prejudices that Syria's new leader had to face were underscored by ʿAwni ʿAbd al-Hadi—Faysal's personal secretary during his brief reign in Syria and one of the founders of the earliest Arabist societies, al-Fatat. When relating his impressions of Faysal, ʿAwni ʿAbd al-Hadi states, for example, that his educational background was no different than that of other Hijazi *ashrāf*, which ʿAbd al-Hadi describes as being quite "limited" since "they were not inclined towards the arts and sciences, and despised both mandatory education and the wooden chairs used in schools."[27] Indeed, adds ʿAbd al-Hadi, Faysal's own private tutor, Safwat al-ʿAwwa, "himself had not achieved an advanced amount of education."[28]

Furthermore ʿAbd al-Hadi claims that Faysal, at the beginning of his political career, was similar to the other "Hijazi *ashrāf*" in that he was "completely ignorant of the sciences of organization and management."[29] He nevertheless adds that Faysal was "unique" in terms of his "intelligence, ability, and awareness."[30] Faysal was thus always able to distinguish the "noble" from the "base" among his followers and associates.

> But he used to believe in keeping the base close to him in order to prevent them from doing harm and keeping the noble close in order to benefit from their good deeds; moreover, he would shower the base with gifts in the mistaken belief that the noble would never abandon him and would follow unconditionally in his footsteps, while the base's loyalty was always contingent upon gifts.[31]

Armed with this gift of "intuitive" tribal wisdom, Faysal was able to sense that

---

[27] Letter written by ʿAwni ʿAbd al-Hadi, in Qāsimīyah, *ʿAwnī ʿAbd al-Hādī,* 20, n. 1.

[28] Ibid.

[29] Ibid.

[30] Ibid.

[31] Ibid.

attempting to realize the Arab nationalists' cherished dream of a united Arab state would not prove as simple an endeavor as these nationalists might have initially hoped. As matters stood, however, Syria was fast becoming Faysal's own personal preserve and primary region of interest; he therefore had to weigh out his options very carefully.

On the international level, Faysal continued to regard himself as a British ally; Britain appeared be the sole source of foreign support for his cause and did not seem to be directly threatening his domain. The same certainly did not apply to France. France's aspirations and interests in Syria were quite explicitly stated and its plans for the region had been repeatedly expressed in no uncertain terms. Moreover, France's cruelty towards the Arabs and Muslims in North Africa was well known, leaving the Syrians with no illusions as to what was in store for them should French rule come to prevail in their region. Faysal himself described French rule in his written statement to the King-Crane Commission thus: "She takes off manliness from the people and prevents it from progress and development as a political body…"[32]

The British were mindful of Faysal's political situation and his abilities to face the challenges ahead. After several interviews with Faysal in Beirut on the eve of his first visit to Europe in November of 1918, Colonel Cornwallis would remark:

> He feels his position somewhat acutely since he is going as a representative of his father, whom he knows not to be very popular in Syria, and without any mandate from his people.[33]

He goes on to state:

> It must be remembered that Feisal has not yet been formally accepted by the people as their future ruler although he has everywhere been well-received and is personally much liked. He is not however sufficiently sure of his position to feel justified in making any final decision without their consent and his advisors, who on the whole are badly chosen, do not possess the confidence of the public.[34]

The French, for their part, did not hide their distrust and resentment of Faysal, whom they perceived as a British-sponsored threat to their plans to dominate Syria. The reports Faysal received about the policies of the French

[32] *Chief Political Officer, Egyptian Expeditionary Force to Foreign Secretary, London, enclosing statement by Amir Faisal to American Commission*, in *Records of the Hashemite Dynasties,* 10: 220.

[33] "Colonel Cornwallis's report on talks with Amir Faisal at Beirut, 19 November 1918" [FO 882/13] text in *Records of the Hashemite Dynasties,* 10: 148.

[34] Ibid., 150.

administration in Lebanon with its open favoritism towards the Maronites, and his own experience with the French authorities first in Beirut and later in Paris, only reinforced his fears and determination to oppose them. As Colonel Cornwallis would comment:

> The French Administration in O.E.T. North has, as you know, failed to earn the approval of the Moslems, who have not been slow in pouring into Feisal's ears the tale of its alleged shortcomings.
>
> The muzzling of the Press, the behaviour of French soldiers and particularly of the Legion d'Orient, the alleged favouring of Maronite at the expense of Mohammedan interests and the rather clumsy French propaganda are all subjects of unfavourable comment. The Military Governor at Tripoli was apparently tactless in his remarks to Sherif Feisal who also thought it odd that the proclamation prohibiting public demonstrations should be published on the day of his arrival. The arbitrary seizure of his car and imprisonment of his chauffeur have also exasperated him.[35]

Faysal's experience with European diplomacy was therefore destined to be fraught with difficulties. Since France constituted the clearest and most immediate threat to his territory, it was only natural that Faysal would perceive it as his main enemy, leading to his denouncing it as the primary obstacle to Arab independence and unity and forming his policies accordingly.

FAYSAL, THE ZIONISTS, AND THE PALESTINE QUESTION

Obsessed with France and its designs on all of Syria, Faysal appeared to regard the Zionists and their ambitions in Palestine as a somewhat secondary issue. He seemed to believe that if the Arabs could rid themselves of the greater French threat in all of Syria, then they could easily come to some understanding with the Jews over that small area called Palestine. Faysal was of course well aware of the substantial political influence the Zionists enjoyed in international circles, and, perhaps more importantly, that they had received full British backing for their endeavors of founding a "national home" in Palestine. Hence, he may have calculated that if he could secure Zionist, and by extension British, support for his cause against France, then Palestine would be an ultimately small price to rid him of the overwhelming French threat to the rest of his Arab domain.

The Zionists, for their part, were eager to come to an understanding with Faysal quite early and hoped to entice him with promises of support, both political and material, for his fledgling Arab State. Fully cognizant of Faysal's

---

[35]Ibid., 148.

predicament and his preoccupation with the prospect of French control over all of Syria, they approached him directly in the hope of convincing him of the mutual benefits that a Jewish "homeland" would have for both Arabs and Jews in the region.

The first such meeting took place between Faysal and Dr. Chaim Weizmann, president of the Zionist delegation in Palestine,[36] on June 4, 1918, at Uhayda, under the auspices of the British, some four months prior to his celebrated march into Damascus. In a letter to Lord Balfour (dated May 30, 1918) immediately preceding his meeting with Faysal, Weizmann states:

> From the political point of view the Arab centre of gravity is not Palestine, but the Hedjaz, really the triangle formed by Mecca, Damascus and Baghdad. I am just setting out on a visit to the son of the King of the Hedjaz.[37] I propose to tell him that if he wants to build up a strong and prosperous Arab kingdom, it is we Jews who will be able to help him, and we only. We can give him the necessary assistance in money and in organizing power. We shall be his neighbours and we do not represent any danger to him, as we are not and never shall be a great power. We are the natural intermediaries between Great Britain and the Hedjaz against becoming a French sphere of influence, the one thing which the Hedjaz people seem to dread. With him I hope to establish a real political entente. But with Arabs of Palestine—in whom, so far as I can gather, the Shereef is little interested—only proper economic relations are necessary; and these will develop in the natural course of things, because they will be essential in our interests as well as in those of the Palestinian Arabs.[38]

At the meeting, Faysal's position was officially noncommittal concerning the prospect of a Jewish "colony" in Palestine; nevertheless, he did seem favorably disposed towards its creation. Indeed, Weizmann's constant lures of Jewish material aid in the development of the prospective Arab kingdom and political support for it in international circles must have been particularly persuasive. Weizmann was also careful to stress Jewish political power in the United States—where he was about to visit—and promised "the influence of the Jews in that country and elsewhere would be used with Dr. Wilson in

---

[36]Chaim Weizmann would later become the president of the World Zionist Organization from 1921-1929 and president of the Jewish Agency for Palestine from 1929 to 1931 and from 1935 to 1946, and was the first President of Israel.

[37]Weizmann left for Aqaba for a meeting with Faysal that same day.

[38]Chaim Weizmann to Arthur J. Balfour, 30 May, 1918 in *The Letters and Papers of Chaim Weizmann*, edited by Meyer Weisgal, Jerusalem, 1977, Vol. VIII, Series A, (Nov 1917-Oct 1918), Letter 208, p. 205.

favour of the Arab movement and the necessity for an Arab country."[39]

In turn, Faysal reiterated the need for Arab and Jewish cooperation but, regarding the question of a Jewish colony, he claimed, "These questions were already the subject of much German and Turkish propaganda and would undoubtedly be misinterpreted by the uneducated Bedouins if openly discussed."[40] He did nevertheless assure Weizmann that "later on when Arab affairs were more consolidated these questions could be brought up."[41] When finally pressed on the issue, Faysal claimed he personally accepted "the possibility of future Jewish claims to Territory in Palestine...but he could not discuss them publicly as he was in no way representing the Arab Government and was greatly afraid of the dangers of enemy propaganda."[42]

Faysal therefore left both the Zionists and the British with the impression that he was willing to acquiesce in their plans for a Jewish homeland in Palestine, albeit for the right price at the right time. Hence, Colonel Joyce subsequently reported in a private letter to Clayton:

> My private opinion of the interview was that Faisal really welcomed Jewish cooperation and indeed considered it essential to future Arab ambitions. I am certain he fully realizes that a Jewish Palestine is a future possibility and I believe though I have no authority for saying so that within bounds he would accept this, if through it Arab expansion further North could be brought about.[43]

Weizmann's impressions of the interview and of the Hijazi Amir were also quite positive; he described them to his wife in a letter a few days later:

> He is the first real Arab nationalist I have met. He is a leader! He is quite intelligent and a very honest man, handsome as a picture! He is not interested in Palestine, but on the other hand, he wants Damascus and the whole of northern Syria. He talked with great animosity against the French, who want to get their hands on Syria. He expects a great deal from collaboration with the Jews! He is contemptuous of the Palestinian Arabs whom he does not even regard as Arabs![44]

---

[39]Report by Colonel Joyce, Special Service, Aqaba, 5 June 1918 [*FO 882/14*], text in *Records of the Hashemite Dynasties*, 10: 34.

[40]Ibid.

[41]Ibid.

[42]Ibid.

[43]Letter from Colonel Joyce, Aqaba, to General Clayton, 5 June 1918 [*FO 882/14*], text in *Records of the Hashemite Dynasties*, 10: 35.

[44]Chaim Weizmann to Vera Weizmann, 17 June, 1918, in *The Letters and Papers of Chaim Weizmann*, Vol. VIII, Series A (Nov 1917-Oct 1918), Letter 213, p. 210.

The Hijazi leadership, as represented by Weizmann's account of the words of Faysal, was clearly perceived to be more concerned with establishing a state in "northern Syria" and warding off French designs on that area, than it was with Zionism, Palestine, or the preservation of "Syrian unity" within the boundaries delineated by the nationalists. It is difficult to gauge the degree that Faysal's stance in this regard is attributable to a measure of *realpolitik* borne of political desperation; genuine ignorance of the local sentiment as to the importance of Palestine to the local population and their attachment to it; or to his disdain for the rights of the Palestinian people "whom he does not even regard as Arabs," thereby rendering them expendable. The fact remains that Faysal appeared willing, albeit privately, to negotiate away what most Syrians would have considered an integral Syrian region from the very outset of their political existence. Indeed, Faysal's alleged objections to openly supporting the foundation of a "Jewish colony" were based upon the bedouin and their disapproval, not the Palestinian or Syrian inhabitants of the region he was setting himself up to rule.

After the meeting, Faysal continued to maintain cordial relations with the Zionists, sending Weizmann his congratulations on the event of the laying of the foundation stone of the Hebrew University in Jerusalem on July 24, 1918, and his regrets for not being able to attend the ceremony in person.[45] To this, Weizmann replied, "I trust we may rely on your sympathy in the establishment of an institution which is designed to promote progress and education for the benefit of all communities alike."[46]

Faysal's congenial attitude encouraged Weizmann to pursue a more formal and binding agreement with the Hashemite leadership regarding the Zionists in Palestine and future relations with the Arabs. For this, he sought the good offices of the British, as Reginald Wingate reported to Balfour from Ramleh:

> The following suggestion...was made to me tentatively and privately a fortnight ago, by Doctor Weizmann...on his return from his visit to the Emir Feisal at Akaba. He proposed that, recognizing the King of the Hedjaz as the head of the Arab Movement, the Zionists, acting as a private organization, should deal directly with him and offer:
>
> > A. Financial and, if required, other assistance for the establishment of the Kingdom of the Hedjaz.
> > B. Support in Europe and America for Syrian political aims and sympathies.

[45] "Late news on ceremony at Hebrew University," *Arab Bulletin*, No. 98, 23 July 1918, in *Records of the Hashemite Dynasties,* 10: 53.

[46] Ibid.

In return for:

> Recognition by the Arabs of Zionist aspirations in Palestine.[47]

Acknowledging that the current political situation in Syria presented "many points of conflict,"[48] Wingate observed:

> At the present moment the Zionists with their great financial resources and political influence seem the most likely to realize their aims. But the Zionists clash with Syrians over the separation of Palestine from Syria, and with the Sherifials over the treatment of the Palestinians who fully realize that equal rights for the Jews and Arabs will tend, sooner or later, to the prejudice of the latter.[49]

He nevertheless concluded quite poignantly, that any such arrangement can

> only be taken into serious consideration if our formal obligations to France respecting Syria are regarded as no longer binding (without prejudice to an offer of good offices in any future direct negotiations between the French and the Arabs), and if all idea of preserving the privileges of the Palestinian Arabs is abandoned. The latter may, I suppose, be taken as implied in His Majesty's Government's original declarations in favour of Zionism: the Anglo-French agreement, if still existent, is certainly out of date.[50]

After Faysal marched into Damascus carrying the Arab banner a few months later, there was no substantial change in his position towards the Zionists, especially since the French threat continued to loom larger than ever. Weizmann was also eager to reach an understanding with the Hashemites and sought to capitalize on the friendly relations he enjoyed with Faysal. Faysal himself appears to have encouraged such an agreement, provided it served his interests and could provide relief from the political and financial burdens he was facing. According to a telegram sent to Weizmann by Dr. Eder reporting on Faysal's situation on October 27, 1918:

> His chief needs at present are immediate loan and financial adviser. His engagements are £200,000 monthly without expectation of income till next harvest. All taxes gathered

[47] Sir Reginald Wingate, Ramleh, to Mr. Balfour, London, 25 June 1918" [*FO 371/3381*], in ibid., 44-5.

[48] Ibid., 46.

[49] Ibid.

[50] Ibid., 47.

> by Turks for this year. Faisal would prefer loan from sources you suggested in your interview with him rather than from elsewhere and your proposed solution of adviser would be acceptable. The other side of policy would be executed but it all must be clearly formulated now. It would be necessary for you or someone with definite instructions and powers to see Faisal, making explicit agreement on lines of your original proposition. Inviting Faisal for celebration on November 2nd probably unable to come as probably too busy.[51]

The ground was thus already being laid for a Hashemite-Zionist understanding, if not formal treaty. The Zionists were willing to provide Faysal and the Hashemites with a much-needed ally willing to recognize Sharif Husayn and Faysal's authority, to promote the Arab and Syrian cause in the West, and provide financial, material, and technical aid to the Hashemite states. In return, however, they wanted control of Palestine and their right to establish a Jewish national home there that was officially recognized by the Hashemites and, by extension, by the Arabs under their domain. An official, binding treaty definitively underling the exact terms of this understanding, which Faysal would be willing to sign, was therefore needed.

Faysal and European Diplomacy

Faysal's travels to Europe and his dealings with the European diplomats—the French in particular—underscored his isolation and the difficulty of his impending task in the coming European peace negotiations. Faysal quickly realized that France was determined to set as many obstacles in his path as it possibly could, that Britain's support was certainly not unconditional, and that, ultimately, he had little power to wield in terms of being able to realize any of his demands, particularly considering how little he knew of European diplomacy.

Before Faysal even set off to Paris, France refused to recognize any authority he might claim, on his or indeed his father's behalf, as equal partners in the coming peace negotiations with regard to Syria and its future. The French were determined to claim Syria as their own, and had accurately estimated that, under the circumstances, Faysal would be forced to rely on British support and consequently remain beholden to British interests. They decided to take the initiative by attempting to prevent Faysal from going to Paris altogether on the grounds that he essentially had no right to be there.

Faysal, himself, seemed unsure of what the exact nature of his "mission" was, not to mention his ability to carry it out successfully. As Colonel Cornwallis reported following his interviews with Faysal in Beirut, immediately before the latter's departure to Europe:

---

[51] "Telegram, General Clayton, Cairo, 27 October 1918" [*CAB 27/35*], in ibid., 54.

> I found him at first in a nervous condition and overweighted by a sense of responsibility.
>
> He fully realizes the weakness of his government and is anxious about leaving it when so much remains to be done.
>
> Without any suggestion from my part he again raised the question of British advisers and begged that something might be done to strengthen the government and inspire public confidence in his absence...
>
> He is frankly frightened about his mission and complained firstly that he had been given no time to prepare himself and secondly that he had received no instructions as to what he was expected to do.[52]

In an effort to strengthen and legitimize his son's position, Sharif Husayn requested that the British give his son formal accreditation as his official representative in Paris. Accordingly, the Foreign Office telegrammed its ambassadors:

> King Hussein has asked His Majesty's Commissioner at Cairo to convey to His Majesty's Government formal ratification of the fact that his son Emir Feisal as proceeding as his representative to Paris. He also asked that similar notification may be made by His Majesty's Government in his name to French Italian and United States Governments.[53]

The French were not impressed, however, and remained firm in their stance. In an immediate response, Lord Derby informed the Foreign Office that the "French Government point out that they were not consulted on this matter and their agent in Syria was not asked for his opinion and they desire to give their point of view before agreeing to the despatch of Emir Feisal or any other Delegate of the King of the Hedjaz."[54]

> Generally Speaking question of participation in Peace Conference must form subject of precise agreement between the Powers...Case of the Kingdom of the Hedjaz (which is not Arab Kingdom and was distinctly limited to Hedjaz by France and England in 1917) is special. Apart from English and French it has not been recognized by the Powers. It is

---

[52] "Colonel Cornwallis's report on talks with Amir Faisal at Beirut, 19 November 1918" [FO 882/13], text in *Records of the Hashemite Dynasties,* 10: 147.

[53] "Telegram from Foreign Office, London to British Ambassadors in Rome, Paris and Washington, 22 November 1918," in ibid., 152.

[54] "Reply from Lord Derby, Paris to Foreign Office, London, 22 November 1918," in ibid., 153.

> therefore not admissible that Emir Feisal should leave Syria on an English ship as a Delegate of King Hussein and of a hypothetical Arab Kingdom.[55]

The French did finally agree to receive Faysal, but only on the clear understanding that:

> Emir Feisal shall be treated on arrival and during his stay as distinguished foreigner, son of King of the Hedjaz; He will be told on disembarking that he has no recognized official title and that his qualification for any purpose remains to be discussed between Allies; that in no case before a formal agreement between Allies can he be admitted as representative of Arabs to any meeting of plenipotentiaries (Congress, Commission, or Committee).[56]

According to ʿAwni ʿAbd al-Hadi's exaggerated account, when Faysal first arrived in Paris in December of 1918, he was supposedly awe-struck, "his eyes saw something he never expected to see,"[57] and "he saw a great world like that of *Yaʾjūj* and *Maʾjūj*[58] bustling with people."[59] While there, however, Faysal was very conscious of the fact that he was being treated more like an exotic "Hijazi prince" rather than a legitimate "politician representing his father at the Peace Conference."[60] Moreover, much to Faysal's dismay he was surprised to find that no one at the Conference was interested in the Arab Question, save Britain and France, the very two powers who sought to divide and rule the area amongst themselves.

His experience in London shortly thereafter was a little more pleasant. Hailed as "Hero of the Arab Epic" by *The Times*, it goes on to describe him as a "tall dignified figure somewhat fairer than the usual Arab type, and is 32 years of age."[61] Proving to be a huge success with the press and the cream of British society, Faysal met with numerous illustrious and eminent personalities, receiving honors and invitations to a number of exclusive parties. As another article by *The Times* illustrates:

---

[55] Ibid. 153-4.

[56] "Mr. Grahame, Paris to Foreign Office, London, 24 November 1918," in ibid., 158.

[57] Qāsimīyah, *ʿAwnī ʿAbd al-Hādī*, 21.

[58] Yājūj and Mājūj or Gog and Magog, "are the names of apocalyptic peoples" mentioned in "Biblical and Qurʾanic eschatology." "Yādjūdj and Mādjūdj," E. Van Donzel and Claudia Ott, in *Encyclopedia of Islam*, 11: 231. (For more on this, see ibid., 231-234.) ʿAbd al-Hadi's use of the names, however, is obviously idiomatic, intended to convey an image of "a mad world beyond imagination."

[59] Qāsimīyah, *ʿAwnī ʿAbd al-Hādī*, 21.

[60] Ibid.

[61] *The Times*, 11 December 1918.

> Prince Feisul, son of the King of the Hedjaz, visited the King at Buckingham Palace yesterday, and was decorated by his Majesty with the Chain of the Royal Victorian Order, Prince Feisul drove to the Palace with his Aide-de-Camp, Brigadier General Nuri Pasha Said, D.S.O. Both wore picturesque native uniform. The Prince acknowledged in grave and dignified fashion the salutes of spectators near the Palace.[62]

While Faysal did appear to have achieved celebrity among the British as a mysterious foreign prince whom the aristocracy sought to showcase at their gatherings, this status unfortunately did not yield much in terms of substantive results for his cause. At this point therefore, whatever support he could receive, from whichever quarter, was deemed desperately welcome.

Faysal at the Peace Conference

Despite their earlier determination to deny him a seat at the Conference, France finally succumbed to the pressures exerted by the British Foreign Office, and Faysal was granted two seats for the Hijazi Arab delegation. The first hearing of the Arab case took place on February 6, 1919, when Faysal's delegation was invited to attend a formal meeting of the conference. In his statement to the conference, dated January 1, 1919, Faysal spoke "as representing my father, who by request of Britain and France, led the Arab rebellion against the Turks."[63]

> I have come to ask that the Arabic-speaking peoples of Asia, from the line Alexandretta-Diyarbekr southward to the Indian Ocean, be recognized as independent sovereign peoples, under the guarantee of the League of Nations. The Hejaz, which is already a sovereign state, and Aden, which is a British dependency are excluded from Arab demand. The confirmation of the states already existing in the area, the adjustment of their boundaries with one another, with the Hejaz, and with the British at Aden, and the formation of such new States as are required, and their boundaries, are matters of arrangement between us, after the wishes of their respective inhabitants have been ascertained. Detailed suggestions in these smaller points will be put forward by my Government when the time comes. I base my request on the principles enunciated by President Wilson (attached)[64] and

---

[62] *The Times,* 13 December 1918.

[63] Quoted in Antonius, *Arab Awakening*, 286.

[64] Attached to the statement was the text of the Second Point of Wilson's Mount Vernon address of July 14, 1918.

> am confident that the Powers will attach more importance to the bodies and souls of the Arabic-speaking peoples than to their own material interests.[65]

In his address to the meeting several days later, Faysal gave a "reasoned amplification" of this statement, in which he stressed Arab rights to freedom, independence, and unity, stating: "We believe our ideal of Arab unity in Asia is justified beyond need of argument";[66] he emphasized the Arabs' role in the war and the sacrifices they endured; and "in courteous but outspoken language, he expressed his condemnation of the Sykes-Picot Agreement."[67]

In his address, Faysal nevertheless does stress that: "The various provinces of Arab Asia—Syria, Irak, Jezireh, Hejaz, Nejd, Yemen—are very different economically and socially, and it is impossible to constrain them into one frame of government."[68]

With regard to Syria, however, he states:

> We believe that Syria, an agricultural and industrial area thickly peopled with sedentary classes, is sufficiently advanced politically to manage her own internal affairs. We feel also that foreign technical advice and help will be a most valuable factor in our national growth. We are willing to help pay for this in cash; we cannot sacrifice for it any part of the freedom we have just won for ourselves by the force of arms.[69]

Although Faysal does not initially list "Palestine" as an independent province apart from Syria when enumerating the various "provinces of Arab Asia," he does discuss its future independently as a unique case.

> In Palestine the enormous majority of people are Arabs. The Jews are very close to Arabs in blood, there is no conflict of character between the two races. In principles we are absolutely at one. Nevertheless, the Arabs cannot risk assuming the responsibility of holding level the scales in the clash of races and religions that have, in this one province, so often involved the world in difficulties. They would wish

---

[65] Antonius, *Arab Awakening,* 286-287.

[66] "Memorandum by the Emir Faisal to Peace Conference, January 1, 1919," [11162/1], in *British Documents on Foreign Affairs,* Part II: Series B, Vol. 15, p. 250. For full text, see ibid., 250-251.

[67] Antonius, *Arab Awakening,* 287.

[68] "Memorandum by the Emir Faisal to Peace Conference, January 1, 1919," [11162/1], in *British Documents on Foreign Affairs,* Part II, Vol. 15, p. 250.

[69] Ibid., 250.

> for the effective super-position of a great trustee, so long as a representative local administration commended itself by actively promoting the material prosperity of the country.[70]

Finally, Faysal thanked the British and the French for their help in the Arab struggle for freedom and independence, asking them that they fulfill their wartime promises and provide the Arabs with genuine, altruistic guidance for their future, for which "we can offer you little but gratitude."[71]

Upon close examination of Faysal's stance, it is clear that in his initial statement he treads very carefully with regard to the issue of Syrian unity and Palestine. He does not mention, let alone condemn, the question of Zionism and its designs to create a state in Palestine, and seems to leave that area open for future negotiations. Indeed, Faysal clearly does not discount the possibility of the "formation of such new States as are required" but leaves the issue of "boundaries" as "matters of arrangement between us," that is, "after the wishes of their respective inhabitants have been ascertained."

The latter part of Faysal's suggestion, in which he stressed the Wilsonian principle of "consent of the governed," would have fallen on deaf ears had it not piqued the interest of the American President, Woodrow Wilson. Taking the proposal to heart, Wilson ended up championing the idea of sending an international commission to the region for that purpose and, as discussed earlier,[72] it was eventually formally adopted by the Peace Conference despite initial British and French resistance.

In his address to the Conference, however, Faysal goes even further. Starting out by properly stating that the "enormous majority" of Palestine's inhabitants are Arab, and carefully stressing that there exists no conflict in principle between Arabs and Jews, he nevertheless makes no claim to Palestine as part of the province of Syria. Indeed, he goes on to practically disown it, by claiming that the Arabs "cannot risk assuming the responsibility" of governing it, and formally requests "the effective super-position of a great trustee."

By separating the question of Syria from that of Palestine at the conference, Faysal had officially laid claim to his own territory—which was "sufficiently advanced politically to manage her own internal affairs" and therefore in no need of "trusteeship," while at the same time appeasing Britain and its Zionist clients. By declaring Palestine a troublesome spot that his administration could not presume to manage, he actually requested that it be left at the mercy of the supervision of a "great trustee" who would be practically free to impose

---

[70] Ibid. Cf. Shukri Ghanim's statement to the Peace Conference on February 13, 1919, in which he declared Palestine to be "incontestably the southern portion of our country," suggesting the creation of a federal Syrian state where the Jews in Palestine "will be represented in the Government in proportion to their numbers." See Chapter 4, above.

[71] Ibid., 251. For full text, see ibid., 250-251.

[72] See Chapter 3, above.

its own plans for the region's future as it saw fit. By conveniently transferring the responsibility for Palestine unto a more able "trustee," Faysal and his administration could thus not be held accountable for what happened to it from this point onwards. Faysal had therefore fulfilled his part of the bargain with both Britain and the Zionists, and left the door open for an understanding between himself and the Zionists.

Faysal-Weizmann Agreement

In early January 1919, Faysal signed the Faysal-Weizmann Agreement which, ʿAwni ʿAbd al-Hadi alleges, T. E. Lawrence "played a despicable role in duping Faysal into signing."[73] Although this treaty did not amount to much in terms of its intended results, it was surrounded by controversy down to the smallest detail. According to the "original copy," for example, the agreement was signed on January 3; nevertheless ʿAbd al-Hadi raises doubts about this date, claiming it was written after that, the proof being that the stipulation inserted by Faysal at the end of the text was dated January 4.[74]

As the name suggests, the agreement was signed by:

> His Royal Highness the Amir Faisal, representing and acting on behalf of the Arab Kingdom of Hejaz, and Dr. Chaim Weizmann, representing and acting on behalf of the Zionist Organisation, mindful of the racial kinship and ancient bonds existing between the Arabs and the Jewish people, and realizing that the surest means of working out the consummation of their national aspirations is through the closest possible collaboration in the development of the Arab State and Palestine, and being desirous further of confirming the good understanding which exists between them.[75]

It is evident from the Faysal-Weizmann Agreement of "January," 1919,[76] that Faysal was initially inclined to come to terms with the Zionists and the Jewish homeland pledged by the British government. As the wording and general tone of the agreement seem to indicate, there was a general optimism about being able to reach an understanding with the Zionists in Palestine as a separate entity, and there is a clear distinction between the "Arab State"

---

[73] Qāsimīyah, *ʿAwnī ʿAbd al-Hādī*, 23.

[74] Ibid. Antonius, who provides a translation of the Agreement, reports similar misgivings, about both Lawrence's "loose and somewhat misleading paraphrase" in what became the standard accepted 'translation' of Faysal's stipulation (written in Arabic) and the given date of the agreement, which "I have queried." He goes on, "from internal evidence in text of Faisal's stipulation, it seems probable that it was signed at a later date, and in any case not earlier than January 4." Antonius, *Arab Awakening*, 437.

[75] Faysal-Weizmann Agreement, in Antonius, *Arab Awakening*, 437-8.

[76] For a full text of the Agreement see ibid., 437-439.

(undoubtedly Faysal's domain) and "Palestine," the conditional preserve of the Zionists.

> The Arab State and Palestine in all their relations and undertakings shall be controlled by the most cordial goodwill and understanding and to this end Arab and Jewish duly accredited agents shall be established and maintained in their respective territories.[77]

The issue of the "definite boundaries" of Palestine and its borders with the "Arab State" was going to be "determined by a Commission to be agreed upon by the parties hereto."[78] Moreover, the prospective Jewish entity in Palestine was going to be founded on the guidelines envisioned by the Balfour Declaration of November 2, 1917.[79]

Despite certain safeguards, such as protecting the "rights" and "economic development" of "Arab peasant and tenant farmers,"[80] "free exercise of religion,"[81] and the guarantee that "the Mohammedan Holy Places shall be under Mohammedan control,"[82] by accepting—if not endorsing—the Balfour Declaration, Faysal was unequivocally agreeing to Palestine falling under undisputed Zionist control, and hence:

> All necessary means shall be taken to encourage and stimulate immigration of Jews into Palestine on a large scale, and as quickly as possible to settle Jewish immigrants upon the land through closer settlement and intensive cultivation of the soil.[83]

Faysal also sought to derive benefit from this Zionist control:

> The Zionist Organisation proposes to send to Palestine a Commission of experts to make a survey of the economic possibilities of the country, and to report upon the best means for its development. The Zionist Organisation will place the aforementioned Commission at the disposal of the Arab State and to report upon the best means for its development.

---

[77] Article I, in ibid., 438.

[78] Article II, ibid.

[79] Article III, for example clearly states: "In the establishment of the Constitution and Administration of Palestine all such measures shall be adopted as will afford the fullest guarantees for carrying into effect the British Government's Declaration of the 2nd of November, 1917." Ibid.

[80] Article IV, ibid.

[81] Article V, ibid.

[82] Article VI, ibid., 439.

[83] Article IV, ibid., 438.

> The Zionist Organisation will use its best efforts to assist the Arab State in providing the means for developing the natural resources and economic possibilities thereof.[84]

The two parties agreed, moreover, to "act in complete accord and harmony in all matters embraced herein before the Peace Congress,"[85] and that any matters of dispute that may arise would be referred to and arbitrated by the British government.[86]

As mentioned earlier,[87] Faysal did add a stipulation (in Arabic) at the end of the agreement, stating:

> Provided the Arabs obtain their independence as demanded in my Memorandum dated the 4th of January, 1919, to the Foreign Office of the Government of Great Britain, I shall concur in the above articles. But if the slightest modification or departure were to be made [*sc.* in relation to the demands of the Memorandum] I shall not then be bound by a single word of the present Agreement which shall be deemed void and of no account or validity, and I shall not be answerable in any way whatsoever.[88]

Faysal's reasons for boldly signing this agreement, as well as adding his stipulation, are understandable. After his initial experience in Europe, Faysal realized that when facing his formidable French foes who were determined to deny him any authority at the conference, he only had Britain's precarious friendship upon which to rely. If he could secure a Zionist alliance therefore, he would be able to utilize their substantial international influence both in the United States and with their British patrons towards his cause.

Appeasing Britain was clearly crucial to Faysal; without British backing, Faysal could not even hope to attend the Peace Conference, let alone acquire his Arab state. Furthermore, if his prospective state did in fact materialize, Britain was also the only power that could effectively secure the new state's independence and maintain the integrity of its borders by preventing France from occupying it entirely. British support and assistance, military, financial, technical, and otherwise, were going to be vital for its continued existence.

Zionist financial and technical support and expertise were of course extremely welcome. Nevertheless, Faysal's added stipulation indicates that he hoped to capitalize on their eagerness to establish their own Zionist state with Arab blessing, and hence benefit from their political influence to add pressure

---

[84] Article VII, ibid. 439.

[85] Article VIII, ibid.

[86] Article IX, ibid.

[87] See n. 74, above.

[88] As translated by Antonius, *Arab Awakening*, 439.

on the Allies to meet his own demands. Consequently, he sought to make Arab peace with the Zionists contingent upon him getting his state according to his own conditions, which, if not met exactly, would render the entire agreement null and void. The treaty, moreover, had the additional safeguard of being secret; if his attempt to strike a bargain with the Zionists did not achieve the desired outcome, it could be conveniently disowned.

As General Clayton reported to Commander Hogarth upon providing him with a copy of the agreement:

> The agreement is of course Secret, and should not be divulged until the parties concerned see fit to do so but it is a useful indication of the lines on which they are working and helps towards determining the attitude taken up in discussions with Arabs.[89]

Faysal's position *vis à vis* the Zionists can be understood from the perspective of a Hijazi prince ultimately representing Hashemite interests; from both the Arab and Syrian nationalist point of view, however, negotiating away any Arab or Syrian land, let alone Palestine, was anathema. What Faysal—the new hero of the Arab cause—was attempting to do was therefore was tantamount to blasphemy. His attempt to hedge his bets by adding a stipulation that this agreement would only be binding if he was awarded his Arab state within certain designated borders, did not disguise nor excuse his willingness to consent to its ultimate conclusion: permitting the Zionists to create their own state in Palestine. The loyalty that Faysal enjoyed among certain sectors of the population of the region, however, was fully contingent upon him fulfilling their national aspirations; any deviation on his part from what they viewed as their "legitimate" goals could easily render him a traitor in their eyes.

As one British Major, J. N. Camp, would remark rather perceptively:

> In my opinion, Dr. Weizmann's agreement with Emir Feisal is not worth the paper it is written on or the energy wasted in the conversation to make it. On the other hand, if it becomes sufficiently known among the Arabs, it will be somewhat of a noose about Feisal's neck, for he will be regarded by the Arab population as a traitor. No greater mistake could be made than to regard Feisal as a representative of Palestinian Arabs (Moslem and Christian natives of Palestine who speak Arabic); he is in favour with them so long as he embodies Arab nationalism and represents their views, but would no longer have any power over them if they thought he had

[89] "General Clayton to Commander Hogarth enclosing copy of agreement between Amir Faisal and Dr. Weizmann, 1 February 1919" [*FO 882/22*], in *Records of the Hashemite Dynasties,* 10: 55.

> made any sort of agreement with Zionists and meant to abide by it. But it seems he is capable of making contradictory agreements with the French, the Zionists and ourselves, of receiving money from all three, and then endeavouring to act as he pleases. This is an additional reason why his agreement with Weizmann is of little or no value.[90]

Despite later claims by his apologists, such as ʿAbd al-Hadi, for example, that the treaty itself was merely a ruse, or a bargaining ploy, to attain honorable Arab nationalist objectives, events would demonstrate that Faysal himself was never fundamentally opposed to the notion of a Jewish state in Palestine.

While at the Peace Conference, Faysal continued to maintain good relations with the Zionists, through their leader, Chaim Weizmann. In a letter to Mr. Balfour on April 9, 1919, Dr. Weizmann would state:

> Between the Arab leaders, as represented by Feisal and ourselves there is complete understanding, and therefore, complete accord. You may have seen the recent letter of Feisal in the course of which he says:
>
> > "We Arabs, especially the educated among us, look with the deepest sympathy on the Zionist movement. Our deputation is fully acquainted with the proposals submitted yesterday by the Zionist Organization to the Peace Conference, and we regard them as moderate and proper. We will do our best in so far as we as are concerned, to help them through, we will wish the Jews a most heart-felt welcome home."
>
> Undoubtedly there is a good deal of honest misunderstanding among the Arabs, and Feisal has undertaken to exert all his influence towards his having his estimate of the Zionist cause and the Zionist proposals as "moderate and proper" shared by his following. I need not dwell upon the difficulties of this educative process and the hearty cooperation that is required between the Arabs and Zionist leaders, but that cooperation is assured between us.[91]

---

[90] Major J. N. Camp, *Arab Movement and Zionism,* Jerusalem, 12.8.19, Enclosure in No. 253, Colonel French (Cairo) to Earl Curzon (Received September 6), C.P.O. 31/110 [125609/2117/44A], No. 253, in *Documents on British Foreign Policy,* 4: 364-5.

[91] Dr. Weizmann to Foreign Secretary, Mr. Balfour, London, 9 April 1919 [*FO 800/216*], text in *Records of the Hashemite Dynasties,* 10: 62-63, quotes in the original.

Despite all his confidence in Faysal, and by extension, his Arab leadership's goodwill towards the Zionists, Weizmann was nevertheless aware of Faysal's limitations and that his position was not fully representative of Syrian public opinion. The Palestinians declared themselves an integral part of the Syrian nation and as vehemently opposed to Zionism and its designs at the First Palestine Congress.[92] Further, the Syrian political scene was bustling with political parties, many of them Egyptian-based, with a clearly defined focus on Syria and Syrian nationalism and, as such, vigorously opposed to ceding any part of what they perceived to be their "homeland."

These parties, as was previously discussed,[93] were not necessarily personally loyal to Faysal, nor that averse to French control if France were to assure them of Syrian unity and eventual independence. While Weizmann may have been confident of Faysal's ability to dispel any "honest misunderstandings" about Zionism among the Arabs under his sway, he recognized that there were others over whom Faysal had little or no control. Consequently, Weizmann was quick to point out:

> We are dealing also with purposeful and organized misunderstanding. Indisputably a vigorous agitation is on foot, especially emanating from Damascus, directed against Jewish interests in Palestine. This has been confirmed by Emir Feisal and Col. Lawrence as well as by the late Sir Mark Sykes—than whom there was no better friend of the Arabs. This agitation has reached such a stage that reports of responsible observers have come to me warning against dangers threatening the Jewish community from organized Arab groups.[94]

Weizmann was also very careful to define friends and allies under these political circumstances. The British and the Zionists had, in his estimation, congruous aims and interests, and so long as Faysal fell in line with them, he could be considered as part of the same camp. The Arab and Syrian nationalist "agitators" and the French, on the other hand, formed an opposing camp, which sought to threaten these "common interests."

> I am more concerned by this agitation because, I venture to say, it is as much anti-British as it is anti-Jewish. During the recent Egyptian difficulties two agitators from Damascus appeared in Palestine on their way to Egypt and, while there, agitated against the British and the Jews, indicating that

[92] See Chapter 2, above.

[93] See Chapter 4, above.

[94] Dr. Weizmann to Foreign Secretary, Mr. Balfour, London, 9 April 1919 [*FO 800/216*], text in *Records of the Hashemite Dynasties,* 10: 63.

> they had come from the Arabs of Damascus to encourage their friends in Egypt and to inform them that Damascus and Palestine would join in the movement...I know you realize that there is great provocation against the Jews in Palestine, a provocation which only intensifies the general unrest in the East. The persistent misrepresentation in the French press here—the continued talk of "Jewish State" when such a claim has been authoritatively repudiated have likewise their disturbing effect in the East...The situation is so serious from both the British and Jewish point of view—and to my mind, their interests in Palestine are inseparable.[95]

Faysal and the American Commission

Overall, Faysal's experience at the Peace Conference was not very positive, and he appeared particularly disheartened with the French attitude. In a letter written to his father, dated February 28, 1919, Faysal states:

> I do not expect any great advantage to result from our conference, owing to the divergence of our interests—the tenacity of the French to their principles on the one hand, and my own tenacity to mine on the other. Their Press is constantly showing hostility towards us, so much so that the "Temps" yesterday published a long article demanding an agreement with England for the definite partition of our country. In the course of the article, it spoke of, and demanded, our separation from that country (Syria); alleging that if we had any authority in it, it would not be long before we stirred up trouble between the French and British governments there. The English are confident in the future and are only awaiting events...[96]

Faysal was nevertheless extremely optimistic about the role that the Americans might play in the negotiations and saw in Wilson the ally that the Arabs desperately needed:

> The Americans, at the head of whom is President Wilson, are in complete agreement with us. They are now showing dislike of the French on account of the greed and covetousness which they observe in them, for the occupation of a country which does not belong to them.
>
> We are waiting the return of President Wilson from

[95] Ibid., 63-4.

[96] "Amir Faisal, Paris to King Hussein, Mecca, 28 February 1919" [*FO 882/22*], in *Records of the Hashemite Dynasties,* 10: 179-180.

> America and when he returns it is expected that he will have obtained the support of the entire American nation, and will defend the rights of nations—particularly weak nations—before the Peace Conference. The situation will then be cleared up and things will be all that can be desired. President Wilson made a speech on his arrival in Boston in which he urged the defense of those lofty ideals for the realization of which the American nation alone entered the war. If he succeeds in his efforts we can then say that the aspirations of the Arabs have been completely attained.[97]

At the end of April 1919, Faysal set sail for Syria on the understanding that an international commission would be sent to the region to determine the wishes of the inhabitants as preliminary for its future policies. The proposal for this commission, initiated and backed by Wilson, was formally adopted and approved by the Council of Four on March 25.

> It is related when news of the decision reached Faisal's ears he drank champagne for the first time, and drank it as though it were water. Then he went for a drive past the headquarters of the American and British Delegations and threw cushions at the Crillon, the Majestic and the Quai d'Orsay, saying that, as he had no bombs, he could only express his feelings in that way.[98]

When Faysal returned to Syria, the political atmosphere had already changed. The First Palestinian Congress had taken place outlining unequivocally Syrian nationalist demands and expressing the clear desire for unity with Syria.[99] By July, the first General Syrian Congress was held reiterating the demands of the Palestinian conference.[100] Faysal's scope for negotiations with the Allies and the Zionists regarding the creation of a Jewish national home in Palestine or any acquiescence in the division of Syria was thereby severely limited.

When describing Faysal's position after his return to Syria in May, Colonel Cornwallis states:

> Feisal stands pledged to the independence program and has received full backing from the notables. This gives him no new official standing...but it is another proof that he stands very high in popular favour at present.[101]

---

[97] Ibid., 180.

[98] Antonius, *Arab Awakening*, 288.

[99] For more on this see Chapter 2, above.

[100] See ibid.

[101] "Report by British Liaison Officer on Political Situation in Arabia," 16 May 1919,

Describing the political situation in Syria and Faysal's attempts to maintain control of it, Cornwallis reports:

> Feisal...dissolved both the "Hizb-el-Istiklal" and the "Ittihad-es-Suri" and stated that there will be no more political parties in O.E.T. East. He knows, however, that it would be easier to dam the Falls of Niagara than to stop the Syrians from talking politics, and he will, therefore, allow discussions to continue in the houses of members. His policy is to bring the Extremists into line and to prevent the creation of an opposition party, and he claims to know everything that is going on.
>
> Feisal has taken the whole of the political campaign into his own hands, and has already sent instructions to all parts of the country...The people have been told to ask for complete independence for Syria and, at the same time, to express a hope that it will be extended to other Arab countries. By this compromise Feisal has reconciled the "Ittihad-es-Suri," which thinks only of Syria, with the pan-Arab empire enthusiasts represented in the "Istikhlal-el-Arabi."[102]

Insofar as the Palestine question was concerned, it was becoming clear to Faysal that Palestine could not be conveniently relinquished and that it was an issue on which he certainly needed to modify his stance.

> Feisal is beginning to realize the difficulties which he will have in reconciling the Palestinians and the Zionists, and no longer treats the question as a minor one. He has abandoned the idea of having a conference here, but intends to ask various notables to visit him separately and endeavour to convert them. He will also try to induce the Zionist Commission to moderate its demands, and will probably propose a conference to the Peace Commission.
>
> Meanwhile Palestinians here are as vehement as before, and Mohamed-es-Saleh-el-Husseini, of Nablus, has been advocating the defence of Arab independence of Palestine by the sword. Abdel Kader-el-Muzghar, also, does not allow his opinions to mellow with time. There was a meeting yesterday in honour of Feisal, at which the speeches aimed at independence and inclusion in the Syrian State. They

---

11562/54(i), in *British Documents on Foreign Affairs,* Part II: Series B, Vol. 1, p. 50.

[102] Ibid.

> were censored beforehand, and contained nothing very objectionable.[103]

The disturbances in Jerusalem in the summer of 1919 and the appointment of Sir Herbert Samuel, a well-known Zionist, as High Commissioner for Palestine only exacerbated the situation, rendering Faysal's position more difficult. Consequently, in an urgent letter sent to the British authorities in Egypt regarding these issues, Faysal was careful to adopt the nationalist line. According to the report sent to the Foreign Office in London:

> He states that the news has had as bad an effect as is possible on the Arabs since it is universally known that Sir Herbert Samuel is a Zionist whose aim is to build a new Jewish State upon the ruins of Palestine, a considerable and integral part of Syria.[104]

Since the Arab nationalists formed the backbone of Faysal's base of support, he could not afford to alienate them by agreeing to anything that was in direct conflict with their demands and aspirations, let alone be construed as traitorous. Faysal must have also genuinely believed that if an international commission were to investigate the demands of the region's inhabitants, they would be convinced of the "justness" of the "Arab cause" and help his case tremendously before the Peace Conference. The Americans now appeared as a glimmer of hope that this cause could finally be presented to the world, thus increasing its chances of being successful.

Seeing the American Commission as his only viable chance to achieve his objectives and regarding the United States as a genuine ally, Faysal placed a great deal of confidence in the Commission and its ability to influence the decisions of the Peace Conference. When rumors had reached Faysal that the decision to divide the region had already been made, that France would control Syria, and the Commission would not be sent, he became very distressed and demanded an immediate meeting with the British authorities.[105] After meeting with Colonels Cornwallis and Joyce, they reported:

> He was very insistent about the Commission coming out... He is still unwilling to accept any compromise as regards an independent Syria. He also showed himself very mistrustful of our Zionist aims, although he declared that he was only

---

[103] Ibid., 51.

[104] "Paraphrase of telegram from High Commissioner for Egypt to Foreign Office, London, 9 June 1919" [*FO 800/23*], in *Records of the Hashemite Dynasties,* 10: 66.

[105] For more on this see Chapter 3, above.

> presenting the point of view of the people of the country to us.[106]

In this tumultuous political atmosphere, seething with anger, fear, and uncertainty, Faysal's political position hung in a very delicate balance. Any action or decision that he took in the international arena would have immediate repercussions on his popularity and support at home. It was therefore very difficult for him to deviate in any official capacity from the guidelines set by the Arab congresses.

In his report on an interview with Michel Lutfallah of the Syrian Unity Party[107] in Cairo, Colonel French stated that Lutfallah "proceeded to enlighten me on the political circumstances and events attending the arrival of the American Commission."[108] Essentially, Lutfallah "declared that his own party—the 'Union Syrienne' were in agreement with Feisal and leading notables on general principle—viz., autonomy as self-governing dominion within the British empire. But they disagreed as to means."[109]

According to French's report on Lutfallah's account of events:

> Feisal...decided to press for a British Mandate for the whole of Syria, hoping to progress via Mandate to the status of self-governing dominion within the British Empire. With this intent he convened a gathering of leaders and expounded his views. This meeting becoming known, a storm of indignation was raised by the Arab Independence Party,[110] and demonstrations were held in the streets. Feisal was branded a traitor and the British were cursed. Machine-guns had to be placed in the streets...Feisal's popularity disappeared, and eventually the formula contained in the statement presented to the American Mission by the Syria Congress was generally adopted.
>
> To restore Feisal's popularity, he, Lotfullah, organized a banquet at which he was followed by Feisal in a speech demanding complete independence and no Mandate. Feisal's

[106] "Brigadier General Clayton to Earl Curzon, General Headquarters, Egyptian Expeditionary Force, June 23, 1919" 11562/63, in *British Documents on Foreign Affairs,* Part II, vol. 1, p. 67.

[107] For a more detailed discussion of this party see Chapter 4, above.

[108] "Report on conversation with Michel Bey Lotfullah, 5 August 1919" [*FO 371/4182*], in *Records of the Hashemite Dynasties,* 10: 228.

[109] Ibid., 228-9.

[110] For more on this party see Chapter 4, above.

> volte-face was well received, and he was now recovering popularity.[111]

When the American Commission did finally come out therefore, Faysal was forced to adopt a clear Arab nationalist line in his demands during his interview with them on July 3, 1919. In his address to the "honorable commission," Faysal claimed to speak "on behalf of the Syrians, being authorized by them by official documents containing over three hundred signatures."[112] Faysal summarized the Syrian people's concerns and demands as follows:

> 1. The fear of colonization and division of their country.
>
> 2. The desire of the Liberty and Independence. The Syrian Country is situated between the boundaries defined as follows:- On the West the Mediterranean, on the East the Euphrates and Al Khabour rivers, on the North the Taurus mountains, on the South the Sinai desert and the Red Sea and the desert of the Hijaz. ...They are fully aware that no existence can there be in the future without the national unity which is the center of their aspirations.[113]

While Faysal constantly addressed the dangers the Syrians were facing with respect to the impending threat of French domination and colonization, and even the issue of separating Lebanon and the Western zone,[114] he did not mention Zionism or the Palestine question directly, alluding to it only in his general demands for Syrian unity and independence. He nevertheless reiterated that:

> The Syrians, both abroad and at home, anxious for their independence and desirous of being masters of their own country, are agreed and determined on Syrian Unity as defined above, and reject whatever infringements of that racial integrity, which requires to be maintained in view of the common economical and moral influence by bonds of union between the various zones with relation to their climatical and topographical conditions and requirements. It is well known that Syria has...been one in fortune and misfortune all through its history, ...the Syrians refuse to give up the

---

[111] "Report on conversation with Michel Bey Lotfullah, 5 August 1919," [*FO 371/4182*], in *Records of the Hashemite Dynasties,* 10: 229.

[112] "Statement by Amir Faisal to the American Commission, 11 July 1919," Chief Political Officer, Egyptian Expeditionary Force to Foreign Secretary, London [*FO 371/4182*], in *Records of the Hashemite Dynasties,* 10: 215.

[113] Ibid.

[114] For full text, see ibid., 215-221.

> solid unity which is...their national existence; and will prefer death determined...of its unity and solidarity.[115]

After his talks with the American Commission, Faysal had an interview with General Clayton the next day, during the course of which "he gave me the gist of what had transpired."[116] Reporting on this interview, General Clayton stated:

> With regard to Syria, no partition of Syria from Palestine on the Western zone would be acceptable as they were nationally one...Zionism he stated some months ago he was prepared to accept in its limited sense of a certain amount of immigration and the retention of the existing Jewish colonies. The wider Zionist aspirations had however, frightened the people of the country and he now finds them determined not to have any form of it. He apparently did not say a great deal on this point or express himself very strongly.[117]

Faysal was consequently in quite an unenviable position. He could not compromise on the unequivocal demands of his own constituents and risk losing their support, he could not afford to alienate the British, nor, for that matter, could he face France's military might. Indeed, as Colonel French would sympathetically comment a month later:

> The situation is exceedingly difficult for the Emir Feisal whom I believe to have made honest attempts to hold the balance between the moderate and extreme sections of the Arabs and who desires to fulfill his promises both to His Majesty's Government and to the Zionists; and this very honesty has to a certain extent undermined his influence which for the moment is probably decreasing rather than increasing.[118]

Unable to fully contain the Arab nationalists and their dominant influence in the country, Faysal hoped to temper their influence by appearing to represent national demands, meanwhile utilizing their power and popular support in his

---

[115]Ibid., 217.

[116]"Major Clayton's account of his interview with Amir Faisal, following the latter's talks with American Commission, 11 July 1919," Chief Political Officer, Egyptian Expeditionary Force to Foreign Secretary, London [*FO 371/4182*], in *Records of the Hashemite Dynasties,* 10: 223; for full text of report see ibid., 223-5.

[117]Ibid., 223-4.

[118]"Colonel French to Earl Curzon, General Headquarters, Egyptian Expeditionary Force, August 30, 1919" 11562/98, in *British Documents on Foreign Affairs,* Part II, vol. 1, p. 93.

negotiations with the Allies. By September, Colonel Meinertzhagen would report:

> My political Officer at Damascus reports volunteers are being voluntarily enrolled and swearing to defend the country against partition without any special reference to any power. Feisal gives an assurance that there will be no trouble at present. Feisal intends the movement to strengthen his case before H.M.G.... Feisal also wishes to repudiate his agreement with Weizmann for fear it may be construed as acquiescence in partition of Syria.[119]

When Faysal was invited back to Paris towards the end of the year, he vacillated. His primary concern, naturally, continued to be France and its persistent determination to occupy all of Syria. The British consequently attempted to arrange a meeting between Faysal, the French, and themselves, in order to reach some sort of understanding before he could proceed to Europe again. This meeting took place in Damascus on September 9, 1919, and was attended by Faysal, Colonel Meinertzhagen the Chief British Political Officer in Damascus, and Marie-Xavier Laforcade the French High Commissioner. During the discussions, in Meinertzhagen's estimation, "effort was made to improve relations between French and Arabs by frank exchange of views."

According to Meinertzhagen, the discussion centered on the following four main points:

> 1. British refusal of Syrian mandate.
> 2. Establishment of Zionism in Palestine
> 3. The Anglo-French 1918 agreement
> 4. The nature of present administration of occupied territory whereby any breach of the peace would bring Faisal into direct conflict with Allies to the (? detriment *sic*) of his cause."[120]

During the course of the meeting, Faysal stressed Syrian unity as a "vital issue"[121] to Laforcade, defining the borders of Syria "from Gaza to the Taurus."[122] Nevertheless, states Meinertzhagen, "he accepted Zionism."[123] It was obvious that Faysal remained more concerned and fearful of the prospect of a French

---

[119] "Colonel Meinertzhagen, Cairo to Foreign Office, London, 3 September 1919" [*FO 608/80*], in *Records of the Hashemite Dynasties,* 10: 67.

[120] Colonel Meinertzhagen, Cairo to Foreign Office, London, 11 September and 12 September 1919, in *Records of the Hashemite Dynasties*, 10: 272.

[121] Ibid.

[122] Ibid.

[123] Ibid.

mandate over Syria, than he was with Zionism or Palestine. In fact, when Laforcade suggested that Syrian unity could be preserved under a French Mandate and inquired what Faysal's objections would be to such a proposal, Faysal replied that a "French Mandate entailed slavery, quoting local instances of French oppression."[124] Faysal did add, however, that the "definite reply to the Syrian question of French mandate would be given," once the British and French gave their assurances that the 1918 agreement would be the "basic principle of the Syrian solution."[125] Faysal's interpretation of this document, adds Meinertzhagen, "is that it implies compliance with Syrian wishes regarding unity of Syria and choice of Mandatory power."[126]

In his private conversations with Meinertzhagen, Faysal spoke more candidly:

> With me personally Feisal freely discussed the situation reaffirming his policy of a united Syria to absolute exclusion of France and everything French...Feisal has regained support of his people. At first sign of the Peace conference handing Syria over to France our political influence over Arabs and Feisal will disappear... Feisal's ultimate aim is an Arab Federation embracing Mesopotamia and a Jewish Palestine all under a British mandate. He is inclined to (? ignore *sic*) British refusal of a Syrian Mandate and intends to force hand of His Majesty's Government in this respect.
>
> General situation becomes increasingly serious though it is not yet acute. French and Arab propaganda which neither party has agreed to limit is an aggravating fact.[127]

Faysal's "ultimate aim," that is, the creation of an Arab Federation under British tutelage, appeared to be his only way out. Nevertheless, so long as Britain refused the mandate for Syria at the Peace conference, a direct confrontation with France appeared almost inevitable.

By September 13, Faysal's worst fears were beginning to materialize. After meeting for several days, Lloyd George and Clemenceau agreed to the evacuation by November 1 of all British troops from Syria and their replacement by French forces "west of the Sykes-Picot line" and Cilicia, while "the garrisons at Damascus, Homs, Hama, and Aleppo will be replaced by an Arab force."[128] Furthermore:

---

[124] Ibid.

[125] Ibid., 273.

[126] Ibid.

[127] Ibid., 274.

[128] "Aide Memoire in regard to the occupation of Syria, Palestine and Mesopotamia pending the decision in regard to Mandates, Paris, September 13, 1919" [*FO 371/4182*],

> After the withdrawal of their forces neither the British Government nor the British Commander-in-Chief shall have any responsibility within the zones from which the Army has retired:
>
> The territories occupied by the British troops will then be Palestine, defined in accordance with its ancient boundaries of Dan to Beersheba, and Mesopotamia, including Mosul, the occupation thus being in harmony with the arrangements concluded in December 1918, between M. Clemenceau and Lloyd George.
>
> The British Government are prepared at any time to discuss the boundaries between Palestine and Syria and between Mesopotamia and Syria. In the event of disagreement in regard to the above boundaries, the British government are prepared to submit the question to the arbitration of a referee appointed by President Wilson.[129]

This agreement, which was accepted by the Conference as an allegedly "purely temporary provisional arrangement for military occupation without prejudice to final settlement of mandate or boundaries,"[130] marked the official and effective severing of Palestine's fate from the rest of Syria. By withdrawing from Syria, moreover, the British had practically abandoned Faysal, who now had to face France and its military on his own. Consequently, Faysal immediately set off for Europe once again.

Despite Faysal's protests to the British requesting "that this proposed engagement…shall be entirely cancelled as it is contrary to the ideals of the League of Nations and is also contrary to our other engagements which were based on national honour"[131] and his pleas that "it would surely be much more advisable to leave the status quo as it is or withdraw all European troops until the final decision,"[132] the writing was already on the wall.

---

in *Records of the Hashemite Dynasties,* 10: 264.

[129]Ibid. For full text, see ibid., 264-265.

[130]"Conclusions of heads of delegations of Allied Powers, War Office, Paris, 15 September 1919" [*FO 371/4182*], in ibid., 266.

[131]"Aide Memoire in regard to the occupation of Syria, Palestine and Mesopotamia pending the decision in regard to Mandates: Reply by His Highness the Emir Feisal to British Prime Minister, London, 21 September, 1919," in ibid., 270; for full text see ibid., 267-271.

[132]Ibid., 271. Also see Faysal's letter to Lloyd George, on October 9, in which he proposes:

That the arrangement arrived at in Paris should be cancelled, or at least its execution suspended.

That the whole question be placed before the Peace Conference for the final settlement

The British Foreign Minister, Earl Curzon, explained to Faysal that he "would appear to be under a misapprehension as to the character of the aide-mémoire"[133] since it "in no sense represents an agreement between the French and British governments."[134] Nevertheless, he pointed out that:

> These proposals—to which they adhere—were worked out by the British Government as soon as they decided that it was impossible for them to continue the occupation of Syria by British troops.[135]

In his own response to Faysal and his proposal, Lloyd George reiterated these points stating:

> I do not think it is necessary for me to discuss again the reasons which have prompted His Majesty's Government in putting forward the proposals contained in the *aide-mémoire*...it does not seem to me that the proposal you now make is practicable. His Majesty's Government have made up their mind that it is impossible for them to continue the occupation of Syria by British troops. Six months ago they announced to the Peace Conference and to yourself that under no circumstances would they accept a mandate for Syria. Their occupation of the country, which involves them in a heavy burden of expense, has been prolonged far beyond their own expectation, in the hopes that the Peace Conference would deal with the question without delay. There is now no prospect of the Peace Conference being able to undertake the discussion of the Turkish problem for some months, and the regrettable illness of President Wilson, without whose participation no final decisions can be arrived at, is likely to delay rather than to hasten the settlement of the problem. It is therefore impossible for His Majesty's Government to withdraw the proposals which they have made for dealing

---

without delay and be considered by the Peace Conference itself, or by a Conference appointed by it (consisting of British, French, and Arab representatives under the presidency of an American chairman), which will discuss the serious question at issue, and render its report to the Peace Conference.

"Amir Faisal to British Prime Minister, 9 October 1919" [*FO 371/4183*], in ibid., 288.

[133] "Earl Curzon to His Highness Sherif Feisal, October 9, 1919" [*F/205/3*, Lloyd George Papers, House of Lords, London], in ibid., 289. For full text see ibid., 289-292.

[134] Ibid.

[135] Ibid.

> with the Syrian problem in the interim period until the Peace Conference can settle it.[136]

Advised to reach an "amicable and satisfactory"[137] understanding with the French, Faysal accordingly began meeting with Clemenceau and a number of French officials in order to determine the dimensions and parameters of Faysal's (and Arab) authority in Syria in relation to the overriding military authority and supervision of France.[138] Palestine no longer figured in this equation since it fell under British control, and was henceforth a British preserve.

Faysal was now in the awkward position of having to maintain the equilibrium between the volatile national sentiment and its demands at home and the political realities that were being dictated by the Peace Conference. Hence, he had to try and balance the nationalist stance of attempting to preserve unity and some semblance of independence as demanded by his constituents; the present political impasse of Britain's refusal to accept the mandate for Syria, thereby eliminating the possibility of keeping Syria united under British tutelage; and the forgone conclusion that he would have to contend with

---

[136] "The Prime Minister of Great Britain to His Highness Sherif Feisal, London, October 10, 1919," in ibid., 293.

[137] Ibid.

[138] See for example the Faysal-Clemenceau Agreement of January 6, 1920. This agreement, which was never ratified, was a reluctant attempt by France and Faysal to negotiate a settlement in late 1919 that aimed at reaching a comprehensive solution over Syria. Encouraged by Britain, these negotiations were largely the result of Britain's conclusion that it could not convince France to forsake its claims to Syria, France's realization of the difficulties involved in imposing its uncontested rule on Syria without the cooperation of the Faysali regime, and Faysal's recognition that he would not be able to face France militarily on his own and his inability to rely on Britain and the United States for support. A compromise agreement was therefore seen as the lesser of evils under the circumstances. The Faysal-Clemenceau Agreement began with the first formal French proposals for a mandate over Syria where the nature of France's future status and role in Syria were discussed. The issues negotiated included certain concessions such as French recognition of Faysal's "semi-independent" Arab state ruling over much of Syria (but definitely excluding Lebanon), French aid for Syria, the Faysali regime's obligation to hire French advisors exclusively, and France's handling of Syria's defense and foreign relations. While the French tried to obtain terms as close to those of the former Sykes-Picot Agreement as possible, the Arabs pushed for more independence, more control over their affairs, and insisted on a parliament. Nevertheless, at the last moment, Faysal did not sign the agreement, whose terms would have been rejected by his Arab nationalist supporters. For more on this see Russell, *The First Modern Arab State,* 117-131; Jan Karl Tanenbaum, "France and the Arab Middle East," *Transactions of the American Philosophical Society*, new ser., vol. 68, no. 7 (1978): 1-50; also, al-Ḥakīm, *Sūriyah wa-al-ʿAhd al-Fayṣalī*; and Khayrīyah Qāsimīyah, *al-Ḥukūmah al-ʿArabīyah fī Dimashq bayna 1918-1920* (Cairo, 1971). For the full terms of the agreement, see Tanenbaum, "France and the Arab Middle East," 44-45.

French supremacy in Syria since Britain and France had already militarily divided Palestine and Syria amongst themselves.

Faysal's stance towards the Zionists at this particular juncture is perhaps best illustrated by his interview with *The Jewish Chronicle* in London on October 3, 1919. At the beginning of the interview, it was suggested to him that the "best solution" for the Arabs and Jews in Palestine would be to call it "the Land of Israel and its inhabitants Israelites,"[139] to which he quickly replied:

> But calling a thing by a name does not alter the thing itself, and Palestine cannot be called the Land of Israel, because it is not in any sense the Land of Israel. Compared to the Arabs there, there are only ten per cent who are Israelites, and it would be far more reasonable to call it the Land of the Arabs, and the Jews there Arabs.[140]

Faysal is also very clear regarding the intentions and aspirations of his leadership and those of his constituents.

> Palestine is and must remain part and parcel of Syria. There is no natural boundary, no frontier between the two countries. What affects one must affect the other. If there is disorder in Palestine there will be disorder in Syria. From the point of view of the Arab, Palestine is a province, not a country, and our intention is to build up an Arab Empire which must consist, as a minimum, of Mesopotamia, Syria, and Palestine. From that we cannot recede.[141]

When discussing Zionism and its aspirations in Palestine, Faysal freely states,

"I have had several conferences with Dr. Weizmann, the able leader of the Zionist movement…He showed me …his proposals, and to those proposals I raise no objection."[142] Noticing that his seemingly contradictory statement apparently confused his interviewer, Faysal quickly explains:

> You seem surprised…and you think there is something inconsistent in my agreeing with Dr. Weizmann's proposals and in what I have said in regard to Arab aspirations respecting Palestine. As I understand, he is working for a regulated immigration into the country, for conditions in which the Jew will have equal rights with the Arab, shall

---

[139] Extract from *The Jewish Chronicle*, 3 October 1919 [*FO 371/4183*], in *Records of the Hashemite Dynasties,* 10: 69. For full article, see ibid., 68-74.

[140] Ibid., 69.

[141] Ibid., 70.

[142] Ibid.

> take part in the government of Palestine, shall have control of Jewish schools, shall have the means of establishing there a Jewish cultural centre, and shall have free use of the Hebrew language. There is nothing to object to in that. Indeed we would welcome the assistance which an immigration of Jews could give us in developing the country.[143]

During the course of the interview, Faysal goes on to explain that Jewish immigration to Palestine would only be feasible in limited numbers—"fifteen hundred per annum"[144]—unless, "of course, you want to set up there a population of beggars, supported by charity."[145] While constantly expressing the Arabs' right and determination to create an Arab Kingdom which must include Palestine as "essential, we believe, to the peace and prosperity of the Near East,"[146] Faysal continues to urge the Zionists to work with him.

> You Jews can do a great work if you would cooperate with us in the formation of this kingdom. Instead of our relying upon any of the great Powers for means of development, for material help, we should like to have the cooperation in these things of the Jewish people. You have the means, and we have the numbers, and when our Arab kingdom is built and set upon firm foundations...then it may be that there would be a concentration of your people into Palestine and that you would make of Palestine a Jewish sub-province of the Arab Kingdom...The number of Christians that there are in Palestine is negligible, so far as our present conversation is concerned. The Jewish people can get everything they desire, such as a Jewish cultural centre, and the Jewish population in Palestine can live its own Jewish life...Although we do not ask the country to be called Arab, and although we are content to let it remain Palestine, still Palestine is in effect the Land of the Arabs, and must remain an integral portion of the new Arab State.[147]

Faysal concludes on a conciliatory note, declaring, "I appreciate quite fully Zionist aspirations, even extreme Zionist aspirations. I quite understand the desire of the Jews to acquire a homeland."[148] And, once again, he goes on to stress:

---

[143] Ibid.

[144] Ibid., 73.

[145] Ibid.

[146] Ibid.

[147] Ibid., 73-74.

[148] Ibid., 74.

> I can only say, and would ask you to impress upon all your people, that we wish Jews to cooperate with us in perfect amity and friendship, for Jews, like ourselves, are Semites. I cannot put it stronger than by repeating: we are cousins; we wish to be brothers.[149]

Despite his attempts to placate the Zionists, no deal with them would be possible unless either both the British and French completely backed away from the region, thus acquiescing in Faysal's independent Arab state which would include Palestine, or the British could be coerced into accepting the mandate for all of Syria, including Palestine, under Faysal's "rule." Considering that the British had already informed Faysal that a Syrian mandate was not going to be a feasible option, and had in effect advised him to reach an understanding with France, any attempted negotiations with the Zionists, while by-passing both the British and the French, were inherently futile. France was going to set its own rules and limitations as to how and whether Faysal would continue to administer Syria. Palestine, ironically at Faysal's own request, was already excluded from the jurisdiction of his administration and was placed under the authority of Britain. It was only a matter of time before the Peace Conference would make British and French control of those areas "official" at the Conference of San Remo in April of 1920.

The nationalists at home, however, were not about to accept this situation and were willing to shed their blood to oppose it. In a secret session held on the evening of Saturday, November 22, 1919, the Syrian Congress "in its capacity as the legal and political representative of the Syrian Arab nation"[150] responded by declaring that, after reviewing the British and French agreement:

> It was incumbent upon the nation…to defend its unity, independence and the honor of its word to the last man, in support of its aspirations and in order to secure its unity, which was being threatened by division, and its independence, which was in danger of being lost. Viewing it as a national obligation …to unify the [national] movement in the country in order to attain its desired objective, [the Congress] sees no alternative but to declare the complete independence of the Syrian region within the boundaries specified by the Syrian Congress to the American Commission, rejecting any form of partition or division [of the Syrian nation] [151]

In this tumultuous atmosphere, Faysal attempted to allay the fears of the

[149] Ibid.

[150] *Jawāb al-Muʾtamar al-Sūrī bi-ittifāq al-ārāʾ fī jalsatihi al-sirrīyah al-maʿqūdah masāʾ al-Sabt, 22 Tishrīn al-Thānī, 1919*, in Qarqūṭ, *al-Mashriq al-ʿArabī*, 91.

[151] Ibid., 91-92; for list of signatories see p. 92.

Syrian and Palestinian populations regarding the future of Palestine. In a statement issued on February 10, 1920, he declared:

> I have understood from the pamphlets that have been distributed in the name of Palestine upon my arrival, that the people are gravely concerned about Palestine [and its future]. However, since Palestine is my right arm, I can guarantee you that I have not forgotten it and will not forget it. I shall endeavor to work for Palestine as I do for Syria and Iraq. You can rest assured that Palestine will be a part of Syria according to the wishes of its inhabitants. Consequently, the people should not rely on what is being broadcast in the media, and the rumors that are being circulated by opportunists.[152]

On March 8, 1920, the Syrian Congress acted on the decision it made in November, a few months earlier.

> We, the members of the Congress, view in our capacity as the true representatives of the entire Syrian nation in all its regions that the only way out of this difficult situation is by relying on our natural and legitimate rights to a free life. From what we have seen, and see every day, of the nation's firm resolve to demand its rights and unity, and to attain that by whatever means necessary, we unanimously declare the independence of our Syrian nation within its natural borders, including Palestine, and its full undisputed sovereignty on the basis of a civilian representative government, which preserves the right of minorities, and reject all Zionist pretensions to create in Palestine a national homeland for the Jews or a place to which they can [freely] immigrate.[153]

The declaration was followed by a written and signed oath of allegiance to Faysal by the "spiritual leaders" of Syria, proclaiming him the constitutional King of Syria "within its natural borders."[154]

By accepting the Syrian crown on these terms, Faysal set himself on the inexorable road to Maysalun. He could not back down from Syrian unity and independence as defined by the Syrian Congress and had to lead the nation

---

[152] "Taṣrīḥ lil-Amīr Fayṣal bi-shaʾn mustaqbal Filasṭīn" 10/2/1920 (al-Kawkab, al-Qāhirah, al-ʿadad 178, 10/2/1920), in *Wathāʾiq al-Ḥarakah al-Waṭanīyah al-Filasṭīnīyah, 1918-1939,* 36.

[153] *Qarār al-Muʾtamar al-Sūrī bi-Iʿlān al-Istiqlāl (al-Ithnayn fī 7 Ādhār, sanat 1920),* in ibid., 95. The declaration goes on to announce Faysal as the choice for the nation's constitutional monarch. For full text, see ibid., 93-96.

[154] *Mubāyaʿat al-Ruʾasāʾ al-Rūḥīyīn li-Fayṣal* in ibid., 96. For a list of the signatories (the heads of eight Christian denominations and the head of the Jews), see ibid.

in their defense, no matter how futile an endeavor that would prove to be. He would subsequently comment to Millerand on May 19, 1920: "The Syrian nation ...will never accept that this inseparable part of its country be given to the Jews."[155]

Conclusion

This chapter has examined Faysal's role in the Palestine question in his capacity as Syria's leader and representative in foreign relations during this formative period in its history. Although the Syrians granted Faysal the mandate to lead and represent them, Faysal himself was in many ways quite unrepresentative of Syrian nationalism and its aspirations. Faysal's understanding of Syrian public opinion and sentiment developed as events unfolded, and he had to rely quite heavily on the Arab nationalists and their support to maintain his popularity.

His own political priorities and personal agenda notwithstanding, Faysal was placed in the near impossible position of having to reconcile the clearly incompatible demands of his constituents with the predetermined plans the Allies had already set for the future of the region. No amount of negotiation, bargaining, or pleading Faysal could muster therefore could have altered the balance in his or Syria's favor at the Peace Conference in any meaningful way. His allies at home and their supporters were determined to seek independence and unity at any cost.

Internationally, Faysal remained faithful to Britain and was hopeful that the British would ultimately come to his aid against France's resolve to seize all of Syria. His British allies, though hesitant to allow the French control of Syria and thus to fulfill their own obligations to France, were nonetheless not about to oppose the French effectively over the issue, content with the compromise which gave Britain control of Palestine and Mesopotamia. Britain, moreover, became quite explicit about its intentions to refuse the Syrian mandate if offered it by the conference.

Insofar as the Zionists and their aspirations were concerned, it is clear that Faysal himself was not fundamentally opposed to the idea of accepting the Balfour Declaration and allowing the establishment of a Jewish homeland in Palestine under negotiated terms. Whether Faysal had hoped to gain diplomatic capital with his British allies through negotiating with the Zionists, or indeed hoped to derive direct benefit from the Zionists themselves by achieving an understanding with them, Faysal did not view them or their designs as particularly threatening. The fact that he was forced to retract all his previous agreements with them and his own statements to the Peace Conference and ultimately proclaim Palestine as an integral part of Syria is more an indication of how strong national sentiment was in that regard, rather than a reflection of Faysal's own beliefs.

---

[155]Russell, *The First Modern Arab State,* 163.

Faysal's initial intentions regarding the Zionists and their national home notwithstanding, circumstances would force him to bow to the nationalist pressure and adopt the nationalist stance of refusing submission to French rule and the division of Syria among the Allies. His attempts to convince, if not coerce, Britain into seeking the mandate for all of Syria as the most beneficial political option for the future of its own empire and the region as a whole, had clearly failed. The result was a stand-off with France in which the French army would ultimately oust the Faysali regime and impose its rule on Syria by military force. Palestine, a British preserve, was severed from the rest of Syria despite the demands of its inhabitants, its future being determined separately by a different mandatory power.

CONCLUSION

The question of Palestine has been one of the most important issues influencing the national and political development of the modern nation-state of Syria. Firmly entrenched within the imagined national boundaries of the "Syrian nation" as the Syrian political community was defining them since its very conception, Palestine ("Southern Syria") and its cause were embedded in the very fabric of Syrian nationalism itself. The Palestine question therefore played a critical role in shaping the evolution of political understanding on the domestic level and became a central pillar of the foreign policy of all Syrian regimes for most of the twentieth century. While the issues of Palestine, Zionism, the creation of the state of Israel in 1948, and the Arab-Israeli conflict have had a tremendous impact on the region as a whole, they struck a deeper chord in Syrian political awareness and understanding than in most other Arab countries, and consequently had a more profound effect on the Syrian nation-state and its evolving nationalist discourse.

The cause of Palestine, the threat of Zionism, unity, and independence were so intricately intertwined into the various Syrian and Arab nationalist ideological perspectives that they continued to influence Syrian political development even as the lines between the different ideological perspectives became steadily more blurred as political realties changed and Palestinian nationalism itself began to take an independent course. When, for example, could the Syrians tackle the Palestinian question as a purely Syrian issue and when should it be deemed an Arab cause affecting Syria like any and every other "Arab region"? Furthermore, was Syria's dedication to Palestine to be justified in terms of the Syrian nation-state's vehement and superior dedication to the general Arab cause or was it an issue where it had an internal stake? Where did the boundaries of it being a Syrian cause cease and its becoming an Arab or distinctly Palestinian cause begin?

The Arab nationalist ideological perspective, for example, in whose development and elucidation Syrian ideologues played a vital role and which, in turn, would dominate Syrian politics and nationalist understandings for decades, proclaimed all Arab "regions" as forming integral parts of one indivisible "Arab nation." Syrian Arab nationalists nevertheless viewed

Palestine as falling entirely within the geographical landscape of the Syrian "region" and not as a distinct region in itself. Unlike Iraq, for whose independence these Syrian Arab nationalists were tirelessly clamoring (albeit as a prelude to future unity with Syria), the question of Palestine and the threat of a prospective Zionist homeland being created there were advocated as a Syrian issue, or rather, as an Arab issue involving the dismemberment and colonization of an integral region of Arab Syria. It was portrayed as an injustice perpetrated against the Arabs in general, and against the Arab inhabitants of the southern part of the "Syrian region" in particular, now being forced to face the prospect of being severed from the rest of Syria and subsequently colonized by a foreign minority.

In order to gain insight into the complexity of the relationship between Syria and the Palestine question and to understand its profound impact on Syria's future political evolution, it becomes necessary to examine all aspects of this relationship, its background, and its development. It is crucial, moreover, to analyze the varying demands and aspirations of the nascent Syrian political community, how these demands were perceived, voiced, justified, and validated, and ultimately, to what extent the notion of "Southern Syria" was pervasive in Syrian nationalist perspectives and consequently, the degree to which it was entrenched in the various Syrian political understandings of what constituted their "nation."

As the map of the prospective "Syrian nation" was being drawn and established by the various nascent political parties, a consensus emerged among political activists, and in the resolutions of the general congresses attended by the proclaimed representatives of the Syrian populace during the period 1918-1920, over what constituted the "Syrian region," defining its borders as:

> The Taurus system on the North; Rafah and a line running from Al Jauf to the south of the Syrian and the Hejazian line to Akaba on the south; the Euphrates and Khabur rivers and a line extending east of Abu Kamal to the east of Al Jauf on the east; and the Mediterranean on the west. [1]

As discussed in the previous chapters, the demand for an independent Syria within these "natural boundaries," was reiterated by all major Syrian political parties whether advocating a Syrian nationalist or an Arab nationalist platform; and it was a central demand in the resolutions of all the Syrian and Palestinian Congresses. The aspiration for a "united Syria" furthermore was unequivocally conveyed to the American King-Crane Commission by the majority of the inhabitants both in the Syrian (O.E.T.A. East) and in the

[1] "Resolution of the General Syrian Congress at Damascus, 2 July 1919," in Hurewitz, *Diplomacy in the Near and Middle East,* 2: 63.

Palestinian (O.E.T.A. South) regions.

The general bitterness and resentment against being deprived of their unity despite the common consensus presented by the resolutions of the Arab Congresses and the various political parties' declarations was made all the more poignant by the Peace Conference sanctioning an official commission of inquiry to the region on the pretense that it was necessary to find out the true wishes of the inhabitants in order to formulate its final decisions.

The discussions and debates regarding the commission took place, moreover, during a very delicate point in Faysal's political tenure upon his return to Syria from the Peace Conference in May 1919.[2] Faysal, at the time, was in the unenviable position of having to face the ire and disappointment of the Syrian and Arab nationalists, many of whom were accusing him of selling the "homeland" to France and the Zionists.[3] The dispatch of the American King-Crane Commission to investigate the situation in the region thus became his only hope. Naively placing too much stock in its effectiveness and ability to influence actual decision-making at the Peace Conference, Faysal made his policies contingent upon it and incorporated it into his list of demands.[4]

Faysal was naturally not the only one who was overly optimistic about the commission, its effectiveness, and its influence. The inhabitants of the region as a whole made great efforts to make representations to this commission and present it with a consistent and unified set of demands. It is clear from the findings of the commission that there was a general consensus over the more encompassing demands and overriding concerns such as the unity and independence of the Syrian region, despite "internal" conflicts over ideological or "nationalist" boundaries, like safeguarding certain economic or political interests, the system of government, and other issues.

In his description of their own preparations for the arrival of the "international commission" in Jerusalem, for example, Khalil al-Sakakini recounts a meeting at Isma^cil Bayk al-Husayni's house on Saturday, April 12, 1919, at which a number of that city's most noted personalities were gathered.[5] The participants at that meeting agreed upon three major demands:

---

[2] See Chapter 3, above.

[3] Muḥammad, *al-Ḥarakah al-Qawmīyah fī Sūriyah,* 48; also ʿĀdil Ismāʿīl, *al-Siyāsah al-Duwalīyah fī al-Sharq al-ʿArabī, 1789-1958* (Beirut, 1964), 5: 28. Muhammad also adds, somewhat apologetically, that this reaction on the part of the nationalists occurred "with the encouragement of British, French, and Zionist intelligence, in an attempt to isolate Faysal and undermine his popularity, thus forcing him to sign whatever offer they presented him with." Muḥammad, *al-Ḥarakah al-Qawmīyah fī Sūriyah*, 48.

[4] See Chapter 3, above.

[5] According to Sakakini, those present were: Hajj Amin al-Husayni, Ishaq Darwish, ʿIzzat Darwazah, Hafiz Kanʿan, Saʿid Affandi al-Husayni, Kamil al-Husayni, Musa Kazim Pasha al-Husayni, ʿArif Basha al-Dajani, ʿAli Affandi Jar Allah, Shaykh Raghib al-Dajani, and Isʿaf Afandi al-Nashashibi. Sakākīnī, *Kadhā Anā,* 175.

> 1. [We demand that] Syria, whose borders extend from the Taurus Mountains to the north and the Suez Canal to the south, become completely independent within the framework of Arab unity.
>
> 2. [We demand that] Palestine, which is an indivisible part of Syria, have domestic autonomy, choosing its governors independently from among its nationals according to the wishes of its people and the needs of the country.
>
> 3. We reject with all our power the Zionists' immigration to and their designs on Palestine, as for the original Jewish [inhabitants] of the country before the war, we consider them nationals, with the same rights and obligations incumbent upon us.[6]

These demands provide an example of the consensus reached over Syrian unity and also illustrate how the issues of Syrian unity and independence, Arab unity, Zionism, Palestine, and, in this particular instance, even certain domestic concerns such as the need to ensure some measure of Palestinian independence with the context of Syrian unity, had become intricately intertwined.

When the Commission did finally arrive in Jerusalem on June 12, the Arab Club (*al-Nādī al-ʿArabī*) and the Literary Club (*al-Muntadá al-Adabī*) greeted it with banners proclaiming quite unambiguously: "We Demand Complete Independence," "Syria is indivisible," "We protest against Zionism and denounce Jewish immigration to our country," and "Long live our Prince Faysal—Syria stretches from the Taurus mountains to the north till the Suez Canal to the south."[7] Nevertheless, adds Sakakini, they were forced to take them all down around 11:00 a.m., following protests and pressure by the British authorities.[8]

Despite all the diplomatic impediments the commission had to face before setting out, and the efforts of the multitudes of delegations to make representations to it, not to mention its conclusive findings regarding the future aspirations of the majority of the region's inhabitants,[9] the King-Crane Commission, as Elie Kedourie put it "manifested itself and went away …its influence on policy was negligible."[10] Gertrude Bell, who was visiting Syria in October, a few months after the departure of the commission, described it as a "criminal deception,"[11] remarking bitterly "nobody, not even the United

[6]Ibid., 175-6.

[7]Ibid., 186.

[8]Ibid.

[9]Ibid.

[10]Elie Kedourie, *England and the Middle East* ([London], [1956]), 147.

[11]Ibid.

States, took any notice of its report."[12]

The blatant disregard for all their claims and aspirations by the Peace Conference and the Allies, without any real moral or legal justification, despite the findings of the American commission, exacerbated the anger and frustration of the Syrian and Arab nationalists. Their efforts to take matters into their own hands and unilaterally declare independence on their own terms led to military confrontation and, ultimately, the violent denial of their claims to unity and independence by force of arms. As T. E. Lawrence would cynically observe:

> Whether they are fit for independence or not remains to be tried. Merit is no qualification for freedom. Bulgars, Afghans and Tahitians have it. Freedom is enjoyed when you are so well armed, or so turbulent, or inhabit a country so thorny that the expense of your neighbour's occupying you is greater than the profit. Feisal's government in Syria has been completely independent for two years, and has maintained public security and public services in its area.[13]

While the issues of "nationalism" and "national interests" became more complicated and confused once the boundaries created by the Allies were officially imposed with the institution of the Mandate System, Palestine continued to play a central role in Syrian political understandings both from Arab and Syrian nationalist perspectives. Under the French Mandate,[14] the Palestine question and the notion of "southern Syria" still featured quite prominently in Syrian political thinking on a variety of levels.[15]

Despite attempts by the Mandate authorities to "crush the national and patriotic movement within Syria,"[16] some political parties continued to advocate vehemently the cause of Syrian unity and independence from exile, a "unity" which clearly included Palestine. The leading organization during this period was the "Syrian-Palestinian Executive Committee" (*al-Lajnah al-Tanfīdhīyah al-Sūrīyah al-Filasṭīnīyah*) which was formed following a congress of Syrian political organizations held in Geneva at the end of August 1921. Most prominent among those attending congress were of members of

---

[12]Ibid.

[13]"Letter to the editor of the *Times*, July 22, 1920" in *The Letters of T. E. Lawrence*, 307.

[14]For a detailed discussion of this period, see Khoury, *Syria and the French Mandate*; also see Stephen Longrigg, *Syria and Lebanon under the French Mandate* (London, 1958); and Elizabeth Thompson, *Colonial Citizens: Republican Rights, Paternal Privilege, and Gender in French Syria and Lebanon* (New York, 2000).

[15]For a discussion of this, see Khoury, "Divided Loyalties."

[16]Muḥammad, *al-Ḥarakah al-Qawmīyah fī Sūriyah*, 72.

the Syrian Unity Party (*Ḥizb al-Ittiḥād al-Sūrī*)[17] who fled to Egypt following the French occupation in 1920, where they established a club from which they exercised their political activities. Also attending were delegates from the Arab Independence Party (*Ḥizb al-Istiqlāl al-ʿArabī*),[18] the Palestinian Delegation (*al-Wafd al-Filasṭīnī*), the Palestinian Council (*al-Lajnah al-Filasṭīnīyah*) all from Egypt, and the Syrian Liberation Party (*Ḥizb Taḥrīr Sūrīyah*) from New York.[19]

The congress concluded with the formation of the Syrian-Palestinian Executive Committee (of the Syrian-Palestinian Congress), which would be headquartered in Egypt. This organization had two main objectives: the liberation of Syria, Palestine, and Lebanon; and the unity of these regions. Exceptionally active in presenting its case in international circles, particularly in the United States and Europe, was the Congress' permanent delegation in Geneva, which consisted of three well-known members: Shakib Arslan, Ihsan al-Jabiri, and Sulayman Kanʿan (later replaced by Riyad al-Sulh).[20] In addition to their diplomatic efforts abroad, this organization became notorious in Syria for practicing various kinds of resistance against the French, violent and nonviolent, ranging from organizing strikes and demonstrations to political assassinations and armed revolt.[21]

Notwithstanding the extremely limited scope afforded them to exercise any form of independent foreign or domestic policy under the Mandate, many Syrian politicians continued to hold fast to the "Southern Syria" notion on an official level for years after the fall of the Faysali regime. In June 1928, for example, the Syrian Constituent Assembly included both Palestine and Lebanon as part of the Syrian state in its draft constitution for the republic. "This position," states Barry Rubin "was accepted by senior National Bloc leaders, many of whom had been Faysal supporters, and by younger militants like Shukri al-Quwwatli."[22]

Syrians, such as Fawzi al-Qawuqji, moreover, played a leading role both in mobilizing public opinion in Syria and on the battlefield in Palestine during the 1936-39 revolt and as part of *jaysh al-inqādh* (the "rescue army") in the Palestine War of 1948. It is patently clear from their assessments[23] not only how much Palestine was viewed as a central "nationalist" concern, but also

[17] For more on this party see Chapter 4, above.

[18] See above.

[19] Muḥammad, *al-Ḥarakah al-Qawmīyah fī Sūriyah*, 72.

[20] For a detailed account of their thought and activities, see *La Nation Arabe,* edited by Shakib Arslan.

[21] Muḥammad, *al-Ḥarakah al-Qawmīyah fī Sūriyah,* 72; also Dāghir, *Mudhakkirāt,* 155-163; and Farzat, *al-Ḥayāh al-Ḥizbīyah fī Sūrīyah*, 86-87.

[22] Barry Rubin, *The Arab States and the Palestine Conflict* (New York, 1981), 35.

[23] For Qawuqji's memoirs, see al-Qāwuqjī, *Filasṭīn fī Mudhakkirāt Fawzī al-Qāwuqjī.*

the extent to which this issue pervaded both the "Syrian" and "Arab" ranges of the nationalist spectrum, and indeed how intertwined these perspectives had become . As Khidr ʿAli Mahfuz, another Syrian marching under Qawuqji's "banner," described the situation in 1936:

> May God have mercy on this poor massacred people... there, in that clearly visible area beyond the river, the River Shariʿah, [the forces of] colonialism have outrageously and unjustly created a border that separates one Arab people from its brother, and forced upon us Arabs the recognition of this oppressive and false state of affairs, a partition between two banks that has divided the Syrian motherland, yes there is a fervent revolution against tyranny and oppression...lives are being lost, homes are being destroyed, orphans suffer, all in order to maintain the freedom of this country and its independence, and the preservation of the Holy places from falling into the criminal hands of insidious Zionism.[24]

In the years to come, the Palestine question would continue to play a dominant role in Syrian politics and political thinking and would feature prominently in the foreign policy decisions of subsequent Syrian regimes. This relationship would continue to evolve, becoming more complex as Palestinian nationalism began to develop independently, and once the geographic boundaries created by the Mandate system became further entrenched, following the creation of the separate nation-states of Syria, Israel, Lebanon, and Jordan in the post-World War II era. This would perhaps cause the actions of certain Syrian regimes to seem contradictory and confusing at different points in time. As Barry Rubin observes:

> It was therefore never quite clear where fraternal support ended and where Syrian ambitions began. While domestic opinion constricted the precarious Baʿth regimes as it had the pre-1948 civilian rulers, Palestinian interests would not be allowed to interfere too far with Syrian aims. PLO activities were tightly controlled within Syria, and the Syrian military opposed any intervention on the PLO's side during its September 1970 war against Jordan. The Syrian army even briefly fought against the PLO when Damascus invaded Lebanon to dampen the civil war there. Yet any break was always prevented by the intertwining of the Palestinian issue and internal politics[25]

[24]Maḥfūẓ, *Taḥta Rāyat al-Qāwuqjī*, 32-33.

[25]Rubin, *The Arab States*, 15-16.

To conclude, during this critical period in their history, at the birth of their "nation," a broad range of Syrian politicians, public representatives, political activists, and ideologues all tirelessly and repeatedly sought to present a clear and consistent set of demands. They utilized their party platforms, congressional resolutions, pamphlets, leaflets, representations to the American Commission, and demonstrations to high-ranking foreign dignitaries visiting the region from all the Great Nations, in order to present their views and aspirations. The demands for a united and independent Syria within very specific boundaries, which clearly included Palestine, were the most central and explicit demands consistently reiterated by all groups. The fact that both these demands (and indeed all other Syrian demands) were blatantly ignored by the Allies and the Peace Conference, and ultimately denied them by force of arms, in complete disregard of all previous assurances and the wishes of the inhabitants themselves, would certainly have a profound impact on politics and political development in Syria for decades to come. The Palestine question constitutes the forcible denial of one of the central demands of the Syrian populace at the moment of the conception of their "nation"—the demand for the unity of their country within its "natural boundaries."

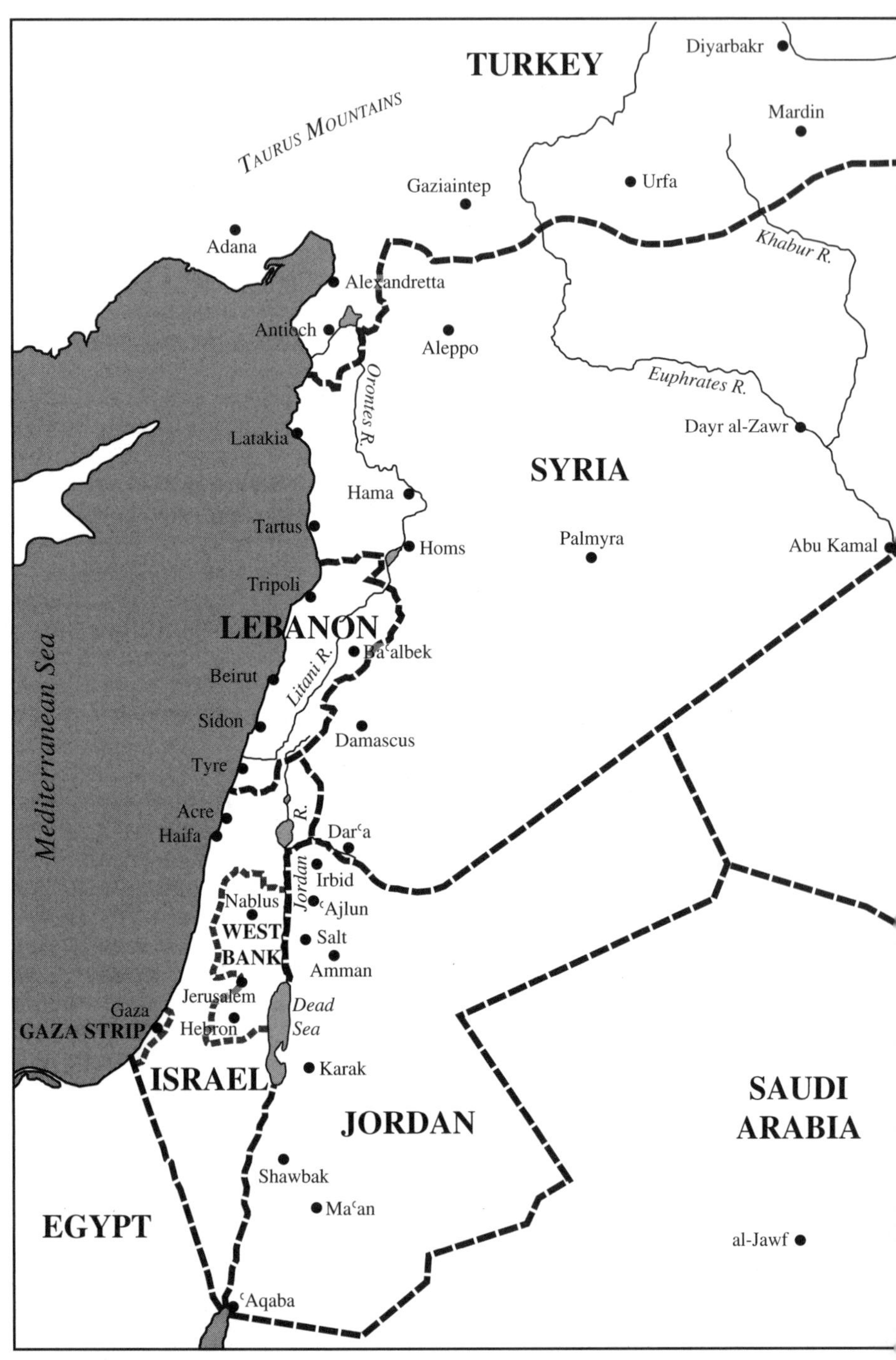

The modern Middle East

L. Urmia
Mosul
Kirkuk
Tigris R.
Hamadan
Kermanshah
IRAN
Baghdad
Karbala
IRAQ
Najaf
Basra
Persia
Gulf
0
50
100 miles

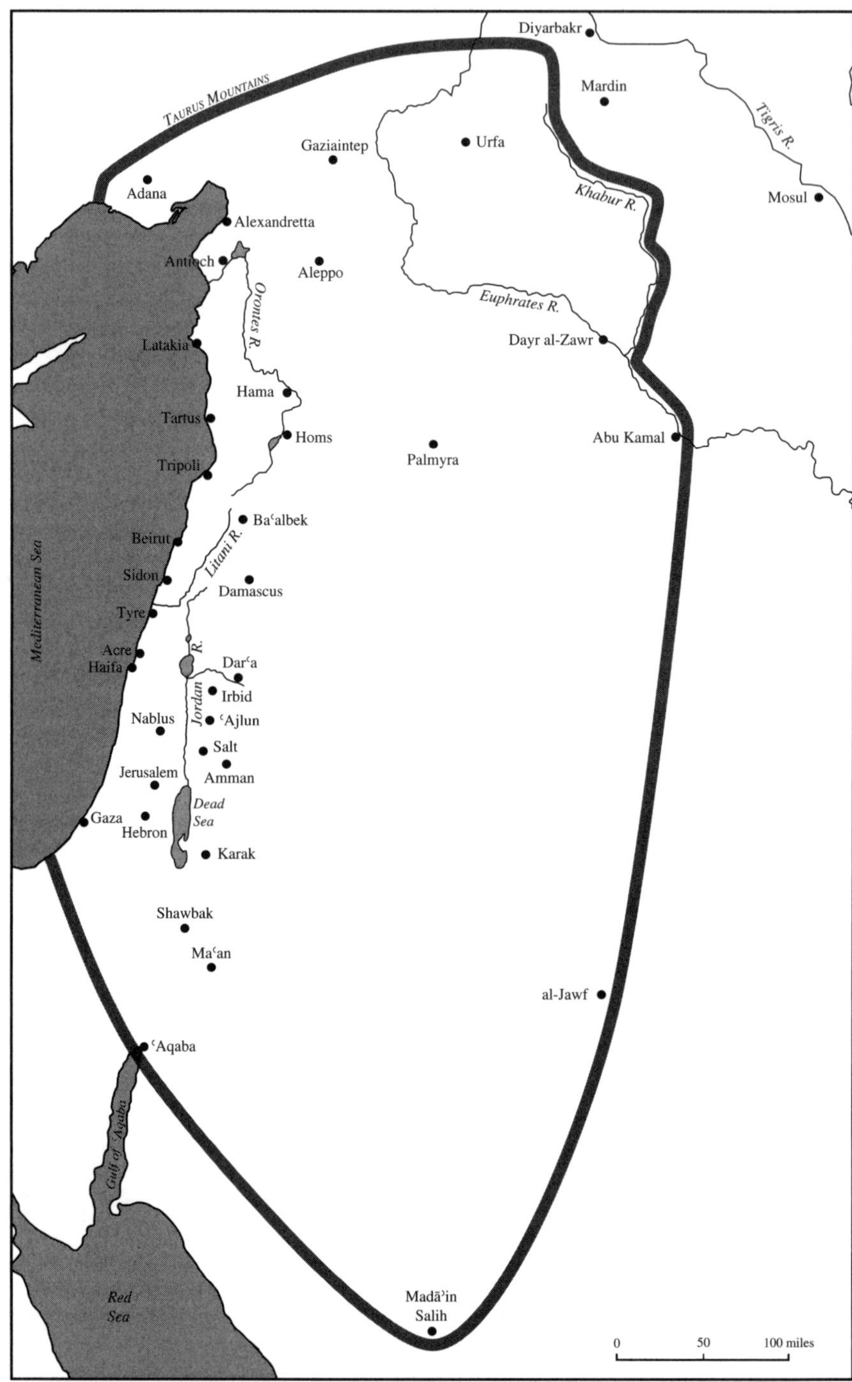

Syria's "natural" boundaries, as delineated by the Syrian and Arab nationalists and confirmed by the Arab congresses

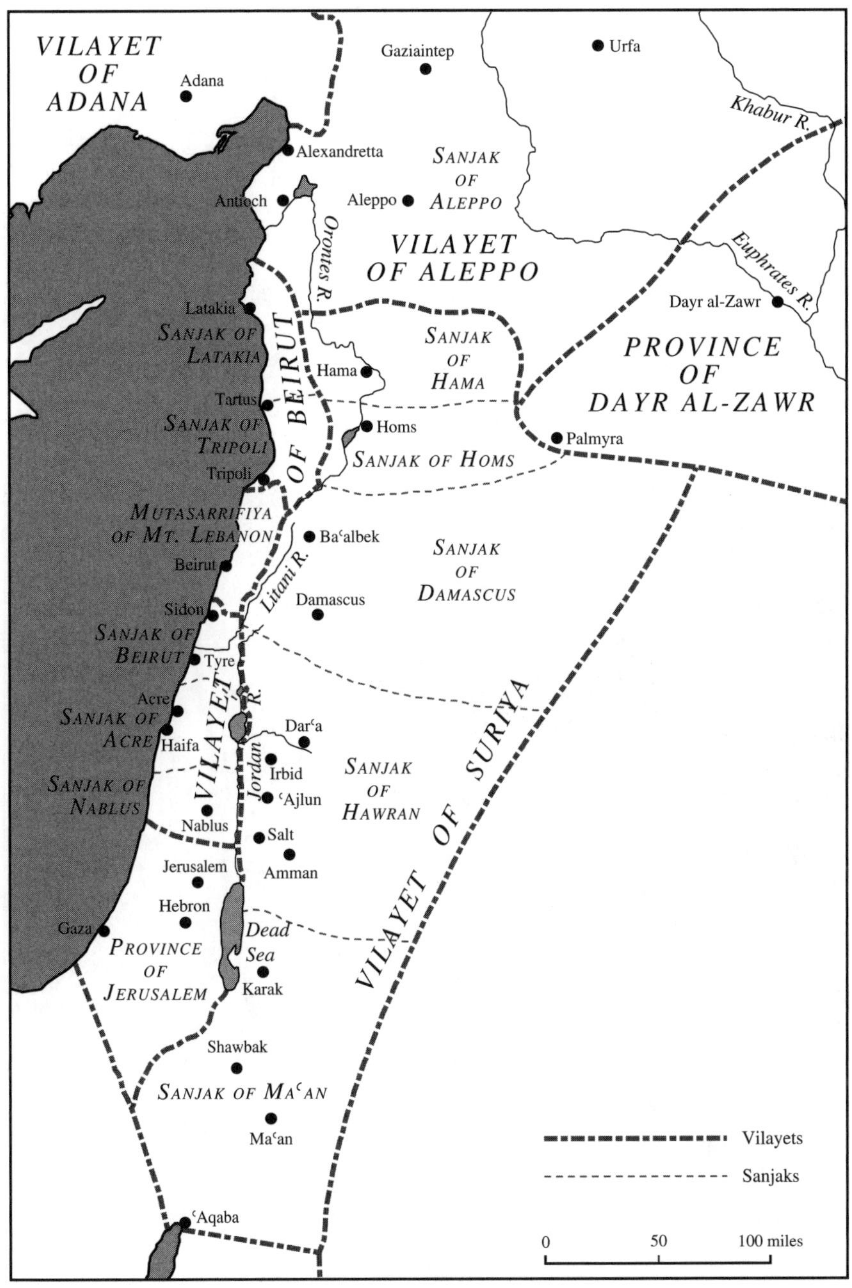

Ottoman administrative divisions

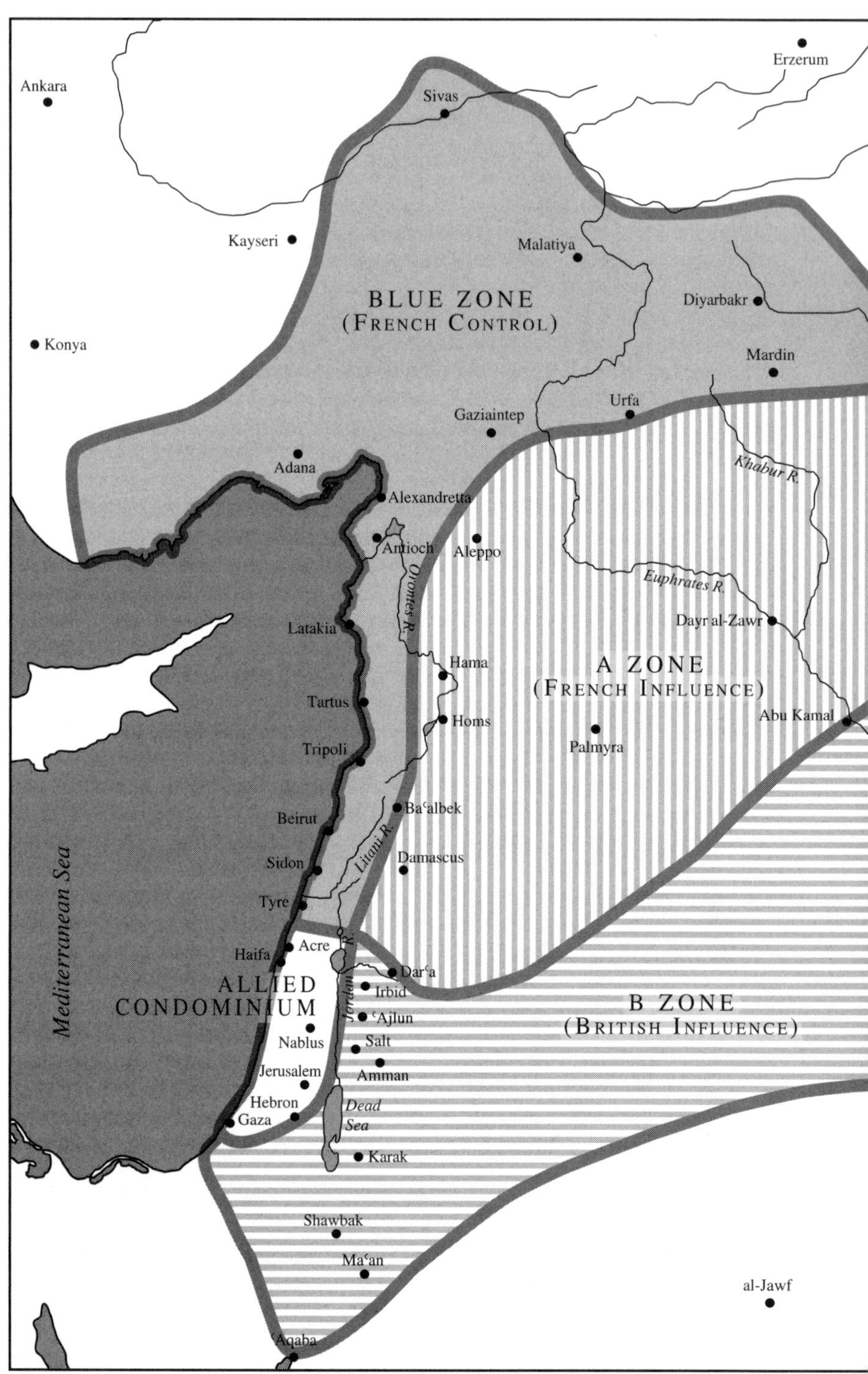

Borders as laid out by the Sykes-Picot agreement

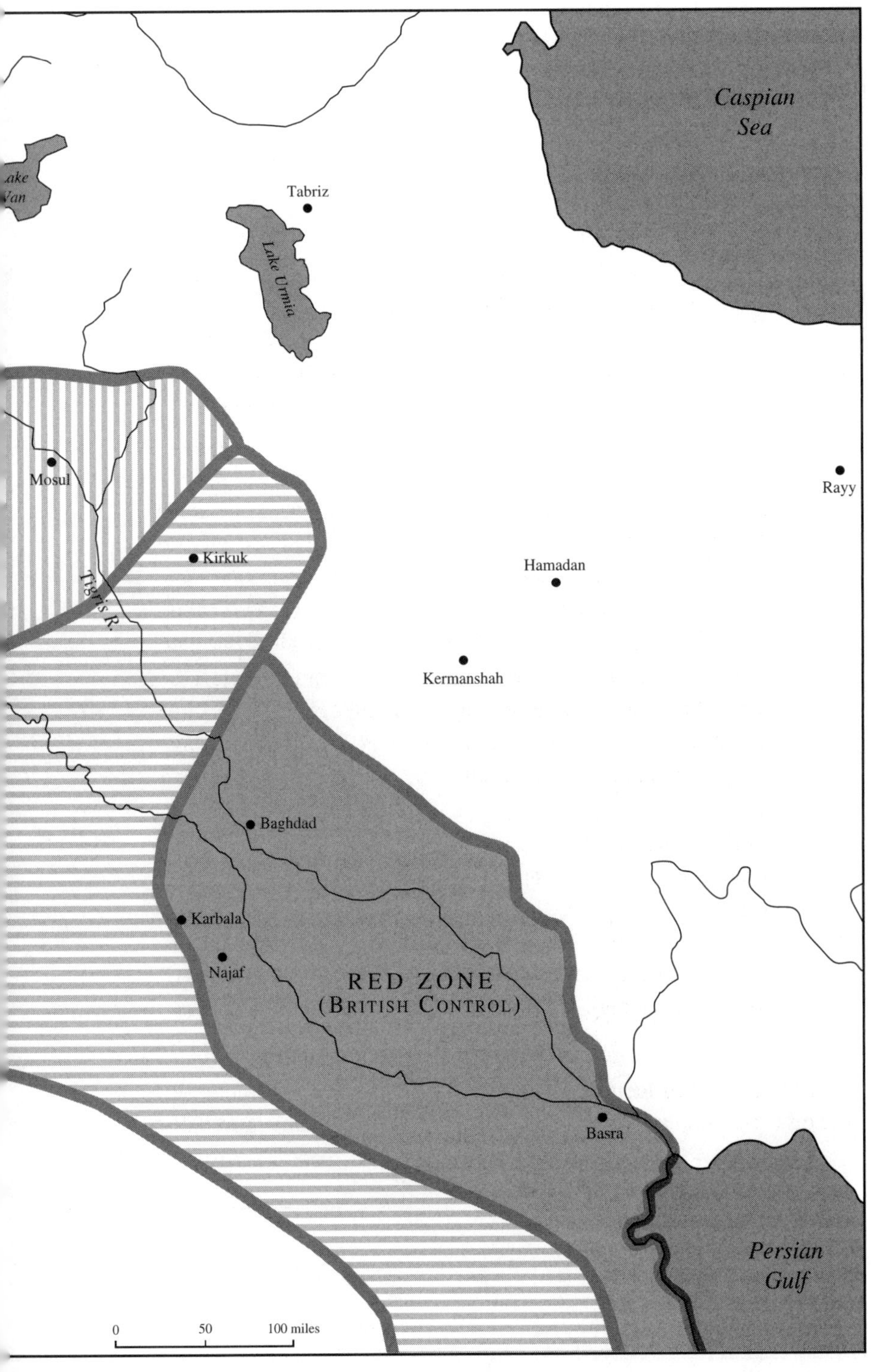
Caspian
Sea
Tabriz
Lake Urmia
Mosul
Kirkuk
Tigris R.
Rayy
Hamadan
Kermanshah
Baghdad
Karbala
Najaf
RED ZONE
(BRITISH CONTROL)
Basra
Persian
Gulf
0
50
100 miles

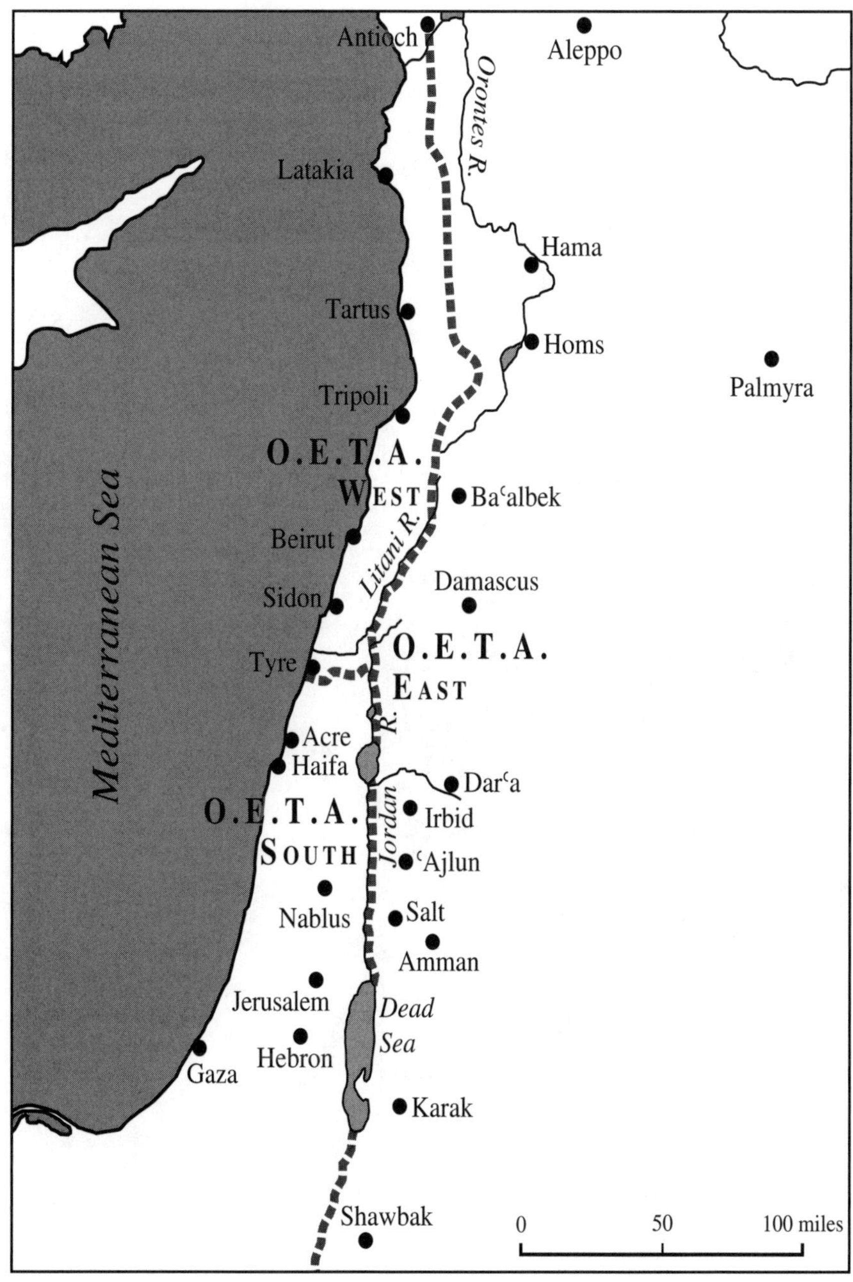

Occupied Enemy Territory Administration (O.E.T.A.) zones, established in October, 1918

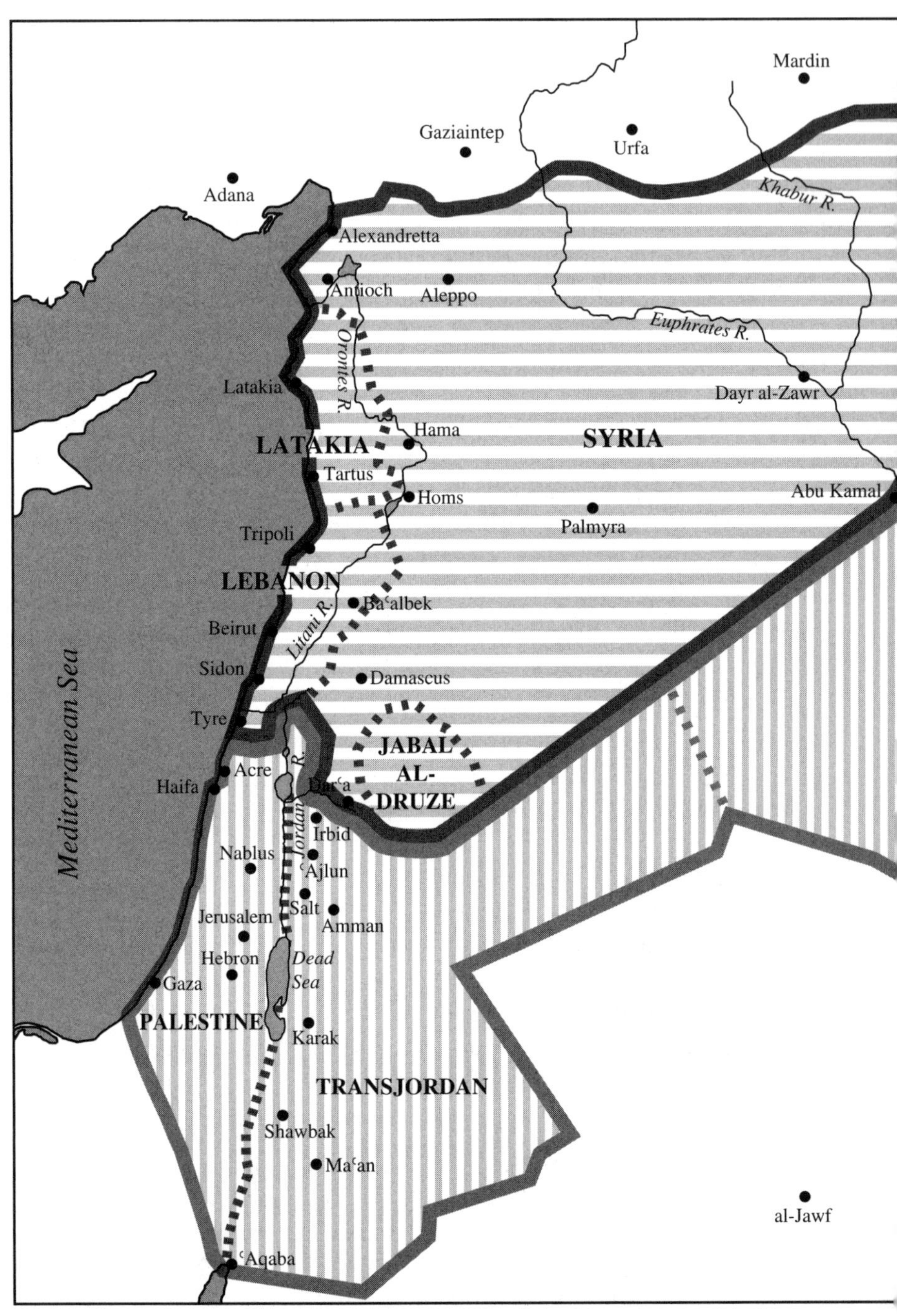

The British and French mandates

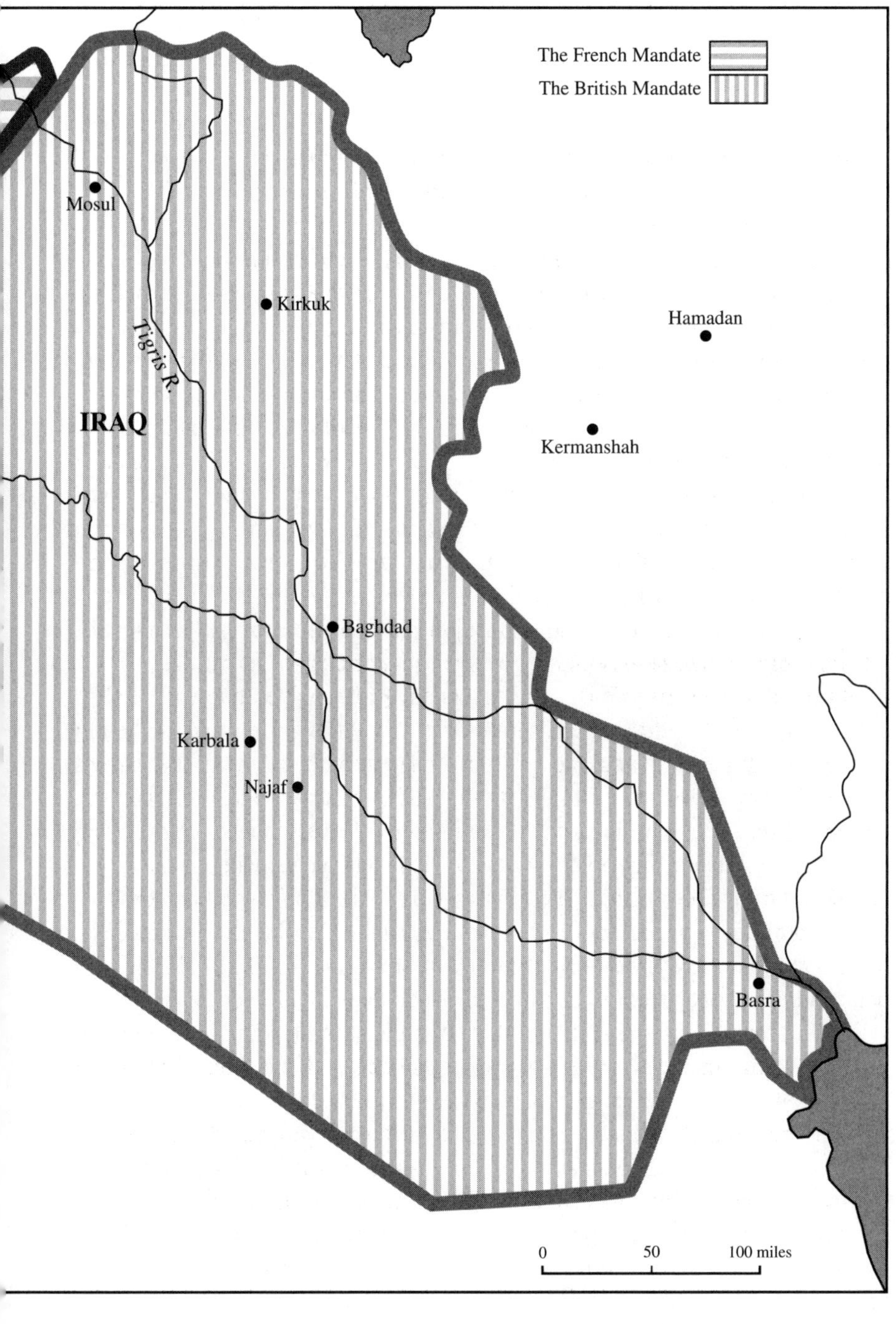
The French Mandate
The British Mandate
Mosul
Kirkuk
Tigris R.
IRAQ
Hamadan
Kermanshah
Baghdad
Karbala
Najaf
Basra
0
50
100 miles

BIBLIOGRAPHY

Primary Sources

Documents (Arabic)

Ḥallāq, Ḥasan, ed. *Filasṭīn fī al-muʾtamarāt al-ʿArabīyah wa-al-dawlīyah: wathaʾiq wa-murāsalāt tunsharu lil-marrah al-ūlá*. Amman: Manshūrāt Rawāʾiʿ Majdalāwī, 1998.

al-Ḥūt, Bayān Nuwayhiḍ, ed. *Wathāʾiq al-Ḥarakah al-Waṭanīyah al-Filasṭīnīyah, 1918-1939: Min Awrāq Akram Zuʿaytir*. Beirut: Muʾassasat al-Dirāsāt al-Filasṭīnīyah, 1979.

Ibīsh, Yūsuf Ḥusayn, and Yūsuf Quzmā Khūrī, eds. *al-Bayānāt al-Wizārīyah al-Sūrīyah wa-Munāqashātuhā fī al-Majlis al-Niyābī, 1918-1958*. Beirut: Turāth, 2000.

Qarqūṭ, Dhūqān, ed. *al-Mashriq al-ʿArabī fī Muwājahat al-Istiʿmār: Qirāʾah fī Tārīkh Sūrīyā al-Muʿāṣir*. [Cairo]: al-Hayʾah al-Miṣrīyah al-ʿĀmmah lil-Kitāb, 1977.

Documents (English and French)

Arslan, Shakib, ed. *La Nation Arabe*. 4 vols. Farnham Common, England: Archive Editions, 1988.

Bidwell, Robin, ed. *British Documents on Foreign Affairs: Reports and Papers from the Foreign Office Confidential Print*. Part II: *From the First to the Second World War;* Series B: *Turkey, Iran, and the Middle East, 1918-1939*. Frederick, Maryland: University Publications of America, 1989.

A Handbook of Syria (Including Palestine): Prepared by the Geographical Section of the Naval Intelligence Division, Naval Staff, Admiralty, London: H. M. Stationery Office, [1920].

Hokayem, Antoine, ed. *Documents diplomatiques français relatifs à l'histoire du Liban et de la Syrie à l'époque du mandat: 1914-1946*. Beirut: Editions univeritaires du Liban; Paris: L'Harmattan, 2003-.

Hurewitz, J. C., ed. *Diplomacy in the Near and Middle East, A Documentary Record*. 2 vols. Princeton, New Jersey: Van Nostrand, 1956.

La Vérité sur la question syrienne. Istanbul: Impr. Tanine, 1916.

Official Documents, Pledges, and Resolutions on Palestine. New York: The Palestine Arab Refugee Office, [1959].

Papers Relating to the Foreign Relations of the United States: The Paris

Peace Conference, 1919. 13 vols. Washington, D.C.: U.S. Govt. Print. Off., 1942-1947.

Rush, Alan de L., ed. *Records of the Hashemite Dynasties: A Twentieth Century Documentary History*. 15 vols. [Slough, U. K.]: Archive Editions, 1995.

Woodward, E. L., and Rohan Butler, eds. *Documents on British Foreign Policy, 1919-1939*. London: Her Majesty's Stationery Office, 1952.

Memoirs and Personal Papers (Arabic)

al-ʿAbbādī, Muḥammad Yūnis, ed. *Mudhakkirāt al-Malik Fayṣal al-Awwal, Malik al-ʿIraq*. Amman: Dar al-Kindī, 2002.

ʿAbd al-Hādī, ʿAwnī. *ʿAwnī ʿAbd al-Hādī: Awrāq Khāṣṣah*. Edited by Khayrīyah Qāsimīyah. Beirut: Munaẓẓamat al-Taḥrīr al-Filasṭīnīyah, Markaz al-Abḥāth, 1974.

ʿAẓm, Khālid. *Mudhakkirāt Khālid al-ʿAẓm*. 4 vols. Beirut: al-Dār al-Muttaḥidah lil-Nashr, 1973.

Bārūdī, Fakhrī. *Awrāq wa-mudhakkirāt Fakhrī al-Bārūdī, 1887-1966: khamsūn ʿāman min ḥayāt al-waṭan*. Edited by Daʿd al-Ḥakīm. Damascus: Wizārat al-Thaqāfah fī al-Jumhūrīyah al-ʿArabīyah al-Sūrīyah, 1999.

Dāghir, Asʿad. *Mudhakkirātī ʿalá Hāmish al-Qaḍīyah al-Arabīyah*. Cairo: Dār al-Qāhirah lil-Ṭibāʿah, 1959.

Darwazah, Muḥammad ʿIzzat. *Ḥawla al-Ḥarakah al-ʿArabīyah al-Ḥadīthah: Tārīkh, wa-Mudhakkirāt, wa-Taʿlīqāt*. 6 vols. Sidon: al-Maṭbaʿah al-ʿAṣrīyah, 1950.

———. *Mudhakkirāt Muḥammad ʿIzzat Darwazah, 1305 H-1404 H / 1887 M-1984 M: sijill ḥāfil bi-masīrat al-ḥarakah al-ʿArabīyah wa-al-qaḍīyah al-Filasṭīnīyah khilala qarn min al-zamān*. 6 vols. Beirut: Dār al-Gharb al-Islāmī, 1993.

Ḥaffār al-Kuzbarī, Salmá. *Luṭfī al-Ḥaffār, 1885-1968: mudhakkirātuh, ḥayātuh wa ʿaṣruh*. Beirut: Riyād al-Rayyis lil-Kutub wa-al-Nashr, 1997.

Ḥakīm, Yūsuf. *Sūriyah wa-al-ʿAhd al-Fayṣalī*. Beirut: Dār al-Nahār lil-Nashr, 1986.

Ḥuṣrī, Abū Khaldūn Sāṭiʿ. *Yawm Maysalūn, ṣafḥah min tārīkh al-ʿArab al-ḥadīth, mudhakkirāt muṣawwarah bi-muqaddimah ʿan tanāzuʿ al-duwal ḥawla al-bilād al-ʿArabīyah wa-mudhayyalah bi-wathāʾiq wa-ṣuwar*. Beirut: Dār al-Ittiḥād, [1965].

Maḥfūẓ, Khiḍr ʿAlī. *Taḥta Rāyat al-Qāwuqjī*. Beirut, 1973.

Qāwuqjī, Fawzī. *Filasṭīn fī Mudhakkirāt Fawzī al-Qāwuqjī 1936-1948*. Edited by Khayrīyah Qāsimīyah. 2 vols. Beirut: Munaẓẓamat al-Taḥrīr al-Filasṭinīyah, Markaz al-Abḥāth, 1975.

Qāsimīyah, Khayrīyah, ed. *al-Raʿīl al-ʿArabī al-awwal: ḥayāt wa-awrāq*

Nabīh wa-ʿĀdil al-ʿAẓmah. [London]: Riyāḍ al-Rayyis, 1991.

Saʿīd, Amīn. *al-Thawrah al-ʿArabīyah al-Kubrá: tārīkh mufaṣṣal jāmiʿ lil-qaḍīyah al-ʿArabīyah fī rubʿ qarn.* 3 vols. Cairo: Maṭbaʿat ʿĪsá al-Bābī al-Ḥalabī, [1934].

Sakākīnī, Khalīl. *Kadhā Anā Yā Dunyā: Yawmāyāt.* Jerusalem: al-Maṭbaʿah al-Tijārīyah, 1955.

Sarrāj, Aḥmad Sāmī. *Min baqīyat al-suyūf: Aḥmad Sāmī al-Sarrāj, 1892-1960: awrāq wa-mudhakkirāt.* Edited by Khayrīyah Qāsimīyah. Damascus: al-Ahālī, 2003.

Memoirs and Personal Papers (English)

Garnett, David, ed. *The Letters of T. E. Lawrence.* New York: Doubleday, Doran, 1939.

Lawrence, T. E. *Revolt in the Desert.* New York: George H. Doran Company, 1927.

———. *Seven Pillars of Wisdom: the complete 1922 text.* Fordingbridge, Hampshire: J. and N. Wilson, 2004.

Litvinoff, Barnet and Meyer Weisgal, eds. *The Letters and Papers of Chaim Weizmann.* 25 volumes. Jerusalem: Israel Universities Press, 1968-.

Meinertzhagen, Richard. *Middle East Diary, 1917-1956.* London: Cresset Press, 1959.

Samuel, Herbert Louis Samuel, Viscount. *Memoirs.* London: Cresset Press, 1945.

Press Articles

The Times, (London), 11 December 1918.

The Times, (London), 13 December 1918.

Secondary Sources

Arabic

ʿAflaq, Michel. *Fī Sabīl al-Baʿth.* Beirut: Dār al-Ṭalīʿah, 1963.

ʿAwaḍ, ʿAbd al-ʿAzīz. *al-Idārah al-ʿUthmānīyah fī Wilāyat Sūrīyah, 1864-1914.* Cairo: Dār al-Maʿārif, 1969.

Farzat, Ḥarb. *al-Ḥayāh al-Ḥizbīyah fī Sūrīyah.* Damascus: Dār al-Ruwwād, 1955.

Haykal, Muḥammad Ḥasanayn. *Mā alladhī jará fī Sūrīyā.* Cairo: al-Dār al-Qawmīyah lil-Ṭibāʿah wa-al-Nashr, 1962.

Ḥuṣrī, Abū Khaldūn Sāṭiʿ. *Abḥāth mukhtārah fī al-qawmīyah al-ʿArabīyah allatī katabahā wa-nasharahā al-muʾallif fī tawārīkh mukhtalifah 1923-1963.* 2 vols. Beirut: Dār al-Quds, [1974?].

———. *Mā hiya al-qawmīyah?: abḥāth wa-dirāsāt ʿalá ḍawʾ al-aḥdāth wa-al-naẓarīyāt*. Beirut: Dār al-ʿIlm lil-Malāyīn, [1963].

———. *Muḥāḍarāt fī nushūʾ al-fikrah al-qawmīyah*. Beirut: Dār al-ʿIlm lil-Malāyīn, 1964.

———. *al-ʿUrūbah bayna duʿātihā wa muʿāriḍihā*. Beirut: Dār al-ʿIlm lil-Malāyīn, 1961.

Ismāʿīl, ʿĀdil. *al-Siyāsah al-Duwalīyah fī al-Sharq al-ʿArabī, 1789-1958*. 2 vols. Beirut: Dār al-Nashr lil-Siyāsah wa-al-Ta'rīkh, 1964.

Kallās, Ghassān. *Yūsuf al-ʿAẓmah Shahīd Maysalūn al-Khālid: safaḥāt min adab Maysalūn*. Damascus: Dār al-Ḥāzim, 2001.

Muḥammad, Najāḥ. *al-Ḥarakah al-Qawmīyah fī Sūriyah min khilāl tārikh tanẓīmatiha al-Siyāsīyah, (1948-1967)*. Part 1. Damascus: Dār al-Baʿth, 1987.

Mūsá, Sulaymān. *al-Ḥarakah al-ʿArabīyah: sirat al-marḥalah al-ūlá lil-nahḍah al-ʿArabīyah al- Ḥadīthah, 1908-1924*. Beirut: Dār al-Nahār, 1977.

———. *al-Thawrah al-ʿArabīyah al-Kubrá: al-ḥarb fī al-Ḥijāz, 1916-1918*. Amman: S. Mūsá, 1989.

Qāsimīyah, Khayrīyah. *al-Ḥukūmah al-ʿArabīyah fī Dimashq bayna 1918-1920*. Cairo: Dar al-Maʿārif, 1971.

Saʿādah, Anṭūn. *al-Āthār al-Kāmilah*. Beirut: ʿUmdat al-Thaqāfah fī al-Ḥizb al-Surī al-Qawmī al-Ijtimāʿī, 1978-1989.

———. *Marāḥil al-Masʾalah al-Filasṭīnīyah, 1921-1949*. Beirut: Manshūrāt ʿUmdat al-Thaqāfah fī al-Ḥizb al-Surī al-Qawmī al-Ijtimāʿī, 1977.

Shahrastān, Mārī Almāz. *al-Muʾtamar al-Sūrī al-ʿĀmm, 1919-1920*. Beirut: Dar Amwaj, 2000.

Shaykhū, Muḥammad ʿIṣmat. *Sūrīyah wa-Qaḍiyat Filasṭīn, 1920-1949*. Damascus: Dār Quṭaybah, 1982.

ʿUlaywī, Hādī Ḥasan. *Fayṣal ibn al-Ḥusayn: muʾassis al-ḥukm al-ʿArabī fī Sūrīyah wa-al-ʿIrāq, 1883-1933*. Beirut: Riyāḍ al-Rayyis lil-Kutub wa-al-Nashr, 2003.

English

Abu Jaber, Kamel. *The Arab Baʿth Socialist Party: History, Ideology and Organization*. [Syracuse, New York]: Syracuse University Press, [1966].

al-Khazendar, Sami. *Jordan and the Palestine Question: The Role of Islamic and Left Forces in Foreign Policy-Making*. Reading, England: Ithaca Press, 1997.

Antonius, George. *The Arab Awakening: the Story of the Arab National Movement*. Beirut: Libraire du Liban, 1969.

Arjomand, Said Amir, ed. *From Nationalism to Revolutionary Islam*. Albany: State University of New York Press, 1984.

Buheiry, Marwan, ed. *Intellectual Life in the Arab East, 1890-1939*. Beirut: American University of Beirut, 1981.

Cleveland, William L. *Islam Against the West: Shakib Arslan and the Campaign for Islamic Nationalism*. Austin: University of Texas Press, 1985.

———. *The Making of an Arab Nationalist: Ottomanism and Arabism in the Life and Thought of Sati' al-Husri*. Princeton, New Jersey: Princeton University Press, 1971.

Cobban, Helena. *The Super Powers and the Syrian-Israeli Conflict*. New York: Praeger, 1991.

Dawn, C. Ernest. *From Ottomanism to Arabism: Essays on the Origins of Arab Nationalism*. Urbana: University of Illinois Press, 1973.

Devlin, John F. *The Ba'th Party: A History from its Origins to 1966*. Stanford: Hoover Institution Press, 1976.

Doran, Michael Scott. *Pan-Arabism before Nasser: Egyptian Power Politics and the Palestine Question*. New York: Oxford University Press, 1999.

Gelvin, James. *Divided Loyalties: Nationalism and Mass Politics in Syria at the Close of Empire*. Berkeley: University of California Press, 1998.

Haddad, William W., and William L. Ochsenwald, eds. *Nationalism in a Non-National State: the Dissolution of the Ottoman Empire*. Columbus: Ohio State University Press, 1977.

Heydemann, Steven. *Authoritarianism in Syria: Institutions and Social Conflict, 1946-1970*. Ithaca: Cornell University Press, 1999.

Hourani, Albert. *Arabic Thought in the Liberal Age, 1798-1939*. New York: Cambridge University Press, 1991.

Howard, Harry N. *An American Inquiry in the Middle East: the King-Crane Commission*. Beirut: [Khayats], 1963.

Jeffries, J. M. N. *Palestine: The Reality*. London: Longmans, Green and Co., 1939.

Kayalı, Hasan. *Arabs and Young Turks: Ottomanism, Arabism, and Islamism in the Ottoman Empire, 1908-1918*. Berkeley: University of California Press, c1997.

Kedourie, Elie. *England and the Middle East*. [London]: Bowes & Bowes, [1956].

———. *In the Anglo-Arab Labyrinth: the McMahon-Husayn Correspondence and its interpretations, 1914-1939*. New York: Cambridge University Press, 1976.

Kerr, Malcolm. *The Arab Cold War: Gamal 'Abd al-Nasir and His Rivals 1958-1970*. London: Oxford University Press, 1971.

Khalidi, Rashid. *British Policy towards Syria and Palestine 1906-1914: A Study of the antecedents of the Hussein-McMahon Correspondence, the Sykes-Picot Agreement and the Balfour Declaration*. London: Ithaca Press, 1980.

———, ed. *The Origins of Arab Nationalism*. New York: Columbia University Press, 1991.

———. *Palestinian Identity: The Construction of Modern National Consciousness*. New York: Columbia University Press, 1997.

Khoury, Philip. *Syria and the French Mandate: the Politics of Arab Nationalism, 1920-1945*. Princeton: Princeton University Press, c1987.

———. *Urban Notables and Arab Nationalism: The Politics of Damascus, 1860-1920*. New York: Cambridge University Press, 1983.

Longrigg, Stephen Hemsley. *Syria and Lebanon under the French Mandate*. London: Oxford University Press, 1958.

Mandel, Neville J. *The Arabs and Zionism before World War I*. Berkeley: University of California Press, 1980.

Ma'oz, Moshe. *Asad: the Sphinx of Damascus: A Political Biography*. New York: Weidenfeld and Nicholson, 1988.

———. *Syria and Israel: From War to Peacemaking*. New York: Clarendon Press, 1995.

Moubayyed, Sami M. *The Politics of Damascus 1920-1946: Urban Notables and the French Mandate*. Damascus: Tlas House, 1999.

Mufti, Malik. *Sovereign Creations: Pan-Arabism and Political Order in Syria and Iraq*. Ithaca: Cornell University Press, 1996.

Muslih, Muhammad. *The Origins of Palestinian Nationalism*. New York: Columbia University Press, 1988.

Petran, Tabitha. *Syria*. London: Ernest Benn Ltd, 1972.

Pipes, Daniel. *Greater Syria: The History of an Ambition*. New York: Oxford University Press, 1990.

Porath, Yehoshua. *The Emergence of the Palestinian-Arab National Movement, 1918-1929*. London: Cass, 1975.

Rabinovitch, Itamar. *The Brink of Peace: The Israeli-Syrian Negotiations*. Princeton: Princeton University Press, c1998.

———. *Syria Under the Baʿth, 1963-1966: The Army-Party Symbiosis*. Jerusalem: Israel Universities Press, [1972].

Rathmell, Andrew. *Secret War in the Middle East: The Covert Struggle for Syria, 1949-1961*. London: Tauris Academic Studies, 1995.

Roberts, David. *The Baʿth and the Creation of Modern Syria*. London: Croom Helm, 1987.

Rubin, Barry. *The Arab States and the Palestine Conflict*. New York: Syracuse

University Press, 1981.

Russell, Malcolm. *The First Modern Arab State: Syria under Faysal, 1918-1920*. Minneapolis: Bibliotheca Islamica, c1985.

Salibi, Kamal. *A House of Many Mansions: The History of Lebanon Reconsidered*. London: I. B. Tauris, 1988.

Schölch, Alexander. *Palestine in Transformation, 1856-1882: Studies in Social, Economic and Political Development*. Washington, D.C.: Institute for Palestine Studies, 1993.

Seale, Patrick. *Asad of Syria: The Struggle for the Middle East*. Berkeley: University of California Press, 1989.

———. *The Struggle for Syria: A Study of Post-War Arab Politics, 1945-1958*. New Haven: Yale University Press, 1986.

Shlaim, Avi. *The Politics of Partition: King Abdullah, the Zionist Movement, and the Partition of Palestine*. New York: Columbia University Press, 1988.

Stein, Leonard. *The Balfour Declaration*. New York: Simon and Schuster, 1961.

Talhami, Ghada. *Syria and the Palestinians: The Clash of Nationalisms*. Gainesville: University Press of Florida, 2001.

Tauber, Eliezer. *The Arab Movements in World War I*. London: Frank Cass, 1993.

Thompson, Elizabeth. *Colonial Citizens: Republican Rights, Paternal Privilege, and Gender in French Syria and Lebanon*. New York: Columbia University Press, 2000.

Tibawi, Abdul Latif. *Anglo-Arab Relations and the question of Palestine, 1914-1921*. London: Luzac, 1977.

Tibi, Bassam. *Arab Nationalism: A Critical Enquiry*. Edited and translated by Marion Farouk-Sluglett and Peter Sluglett. New York: St. Martin's Press, 1981.

Torrey, Gordon H. *Syrian Politics and the Military, 1945-1958*. [Columbus]: Ohio State University, 1964.

Van Dam, Nikolaos. *The Struggle for Power in Syria: Politics and Society Under Asad and the Baʿth Party*. New York: I. B. Tauris, 1996.

Wedeen, Lisa. *Ambiguities of Domination: Politics, Rhetoric, and Symbols in Contemporary Syria*. Chicago: University of Chicago Press, 1999.

Wilson, Mary C. *King Abdullah, Britain, and the Making of Jordan*. New York: Cambridge University Press, 1987.

Zeine, Zeine N. *The Emergence of Arab Nationalism; With a Background Study of Arab-Turkish Relations in the Near East*. Delmar, N.Y.: Caravan Books, [1973].

Articles

Khalidi, Rashid. "Ottomanism and Arabism in Syria before 1914: A Reassessment." In *The Origins of Arab Nationalism*, edited by Rashid Khalidi. New York: Columbia University Press, 1991.

———. "Social Factors in the Rise of the Arab Movement in Syria." In *From Nationalism to Revolutionary Islam*, edited by Said Amir Arjomand, Albany: State University of New York Press, 1984.

Khoury, Philip. "Divided Loyalties? Syria and the Question of Palestine, 1919-1939." *Middle Eastern Studies* 21 (July 1985).

Tanenbaum, Jan Karl. "France and the Arab Middle East." *Transactions of the American Philosophical Society*, new ser., 68, no.7 (1978).

Tauber, Eliezer. "Agreement between the Syrian National Party and the Zionist Movement, March 1920." *Cathedra* (September 2000).

Encyclopaedia of Islam, 2nd ed., s.v. "al-Shām."

Encyclopedia of Islam, 2nd ed., s.v. "Yādjūdj and Mādjūdj."

INDEX